THE SECOND WORLD WAR EX CENTRE

http://www.war-experience.org/

Our mission: To collect and encourage access to the surviving testimony of men and women who lived through the years of the Second World War and to ensure that different audiences share and learn from the personal recollections preserved in the collection.

Saving personal experiences of wartime

The Centre's new leaflets, kindly sponsored by Maria Mallaband Care Group, are now available. To find out more about how we preserve and share wartime memories, visit our websire for a general information leaflet. There are many ways you can help us: by donating memories of wartime life, becoming a volunteer or making a financial gift to support our urgent work

Registered Charity No.1072965
The Second World War Experience Centre is a company limited by guarantee and registered in England and Wales, number 3613847.
Registered Office: 2 Feast Field (off Town St), Horsforth, Leeds, West Yorkshire LS18 4TJ

As a matter of policy and to protect privacy, the Second World War Experience Centre cannot forward personal enquiries to anyone included on the History and Collections pages of the Site.

Disclaimer Notice and Collecting Statistics – Your Privacy
Accessibility: we strive to make the website as accessible as possible.
If you have any problems using the website please email The Second World War Experience Centre
Home Page – About Us – Collections – History – Education
Journal – Research Help – Support Us – Search
Website Design by Jackson Web Services

"The titanic conflict that was the Second World War is again being played out as we pass the 70th anniversary of its declaration. But those with first hand memories of that decisive battle for freedom are inevitably dwindling and will soon be gone.

Here then is a first hand account of one man's war seen through his eyes and that of a Signaller Wren. It makes fascinating and moving reading and adds invaluable colour to the ways in which the war affected and involved ordinary people."

Rt Hon Lord Robertson of Port Ellen KT GCMG HonFRSE PC
Secretary of State for Defence 1997–1999, Secretary General, NATO 1999–2004

The Signaller Wren

Mick Stuart

ARTHUR H. STOCKWELL LTD
Torrs Park   Ilfracombe   Devon
Established 1898
www.ahstockwell.co.uk

www.bothymedia.co.uk

*British Library Cataloguing-in-Publication Data.
A catalogue record for this book is available
from the British Library.*

The author is solely responsibile
for the accuracy of events recorded in this book.

ISBN 978-0-7223-3969-5

*Printed, bound and published by
Arthur H. Stockwell Ltd
Torrs Park   Ilfracombe
Devon*

Author's note

MAY 2007

It is with some disbelief that precisely sixty years have elapsed since that train pulled out from the quay-side platform with a full complement of service people. I am surprised that I am here at all and that I have lived so long. I have survived all the demands made of my frail and small frame and come out of it not wanting. Somehow my mind has remained, most of the time, in control.

It occurs to me that had I not returned from the war, my remains would have been identified by the scar on the sole of my foot, my parents would have received the telegram that was the saddest of all events during the war, then Marie would have partied on. She would have played Mahler or Rakhmaninov on her small grand for someone else most happily and yet she would not have got her life quite right.

Ann, I imagine perfectly reasonably, would have assumed the role of "war widow" for an appropriate number of months and genuinely mourned my going. Then, in her inimitable style, she would have braved this unfair world and run the rest of her life most admirably.

Don't you agree?

Mick

. . . with heartfelt thanks to ANN,
Ordinary Wren of the Royal Navy
while manning the Signal Tower in
H. M. Dockyard, Rosyth, The Forth,
for part of the 1939 — 1945 war,
she wrote all these letters
to a matelot after he was
transferred from the Royal Navy
to the Indian Army during the war.
. . . also to Jane
for keeping an Orderly House whilst
Wendy was doing the typing
and Zia from Pakistan who coaxed the pc
. . . my thanks.

Mick.
January 2009

CONTENTS

PART 1
British Royal Navy

We Joined the Navy

War and an Alien

Hostilities Only

Brown Paper and String

Messing and High Places

Instructors and Gun Drill

Visual Signalling and Wren Ann

Train Travel and All at Sea

Swinging the Lead

Man Overboard

Spitkids and Stoking

Boiler Clean and Shore Leave

Extra Rations

Leave Well – Not Alone

Bombed But Not Broken

Boarded Out – Not Cricket

Polished Performance

Panic Stations

Happy Memories

At a Loose End

Farewell – Hello

WE JOINED THE NAVY

Ordinary Wren "Ann" was a signaller at the Dockyard Signal Station at Rosyth, on the Forth estuary, in Scotland, for part of the 1939–1945 war. She would have been very familiar with the crossing of the Forth estuary by naval picket boat – plying from Hawes Pier near South Queensferry to Rosyth Dockyard.

Communication between all ships, and to shore through the signal station, was by VISUAL means alone. It was before the days of speech radio and walkie-talkies.

Rosyth Dockyard pencil drawing by Lambe given to my father in 1918

Signallers on night watches were provided with ample opportunity to maintain correspondence with family and friends. We enjoyed receiving Wren Ann's letters.

Many years previously; it would have been about 1935. A picket boat waited for us at Hawes Pier. It was painted very pure white and it had a funnel of polished brass that shone golden in the bright sunshine. To the east were the three large humps of the Forth Rail Bridge. Today was my birthday and this was my treat. Tea in the wardroom aboard HMS Hood.

HMS Hood and Nelson at anchor in the Forth. Photograph from the Scotsman *newspaper.*

H.M.S Hood and H.M.S. Nelson at anchor east of the Forth Bridge

3

My mother was helped down by the leading hand or at least by an able bodied seaman. She wore her brown coat and a brown felt head-hugging hat with the brim turned up at the front. It would have been called nigger brown in the shops in those days. She wore a fur stole too.

The stoker stoked and red ashes fell to the ash box. The engine chuffed and the little white boat with its bright polished funnel made its way across the wide Forth estuary. We came alongside the impressive vast grey side of the Hood; on the starboard side. The ship's head was to sea on a flood tide.

It was a long way up the series of steps. We arrived at the quarter deck. I doubt if we were piped aboard – that is reserved for flag officers. It must have been a painful experience for my father, like them, he had been assured of such a career, having been in the Navy since the age of twelve and a half; through "Osborne" and "Dartmouth". His contemporaries who remained in the service after the Geddes Axe were now flag officers, commanders and serving in ships like these. His only hope now to fulfil the dreams that were once his, was through me – a nine year old blue eyed boy with fair curly hair.

Silhouette – at age of three 1928.

A well dressed man was tucked under the side of the broad sweep of the stairs in Jenners shop in Princes Street in Edinburgh. For a small payment he produced silhouettes from black paper.

Some years later I asked my mother why someone like him should want to do such a thing. She explained that life was hard for many who had served in the war and that he was only trying to earn something of a living. There was the general strike in 1926 and poverty was quite common. My father found himself without security. Without skills that were of use in civilian life. There were always management posts in faraway parts of the Empire. He went to a tea estate in Assam, miles from anyone, among the Nagas. He enlisted in the Assam Light Horse. Well! He did have a pony and a sword

I remember the ward room of HMS Hood. It was intimidating, spacious, dark leather. We sat on a long leather upholstered bench seat and tea was served on a small low table. We were waited on by an immaculate steward in whites. It was ritzy and quiet, peaceful.

My father had been thoroughly institutionalised. I knew that he never forgave fate for the blow it had dealt him. His place was here amongst commanders and lieutenants – seated at these long parallel tables lined with plush individual dark leather chairs. His napkin rolled and pigeon holed. His duties defined and the future for his family secure.

This was the sleekest, longest, most massive battleship in the world. But an international agreement, post 1918, had limited its weight. Men and ships alike had been slimmed down. What had been gained in guns and overall length, the Hood had sacrificed in protective armour. Less than adequately protected it received a direct hit in a magazine and the twenty one year old ship quickly sank off the coast of Greenland. There were very few survivors. That was 1941 on 25th May, quite early on in a long war.

After two days, having been pursued by our destroyers and aircraft with torpedoes, the German "Bismark", which had sunk the Hood, was itself sunk by our cruiser the "Dorsetshire".

I believe that I would not have enjoyed life in the navy. I was not then able to articulate such matters but I held quite strong views from an early age. I was far too much a challenger and not sufficiently a conformist.

It may be natural for some fathers to seek to fulfil their own failed ambitions through a son. I did not wish to join the navy. I was not asked. I did as I was told. It did become apparent, very much in retrospect, that every effort was being made to prove to me the great privilege and desirability of a career in the navy.

Some of the best of Britain's might in the 1930s.

I received postcards of the ships that my father would have wished to join and Dinky toy models of them too. A year or so after "the tea party" I was presented to the admirals, at Admiralty Arch in London. There, in rooms with strange shaped windows over the arch and in larger rooms behind, I was interviewed, observed and made to write an essay. I must have wasted everyone's time and my father's money in getting me there. But perhaps the navy paid expenses.

At the age of twelve I cut my foot on a broken glass bottle. It happened as I ran into the sea on a hot sunny day on Leim shore in the Isle of Gigha where we lived part of the time. My father's concern with the surgeon who mended me was "would the injury be likely to bar my entry to the Royal Navy." "Probably", was the verdict.

WAR AND AN ALIEN

Then the next war started. My father was reinstated – in uniform – and he forgot about his ambitions for me. Perhaps with pleadings by mother he began to seek ways of keeping me out of the fighting forces – a reserved occupation. A student of medicine or veterinary science.

We were on Gigha the day that war was declared. There was a violent storm. The sea raged and, although more than a quarter of a mile from the sea, my sister reported that her long hair tasted salty with sea spray. We had to walk three miles to the post office to collect the recharged accumulator so that we might tune in the wireless to hear the fateful news "there exists therefore a state of war between us."

It took some time in the strong wind to tie down a rug with stack rope over the small skylight above the stairs. My father was convinced that German bombers would see our candles and small wick lamps as we went up to the bedrooms; and they would bomb us.

It was on a previous leave that he received a strange commission – in the line of duty. On reporting to Admiralty House (Rosyth) to collect a travel warrant, he asked that it be made out to "The Isle of Gigha." The wren asked him to wait saying that she thought that the Admiral would wish to see him. It transpired that the owner of Gigha was a German who would have to be interned as an alien. So we travelled, shadowed by two men who apparently were not supposed to know us. They were to change into their uniforms, and after my father had served the necessary apprehending statement, they conducted the man, handcuffed presumably, to the Isle of Man where camps were set up for aliens. It was rumoured, as of course it would be, that he intended signalling to U–boats. Perhaps he had.

The game "Jutland" has probably had several names. I knew it as "Battleships" but did it start in the navy after the battle of Jutland?

It was at that battle, off Denmark, that my father at the age of sixteen served as a midshipman. He later made a pencil drawing of the foretop of HMS Valiant, the destroyer, from which he observed the retreat of the German navy and saw the sea fill with dead and drowning men.

HOSTILITIES ONLY

My turn in the Crow's nest was soon to come. Of course I passed the medical. They counted, when it became time for me to enlist, my two legs, two arms and two eyes – and I was in. I was needed. There was not a single comment about the scar on the sole of my left foot. It was reluctantly recorded on my papers as an identification feature. Presumably after death!

There was a need – "just the type we're looking for" they said. So I was signed on as c/w (commission and warrant) ordinary seaman with prospects for promotion. We were to join a fairly fast moving conveyer belt, an assembly line; much as do shells and bombs in a munitions factory that, when complete, are delivered to the battle. When we were uniformly prepared to behave predictably to orders given, we would become officers of the Royal Naval Volunteer Reserve – the wavy navy.

BROWN PAPER AND STRING

There were many cruel moments during the war. One of the more sad must have been the arrival of the brown paper parcel in the post.

We had arrived by train at Harwich – it seemed. It was very dark. It was winter. It was cold and a little damp. There were no lights of course. The sea was black and some land beyond was black. The sky seemed not much less black. Like a gathering of cattle from a Hebridean island for the sea journey to mainland market, we were herded into a vessel at the quayside. I remember neither food nor sleep but became conscious once more at the main store.

Into our extended hands was thrust folded brown paper and a pre-prepared length of string. Then item by item we a-heaped in our arms a complete seaman's kit. That cap, the ribbon bearing "HMS". No ship's names for security reasons during the war. I was on His Majesty's Service and I was C/JX 658807. The "C" signified that my home port was Chatham.

Before we could leave the store, we took our boots to an anvil and, with iron punches, hammered our name and initials into the leather ankle at the top of each boot. I asked; "What's the brown paper for."

"That's to wrap your civvy clothes. You post them home." It may have become a very treasured possession.

Stencils and black goo identified our hammocks, mattress and kit bag. The respirator strap and the navy blue inflatable life jacket were lettered in white. We would wear the rubber ring, deflated of course, at all times at sea.

MESSING

Our mess and sleeping quarters was a wide and long space in which about twenty of us lived. This was almost the last time, that I slept in a bed during my whole time in the navy. The floor was of bare polished wood. A long servery hot plate ran across one end, behind which a large window looked out onto – the mast, parade and recreation areas. In peacetime, I supposed, it would have been a holiday camp – it was Shotley. It was HMS Ganges.

We devised a method of reducing the cockroach population. We soon discovered, or someone knew, that they came out in the dark. The killer squad armed itself with rolled up newspapers and crept up to the serving table which housed a large area of metal hot plates. When everyone was in position, the lights were switched on from the other end of the room. We believed that we were reducing the insect population faster than it could breed replacements. When we left they were not extinct. There were always about fifty foraging for crumbs.

Long handled swivel headed polishing blocks were used to keep the floor shiny clean. Spotless. The heavy cloth covered head travelled through about twelve feet – six to each side – as we pulled and swung one way and then the other. Mostly our instructors were Chief Petty Officers and they disciplined us most thoroughly, very firmly and often with verbally brutal methods. The floor was immaculate.

HIGH PLACES

It was compulsory to go over the mast. It was unbelievably tall. It was frightening. We shinned up the rigging on what seemed to be the starboard side to the top yard arm. Across and then gratefully down the other side. I do not remember how often we had to do it. There was one amongst us who excelled; he made it to the top of the flag pole at the mast's head, then climbed onto the small disc on top and held his arms out – unsupported. He also claimed to be severely mentally disturbed. He was still in the sick bay at Chatham Barracks when I left the navy on completion of my training. The navy decided that they could not release him until they had cured him. He believed that the worse he became the sooner that he would be released. An impasse had been reached.

INSTRUCTORS

Petty Officers were mostly good – but, Chief Petty Officers who trained us were not only expert at their skills, they were quite exceptionally brilliant instructors. Their humour held, even with the most trying and insufferable young cadets. We repeatedly did as we were shown until we had achieved a great sense of pride in doing each task really well. Effective and unquestioning response at all times makes for a reliable fighting force – with the necessary skills.

We kept swear scores for CPOs. I had come from a protected background and this was one way that I could come to terms with language that was over punctuated with obscenities. The f's and c's and b's were ticked off and totalled. Close attention to the scoring sometimes distracted attention from the training content. The winner by a massive margin was the CPO who instructed us on ship identification. In a darkened room we peered at the silhouettes of broadsides and angles of ships (f...... ships) in various light levels. I began to hope that when I was at sea and responsible for important decisions that there would always be someone with me to provide a second opinion; dimensions, distances, masts, funnels, guns, superstructure. It was sometimes the practice in war to erect false superstructure to misrepresent the identity of a ship. We concentrated on German and British ships; from battleships to minesweepers and even tugs.

GUN DRILL

We did quite a bit of foot drill, but not as much as the army does. The real drill, to establish unquestioning response, was – gun drill. A row of six-inch guns lined one of the training sheds; their barrels were massive and long and aimed, when the shutters were open, out to sea. It was realistic. Eight hands comprised a gun crew. Each member had his own task at any one time but we had to move round repeatedly until everyone was conversant with all of them. A rhythm developed as one task after the other was executed. No task could be omitted between the firing of a round and the next.

The breach is opened after a shell is fired. There will still be burning cordite within so the gun must be swabbed out with a wet mop. Sparks are doused or the next cordite charge will ignite and that would kill half or at least several of the gun crew. The mop head rests in a bath of water between applications; on opening the breech, after firing and dowsing, the next round is placed in and two of the crew force it home firmly. Next a vast chunk of cordite as long as your arm, and much thicker, goes in. This is followed by a one ounce gun cotton charge. Lastly the detonator. When the two aimers, one horizontal and the other vertical shout that they are on target, the gun is fired.

We exercised endlessly amidst great noise, shouted commands, explosions and smoke. A crew member was removed periodically and laid "dead" on the deck whilst the rest substituted for the missing number and kept the gun firing. Only when the loud clanging of the check-fire gong sounded did one stop. The order "Check, check, check", had to be shouted as loudly as possible to make it heard. There was that amount of noise. I had almost begun to imagine myself in battle on the Victory – but I'm sure that then they had muzzle loaders. Our instructors might not have been to sea since the end of sailing ships. One of the shells, 100 pounds in weight, rolled on to the fingers of a cadet. He was sick listed for weeks.

The reason for the loss of the Hood, and indeed several dreadnought battleships at Jutland in the previous war, may well have been the result of a practice learnt during training – healthy competition between ships. The cordite is stored in the bowels of the ship as far away as possible from the action. Hoists bring it to the guns. At each deck level there are shutters which close and prevent sparks descending to the explosive stocks. Such was the competitive spirit between ship's companies that some of them were stock piling cordite ahead of its need. Ignited in the gun turret the blast would travel down the hoist, passing other cordite on its way up, to reach the huge explosive stocks below. The ships blew themselves up.

..... AND THERE IS NOT TIME TO LEARN THEN.

VISUAL SIGNALLING AND WREN ANN

As the speed of the little flashing light at the other side of the room increases, one's mind holds hard to its meaning, to each letter and numeral. If the concentration lapses, at all, then two or three letters may be lost or misread. Why should I have trouble with "Q" and "J". They made me hesitate.

Learning opposites (pairs), and runs, was a great help. "G" and "W" will remain as a pair and became a fact of life. Then there's , A and N. P and X . The "runs" – E I S H and T M O.

Everyone knows the Victory signal (V). Beethoven's 5th, I believe, was the music which repeatedly uses the Morse for V and the BBC's call sign on a wavelength not transmitting at the time was a continuous, low, slow drum beat of "dot dot dot dash". It must have been unnerving for Germans whose duty it was to monitor our broadcasts. And Beethoven was German!

Not once in all of my naval training did I come across verbal wireless communication. Wireless telegraphy used Morse. No voice. The navy communicated visually; by Morse lamp and by semaphore; and with flags and pendants. Ann trained at Cabbala and became a signaller. She kept watches in the Dockyard Signal Station at HM Dockyard, Rosyth in the Forth, not too far from Edinburgh, and in sight of her home, but on the other side of the river. I believe that she and I knew each other before we joined the navy. I no longer remember how or where we met. By the time she was demobbed , fairly soon after the war ended, she stated that "visual signalling is now a thing of the past." Presumably radio took over.

By that time her letters were coming to me in the Himalayan foot hills where we were relying on Morse; by flag, lamp and heliograph. We did have some radio sets, but they were extremely heavy. Batteries were very heavy. A wireless between units on the ground, (platoons, or companies), was the heaviest load that a single man could carry. A mule carried a single larger wireless and its accumulators for communication with divisional HQ, sometimes a few hundred miles away. But we were often out of range or in a dead area.

TRAIN TRAVEL

Mostly in our training days we travelled about Britain by train. Ditty box only for short leave. Hammock and kit bag and ditty box when moving to a new establishment, ship or shore. All our worldly possessions. We had no civvy clothes ever – only regulation issue, everything.

It was nigh impossible to negotiate the London underground with the full load. I remember the looks of sympathy on the faces of civilians. Hammock over a shoulder and holding the ditty box, the other hand lugging the kit bag. Fortunately the navy provided trucks to and from main line stations.

Trains were forever packed, dirty and dark. Windows were pasted over with paper to prevent flying glass if we were bombed, and to prevent the dim lights being seen from the air. It was too dark to read on the train at night. It was not uncommon, due to the lack of seats, to be heaped on the corridor floor, a mixture of uniforms representing – army, navy and air force and there might be an ATS girl or two sometimes. The corridor ran down the length of a carriage and each compartment had to be entered by a sliding door. There were luggage racks above the seats in each compartment. I tried sleeping in the rack on two occasions when there was no room on the seats, but the supporting brackets cut into me, and my greatcoat buttons became pulled off by the netting as I turned over. It was usually quite cold.

At Preston Station there was one young WVS girl helping the dear mums and grannies who served tea to every train that came in – day, and right through the night. It could be extremely cold – a bitter wind off the Irish Sea sometimes – at 2 a.m. in the winter. There were urns of hot water and large pots of tea on a table, on the unprotected draughty platform, and an extreme shortage of mugs. It was necessary to take one's own mug.

As the train slowed, the station master droned in a low funereal voice " . . . Preston, ...Preston." There was a rush of a thousand, mostly men, on to the platform. The young WVS girl found a jam jar for me and poured me a tea. It was always with milk and sugar. I do not think anyone made tea any other way during the war. She was there on three occasions. Voluntary work was prodigious and persistent.

ALL AT SEA

There was the *Diomede*, the *Dauntless* and there was *Corinthian*. Principles remain the same whatever is the ship but it must have been highly motivating to spend one's training spell at sea in one of the beautiful cruisers. The *Corinthian*, was an ex banana boat with its holds, it was said, filled with millions of ping pong balls to keep it afloat if it should be holed. That was my ship.

The time at sea was a survival course as well. Hardly any sleep and masses of demanding physical work really sorted us out. At least everyone passed, I believe. The Normandy landings (D-Day) were prepared for but the date was as yet unknown. We were on a conveyer belt, non stop, that one day must become switched off. Sleepless graft with first class training, ship board behaviour, seamanship skills, navigation and some weaponry. It made a man of me.

My mess was forward on the port side. I was port watch. My hammock was slung, when in use, laterally far forward and very near the bow of the ship. My watches were Middle and Afternoon. Whatever else was happening during my watches I was on duty somewhere. Keyboard sentry (when I fell asleep standing leaning against the bulk head and I still kept hold of my rifle), on look out, as assistant stoker in the boiler room (it was a coal burning ship), captain of the heads (cleaning the loos), as crows nest lookout (up the mast in an elongated bucket with a pair of binoculars).

Whilst the CPO instructors insisted on discipline that was unrelenting, I do believe that they had great respect for these young boys who entered so enthusiastically into every activity. Nearly all of us were eighteen years old. The RNVR trained and lost very many officers in convoy escorts across the Atlantic and on extremely uncomfortable escort duty to North Russia. Russia was unexpectedly attacked by Germany in June 1941 and became our ally. Marie's brother was one such who was so affected by his experience at sea in the Atlantic that he became permanently invalided. Marie used to play some Mahler for me on her small grand.

Much of the work was physically demanding. Some of us were more able than others. I remember that I would vie with others for the most "press ups" and "pull ups".

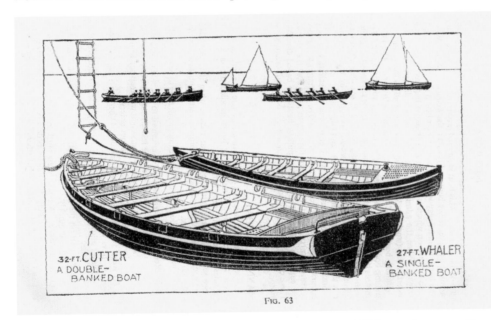

32-FT. CUTTER
A DOUBLE-BANKED BOAT

27-FT. WHALER
A SINGLE-BANKED BOAT

FIG. 63

A whaler is a rather cumbersome wooden boat used extensively in the navy and presumably hand made by the hundred at one time. It was heavy, a reliable survivor and its oars were like slim tree trunks. It took all of our power to wield an oar effectively. We even had races – port versus starboard watch – but such races could never be called sprints – it was like propelling a dead whale through the water. But nobly so.

Having returned to the ship, the petty officer would make us shin up the ropes, back on to the deck – fall in, and report all present and correct. Only then to send us back down, and it was a long way, thirty to forty feet, to the whaler. Then we had to climb up again. That done, the whaler was hooked on and we had to work as a team with blocks and tackle to haul the boat up out of the water, and bring it inboard, to make it secure once more in the ship.

The main reason for our time at sea was more advanced. Navigation opportunistically indulged. There was a row of tables aft, with awnings but no other protection from the elements. In old sailing ships the superior quarters were in the "poop". A high decked block in the stern. If the seas were heavy and came over the stern, the ship was said to have been pooped. We were! I believe that no one and nothing was washed overboard.

13

We became adept at plotting our course, laying off on the charts the directions and distances. We did fixes – dead reckoning, allowing for current, tidal stream and wind; bearings and distances, cross bearings, running fixes and by sounding.

SWINGING THE LEAD

"Sounding" is the term used to describe measuring the depth of the water. Charts usually provide accurate soundings. I did my trick in the chains – various duties are collectively called "tricks"; at the wheel, look out, in the chains. Towards the fo'c's'le and standing out proud of the deck was a platform surrounded by chains. The leadsman stands on the platform "in the chains" and gathers an increasing pendulum action with the lead which is attached to the end of the line. Finally when the momentum is adequate the lead is swung once or twice in a full circle overhead and then launched forward. The lead sinks to the bottom and should touch bottom when the line is vertical.

The line is marked by strips of leather, coloured bunting and knots to indicate fathoms. The lead has a hollow in its base for tallow that picks up a sample of the sea bed; sand, mud. The leadsman shouts to the bridge "By the mark" then the number – if it is indeed a mark. Or "Deep" , then the number if it is between marks. "Deep" is said in a deep voice – and it is hoped that the bridge can hear and distinguish between "marks" and "deeps" correctly.

MAN OVERBOARD

I was at the end of the boom. I dropped the scrubber. I was astride the boom with a bucket of water and now without a brush. It would take minutes to edge myself along the boom, back to the deck to collect another. The Petty Officer in charge would see me. I would receive a dreadful dressing down – perhaps some horrific punishment and I was already suffering exhaustion and lack of sleep. I shouted to my oppo on deck – "Quick – throw me another scrubber." He did, and fortunately I managed to catch it although I was facing out to sea and some fifteen to twenty feet away. It was his accurate throw that did it!

On a somewhat similar occasion someone lost his cap. It was soon dropping astern of us on a flat calm sea. The bridge decided to make it an exercise in "Man Overboard". The helm went over. The shout went out, and the duty sea boat's crew called to station. The motor launch was lowered, the crew descended, but the engine failed to start. The cap was still in sight. It was decided that the skiff should be sent. Small and fast, there were no such things as outboard motors then, it nearly reached the cap when its engine died. So the duty crew and lowerers for a whaler were called. They rowed impressively, collected the cap, took the skiff in tow and returned. Sea boats' crews were never detailed for tricks. They had to be freely available and be easily mustered when called. They were required to be employed near at hand when it was their watch.

SPITKIDS AND STOKING

A hand from each part of the ship is detailed for the spitkid party. It is his duty when "place spitkids" is piped to put the spitkid out in position. He has to clean and stow it at "out pipes". There is the story of the ship whose watches, port and starboard, were running very close in inspection marks. The inspecting officer one day could not put a single mark between them. They were neck and neck. Equal marks for everything. It was a proud ship. The officer decided in the end in favour of the watch that had the brightest, cleanest spitkid. He had done the port side and ordered that its spitkid be brought through beside the one in the starboard mess deck. It transpired that the ship kept one spitkid for inspections. As the inspecting party moved round, the clean spitkid would be moved across to the other mess. It was still a draw – but both spitkids had to be clean thereafter.

Corinthian was a coal burner. She had large boilers and vast coal bunkers down both sides entered by doors from the boiler room. The coal was shovelled down towards the doors, then through to the boiler room floor and finally into the boiler. With long handled shovels the coal was lifted, swung round and then propelled with great conviction and muscle power to the very back of the boiler – through not too wide an opening. The chief stoker was insistent about each shovel-full making it to the very back of the boiler. I was more adept at such tasks than some of my colleagues.

BOILER CLEAN AND SHORE LEAVE

I knew when I went to sleep that we would be tied up in Leith docks. We were in for a boiler clean. There was to be no hurry for once to "rise and shine". I could sleep in. I did. It had gone quiet, some of the others had "lashed up and stowed" and left. Then strange noises made me stir. I pulled down the edge of my hammock – it cocooned me unlike some matelots who used wood stretchers to hold open both ends of the hammock. I peered out, then quickly retreated. The mess was swarming with women! Big burly ones in navy blue boiler suits or dungarees. I had to wait until they left; across to the starboard mess. They were welding brackets on the bulk heads to take new style fire extinguishers. There was a minor emergency when the welding torch set fire to something on the reverse side of a bulk head. Then I lashed up and stowed. There was a neat way of folding in one's single blanket, mattress and the lanyards; then lashing it all the way down with all seven turns equidistant, tight and firm. They were stowed on end in a locker and it was not difficult to withdraw one's own hammock.

Mornings started with "wakey, wakey"; "Rise and shine". Then "Lash up and stow". Sometimes "Show a leg" which is said to have come from sailing ships with women on board and gender was determined by a leg. The seamanship manual says simply that it was "an exclamation used in turning the watch out at night."

As a child I was brought up with the scran bag. Items left lying about were put in it. Items were reclaimed by forfeiting the Saturday penny. I now learnt that it was a naval tradition and the custom in the navy was to offer a piece of soap to reclaim one's possession.

Spells were set aside in the navy as "make do and mend". All those little tasks. Catching up with one's repairs to clothes; buttons, darning and polishing. We were issued with a "hussif" (derived from housewife). It was a linen roll-up "tidy" and contained needles, thread, spare buttons and other items.

Mostly life at sea for us was unending hard work. My middle and afternoon watchkeeping meant trying to get some sleep between the evening meal and midnight, and it was not always at all quiet until about 10 p.m. (2200). On duty from midnight until 4 a.m. (0400). A short sleep until 6.30 a.m. (0630). On deck, bell bottoms rolled up to the knees; bare feet and scrub the wooden deck with long handled scrubbers – with hosed cold North Sea water. I suppose it did us and the deck a great deal of good. Our watch did the port side deck – end to end, then dress fully and breakfast. The rest of the day was spent training.

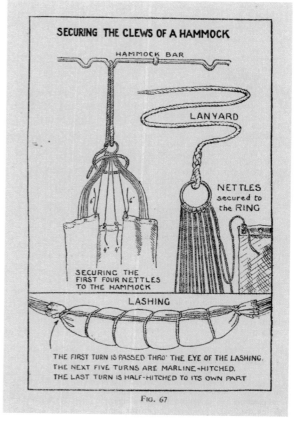

SECURING THE CLEWS OF A HAMMOCK

HAMMOCK BAR

LANYARD

NETTLES secured to the RING

SECURING THE FIRST FOUR NETTLES TO THE HAMMOCK

LASHING

THE FIRST TURN IS PASSED THRO' THE EYE OF THE LASHING.
THE NEXT FIVE TURNS ARE MARLINE-HITCHED.
THE LAST TURN IS HALF-HITCHED TO ITS OWN PART

FIG. 67

It is no wonder that I fell asleep at strange times – I have been able to sleep anywhere since my naval days – on the floor, outside in the open. The only requirement is something on which to rest my head – a boot will suffice if nothing else is to hand. For some seconds I was asleep on key board sentry, leaning against the bulk head, and I did not drop the rifle I was holding. I remember awakening as a door handle rattled as someone came in. I slept briefly in the crow's nest up the mast. In the metal bucket one half stood, leaned and scanned the horizon every three minutes and reported to the bridge – through a voice pipe. Just a pipe. It had a whistle plug which one blew and the other end responded. I wonder how long I had been asleep when they asked me if there was anything to report.

Once when I was stoking, I was moving coal down towards the door to the boiler room, I grabbed a short snooze on top of the coal. The chief stoker was not too abusive when he caught me. I am sure he knew that we were being very heavily worked.

Once the women welders had finished and left I was up, smartly dressed, and joined a shore leave party. We were moored head on – bow to quay – between two other ships. There was the longest ever gang plank from the prow to the shore. It was a treacherous long walk on a bouncing plank with not much of a hand rail. Only one of us at a time descended. Ahead of me a Petty Officer was half way down when his ditty box lid opened and there was a cascade of nutty ration – a couple of dozen bars of chocolate, toffee and gums. I suffered for him. He must have taken weeks to save such a collection – for his girl, wife or children. The sad little bars were airborne for some time and then landed on the surface of the water – and eventually sank out of sight. Not a word was said.

For me a short tram ride from the docks, up Leith Walk and then only a block or two away to our Edinburgh home. There was no one there. The house was deserted. The telephone rang. My parents were away, busy, and my mother was ill around those years. It is possible that they were still in the Isle of Man where my father was "Jimmy the One" – First Lieutenant – in HMS *Valkyrie*, the radar training ship. In those days called "RDF" – Radio Direction Funding. Ann's parents too were often away. Her mother was in the ATS (an officer, I think). Ann's father worked, of course, and did nights on Fire Watching with Civil Defence. Everyone made much effort during the war.

I answered the phone. Edinburgh 26778 was our number. We were all forbidden to touch it when it was first installed, and I retained something between respect and fear for the instrument. It was Ann. Her first words: "You're playing badminton this afternoon," she said. "How did you know I was at home?" I asked. "I was on watch in the Signal Tower when your ship came in, and," she added, "you're taking me out to dinner tonight." "Yes," I queried. "Yes," she said. "Right. You'll be saying we need a carm" I retorted jokingly. Then she said perfectly seriously, "Yes, we do!"

I found the garage key hanging near the telephone in the cloakroom. I found the garage a block away behind in the mews. The car looked OK. An Austin Sixteen; navy blue, dark grey canvas hood and celluloid windows. I checked the petrol. There was some in it. Good!

The left pedal is the clutch and is depressed when changing between gears. The other two pedals were used alternately to accelerate or brake. I knew that one had to engage the clutch gently to effect a smooth start. I slid back the heavy black hung doors that had been there since the coach and horses when the coachman left. The car glided out – in reverse.

I went six times round the three sections of Queen Street Gardens. Up and down the intersections which are extensions of Castle, Hanover and Frederick Streets. Along the flat of Northumberland Avenue and around Abercromby Place. I felt sufficiently confident to convey my passenger with impressive nonchalance. The car's number plate was an Edinburgh registration; FS 7706. Oh! How I wish I had that car now. Six cylinders. But then, come to think of it, its speed was limited, and we sometimes had to stop on a long hill, such as "Rest and be Thankful" which had endless hairpin bends, on our way to the west coast. There was a horse trough half way up where we used to stop to fill the radiator. And it was often so cold that my mother needed her fur foot warmer with a hot water bottle in it. There was very little traffic about in Edinburgh on the day I learned to drive.

We played badminton at Roseburn – near Murrayfield. Then back to Ann's house at Barnton for a change. We motored to Cramond Inn; not Cramond Brig Hotel on the main road, but the little Inn at the estuary of the Almond River which ran into the Forth. There was a ferry man there. He had a small clinker built boat and for a few pennies would row people across. It saved a long walk up to the main road to cross the river.

Before dinner we walked the shore of the Forth. The tide was partially out. Across the other side, in the distance was Rosyth where Ann was stationed – as a signaller. We kicked pebbles and examined under bladder wrack for crawly beasties. We were good company for one another. We dined on lobster.

Ordinary Wren Ann made the crossing of the Forth to Rosyth Dockyard in a naval boat, sometimes almost daily. She was one of the team that provided continuous communication with all the ships – by Morse. I wonder if she knew semaphore as well. She never mentioned it.

I was becoming fairly expert in both Morse and semaphore. I was on a veritable conveyor belt – youths, all male of course – that would provide the reasonably competent officers to see the craft across the channel in the assault upon Hitler's continental bastion in Europe. It would take place somewhere on the northern shores of France, Belgium, Holland – perhaps even Denmark.

We were disciplined. We were drilled. We were shaped. It was all fast, action packed, skill honed, but never less than thorough. We would be needed when the time came. Who can say that I would have – that any of us would have – disported ourselves in a satisfactory manner under fire when faced with serious violent opposition. Many did. Many had done. We later learnt, much later, that the Normandy landings went ahead without us, and evidently with fewer losses than anticipated.

EXTRA RATIONS

We hove to. The ship's engines idled. The reason could be seen, distantly. A mine was adrift, floating several hundred yards away. Obviously we could not go too close. It might explode at any time. There were mines which had horns which if touched exploded them. There were ones which were magnetic or even a vibration might set one off. The Captain, or Officer of the Watch, ordered a marine, or was it a Petty Officer, to bring a rifle – he failed to explode it. We do not know what sort of shot he was anyway. To hit one of its horns, which were visible, at that range would have been nigh impossible.

We were required to experience the use, application and effect of depth charges. There were two throwers aft on each side and two rails to drop them over the stern, a typical pattern to try to surround a submarine. But the Corinthian could only do 16 knots – so we were required to prepare in advance of an attack. We had to get steam up to do full speed or we endangered our own vessel by splitting her seams. One demonstration was enough. Full speed ahead. Set the depth – fairly deep. Over the stern. Wait. The sea erupted. A large elliptical violent white gash appeared under water and then a plume flew upwards. We sent the duty sea boat out to pick up the cod which floated on the surface

View of the bridge of a modern battleship, showing the general lay-out of instruments, from a photograph reproduced by the courtesy of Mr. Charles E. Brown.

[*See* Chapters VIII, IX and

They played music to us over the tannoy when all hands (apart from the duty watch) were stood down. I remember only Vera Lynn singing for us. In one of her songs there was a long slow sigh. It seemed that the ship missed a heart beat, shuddered, slowed imperceptibly and then recovered. Perhaps it was we who sighed.

Somewhere between Scapa Flow and the Forth we encountered serious fog. The Diomede led with Dauntless following and we came astern. In line ahead. I was "look out" port side aft on the Oerlikon gun. This was a lively gun with quite large shells. It could be loaded with varying rounds, explosive and tracer. Around the muzzle was a set of concentric rings to assist with "aiming off" for aircraft speed and direction. I was always convinced that I made exactly the correct allowances on a practice at a towed target, but I was not greatly praised for it.

We were peering through thick fog. I was unable to see the bow of our own vessel. There was a look out, specially posted there, carefully watching for a view of the Dauntless or at least the disturbance, the wake, in the sea. I looked down at the sea passing below me, we must have been doing about 10 knots only, and in the waves playing alongside us – very close to the ship's side – was what looked like a racing dolphin. It was the paravane trailed by the Dauntless ahead of us. A quick buzz to the bridge brought our speed down. Hopefully the bow lookout was able to spot

19

it so that we could thereafter keep station more safely.

I had gone off watch. Slung my hammock and gone to sleep. It was as quiet as a ship under way can be. Nothing bothered me. I was content after a day well spent. Suddenly, without any warning, not even a change in engine revs, there was the most frightening noise. I was not prepared. We had dropped anchor. The anchor chain was the other side of metal plates which were only feet from my head. As the anchor plunged and the cable paid out – all the links were thrashing about inside the chain locker. Each link of that chain would be heavier than I could lift. My heart settled down.

It was dark and the fog had been just too much. We were in Cromarty Firth – off Invergordon. How we made it there with poor vision I did not understand. But we did. But, then, I wonder. There was a little secret room built on the boat deck. The operators came and went and kept the door locked. We were not to know what it did. It was very secret. It was the RDF. (Radio Direction Finding). Later it became called radar. It was possible that the RDF operator was able to discern the shore line on his screen and keep the bridge informed. We did not know of such things in those days.

LEAVE WELL – NOT ALONE

I have to give my father full credit for making my next leave go so well. I have no idea how it all came about. He and I had been in Gigha and we had arranged somehow (there was only one telephone on Gigha – the telephone box – "Gigha 1") to pick up Ann on the way back to Edinburgh. And she was there – in Argyll at the lodge – on her own and on leave too. All three of us in the navy and on leave at the same time. Fate, good luck, or contrived, I shall never know.

My father left me at the lodge with Ann. He then took himself off to Dunoon for the night on the pretext that he had to see someone there. It was late afternoon. The lodge nestled beside trees. Shrubs, azaleas and rhododendrons, a small lawn and some well filled borders set off the grey stone low building in a welcoming way. I remember that the windows were quite small and that it was not at all light. I do not remember if there was electricity. Probably not. We were so used to oil lamps. We had dined on sea trout steaks which Ann prepared most expertly. We dined alone. I had my own neat little bedroom – of course.

The fish had come from a pool in the river. A pool large enough for the keeper to make several draws with us in the small rowing boat. Trees hung over the deep pool and we circled the quiet water until we had netted sufficient fish, around six pounds each, to make up a box for sale next day in Dunoon. But the keeper saw to all of that.

The morning dawned cheerfully bright. My father arrived with the car. We put the hood down and removed the yellowing celluloid windows because they rattled.

We wrapped my father, in his overcoat, in a blanket and settled him back, a little sideways, on the back seat.

He slept much of the journey. We were all in civvies. We were all in the navy – a wren, a seaman and a Lieutenant Commander in the back. Ann had at one time seemed as if she might come to attention and salute when spoken to by my father. Today we were all very relaxed. The wind played with Ann's hair at the left side of her headscarf. She smiled her broad comfortable smile with that sideways look that was distinctly hers. The car probably did 50 mph. It was unnecessary and unfair on the car to go to 60 mph but I remember that it had done so some years before. Three of us – all in the navy. All, remarkably, on leave together and now all returning to our various duties.

On some other occasion I was on leave. Again there was no one at home except that my sister was around and due to depart to boarding school. Ann's brother too would be returning to school. We agreed to take the two young ones out to dinner on their last night.

We had Ann's family table at the Waverley Steps Grill Room in the N B Hotel. The family sherry – the special treatment – the coffee cups warmed with hot water before pouring. It was a very special dinner. After all, Ann's family had almost owned the N B Railway at one time or something like that. That the government was renting all British railways and London Underground for £43 million per annum made no difference to the way the staff behaved towards us. Next morning we met at the Waverley Station to see the young ones off – on different trains – I recall. Ann and I had both been sewing on name tapes before packing the trunks at each of our homes.

GONE TO GROUND

The relentless conveyer belt continued – at pace. We were housed in the underground car park on Brighton sea front. We were treated to a serious over supply of Spam whilst there. However, I do not remember ever finding the food in the navy other than good and adequate. Here we carried trays to tables, I think. Were things looking up, one thought. We slept in bunk beds. A mass of us were spread over a large area. Perhaps, fifty or more of us. On concrete floors – space for forty or fifty cars. The room was also used for instruction such as Morse reading exercises.

The sea front was a tangle of barbed wire and spikes to deter a German invasion. And mined too. We could not enter the beach nor swim in the sea. Several of us frequented the ice rink. The family of a girl I met on the ice took me to the theatre, to a variety concert. They had a small shop in Portslade or Shoreham-on-Sea. I was to go there soon for small ship handling in the narrow deserted harbour.

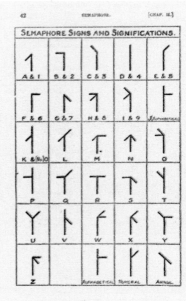

Backing on to the sea, with high hopper windows near the ceiling, was the navigation lecture room. A very realistic exercise took place one day when a storm was raging outside. The instructor pushed the tables about, let off thunder flashes and the wild sea actually came in through the windows above our heads whilst we plotted courses on charts.

PLATE I.   To face page 206

	A **Steam Vessel under way**, showing Masthead, Port, and Starboard Side Lights. (Masthead visible 5 miles. Side Lights 2 miles); or **Steam Fishing Vessel, shooting or towing lines.**
	A **Steam Vessel under way**, showing the additional Masthead Light aft, also the usual Masthead, Port, and Starboard Side Lights. (Masthead visible 5 miles. Side Lights 2 miles).
	A **Steam Vessel towing another vessel**, showing 2 Masthead Lights, vertical, also the Port and Starboard Side Lights. (Visible 2 miles).
	A **Steam Vessel towing more than one vessel**, when the length of tow exceeds 600 feet, showing 3 Masthead Lights, also the Port and Starboard Side Lights.
	A **Vessel not under command**, through accident, not making way through the water, showing 2 Red Lights, vertical, one over the other. (Visible 2 miles).
	A **Vessel not under command**, but making way through the water, showing 2 Red all-round Lights, vertical, and usual Side Lights. (Visible 2 miles).
	A **Vessel not under command by day**, showing 2 Black Balls or Shapes, vertical, each two feet in diameter.
	A **Vessel employed repairing or laying telegraph cables, making way through the water**, not under command, showing Red-White-Red Lights, vertical, usual Side Lights. (Visible 2 miles).
	A **Vessel employed repairing or laying telegraph cables but not making way through the water**, not under command, showing Red-White-Red Lights, vertical. (Visible 2 miles).

L.88. 751-9517

Models of warships' bows and fore decks gave us opportunities to go through, in miniature, the motions of reeving an anchor. It is no mean business controlling the colossal weights of anchors and their chains. Because of their size and weight they require most careful handling.

Morse and semaphore continued. My Morse by lamp reached about twelve words per minute. I did not find that it came naturally or easily. It required concentration.

There was a small room given to damage limitation. Baulks, bars, boards and bits and pieces, nearly filled it. I probably excel at inventive solutions in times of need – what a boss of mine once called most "indigenous" – but I have never felt comfortable with contrived exercises.

We levered, wedged, propped and patched an imaginary hole in a ship's side. A dry run, one might say, without the sea rushing in.

Communication remained an important subject. In addition to Morse and semaphore there were flags and pendants. They were in regular use with bigger ships. A very quick method of intimating orders to a flotilla – so that all would turn together on the hoisting and dipping of the flags.

Ships at sea are required to identify themselves and to indicate, for safety reasons, what they are doing. They have navigation lights at night. A trick question by one of the CPOs was:- "You are travelling south in the English Channel at night and you see ahead of you a single red light surmounted by two white lights, one above the other – what is it?"

The answer is, "A house in France with two rooms occupied."

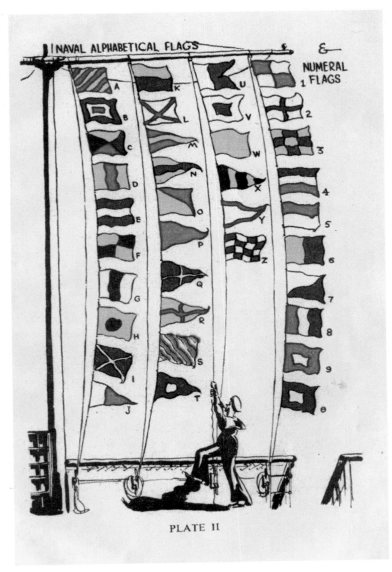

NAVAL ALPHABETICAL FLAGS

NUMERAL FLAGS

PLATE II

BOMBED BUT NOT BROKEN

We could not go too far on a "48". Victor invited me to his home in Hampstead. On one leave bombs had landed all around and huge piles of broken glass were all the way down the middle of the road awaiting collection. Both Victor's brothers were in the forces; both commissioned officers. One a marine and the other in the air force. It was a Jewish home, and one knew it. Mother was central to the family and much loved and Dad greatly respected. I was so well looked after. It was an oasis in an otherwise Spartan and rather brutal existence. Father was in the Civil Defence – we played ping-pong at their HQ at the bottom of the road. It was thoroughly sand bagged all around. Figures in tin-hats, gas masks slung, busied in and out of the darkened streets. All intent on duty.

When it came to the end of our training Victor was, like others, discarded. He took much personal shame for not upholding the family tradition. He should not have done so. Had we been a few months older, he might well have lost his life during the Normandy landings. The requirements of the Admiralty took precedence over the adequacy of us its recruits.

BOARDED OUT – NOT CRICKET

The navy solved a dhobying problem when we were boarded out with landladies. They sent our clothes to a laundry in Brighton. The neat parcels were returned with notes of the laundry girls' names and telephone numbers slipped between the clothes.

We were in Hove. One tends to be organised by alphabetical order. I was with a cadet whose name began with "T". I have forgotten his name now! The digs was a red brick terraced house in Cromwell Road. It belonged to an aging woman who had a dog that was older – and rather mangy or hairless in patches – and not too friendly. I cannot say that I enjoyed any of my stay there, but it was convenient. We had to walk only a short distance to Hove Cricket Club where we endlessly wheeled tea trolleys about on the grass. We laid off plots and fixes and practised all the ways of ensuring that a ship was where it was intended it should be. Silly mid off or at long leg!

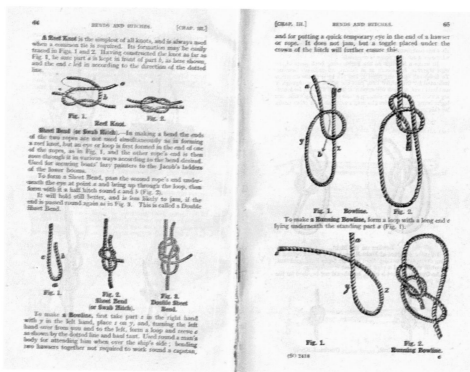

Razor blades were in short supply. My friend had a little curved glass mould. We rubbed safety blades backwards and forwards to sharpen them. It was a 'godsend'.

I knew my knots – from Boy Scout days and from practice on the farm. I put these to good use on many occasions. Clove hitch, reef knot, sheet bend, bowline.

In the navy they were called "bends" and "hitches". Strange that the reef knot came in the group called bends and hitches. Knots were paired with splices. I took some pride in making neat splices, back splices and eye splices.

POLISHED PERFORMANCE

And so further along the conveyor belt – we had a spell at Lancing College. Now waited upon in the dining hall we learned to roll our napkins but not to pass the port yet. We trained all the time.

Left behind in Brighton – at Horne's or Morris Angel or perhaps it was Silvers in Hove – my uniform hung on a rail. My peak cap fitted. The suit was made – the wavy gold braid applied on the sleeves – only the hem of the jacket was yet to be turned up and sewn where the chalk mark decreed. We had practised the march past on the sea front to a stirring march on a gramophone record. The line held straight, the smart eyes right, the best cadet chosen in the lead saluting.

The Normandy landing had taken place. There were no apparent changes yet. We, the nation, the Admiralty confidently and Eisenhower probably, expected success. Casualties there would be, expected but not predicted with any accuracy; unstated, unknown, not declared. Four thousand ships and smaller craft too (the greatest ever armada) were on their way across the channel on the night of D-Day.

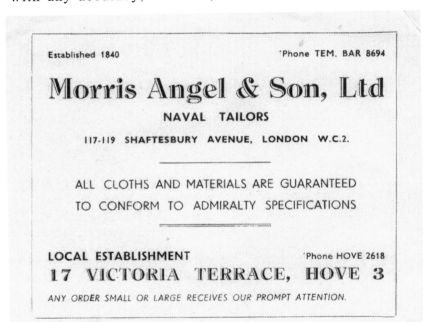

Advertisement in "The Wave". HMS King Alfred *magazine April 1944.*

Many HMS *King Alfred* commissioned RNVR officers lost their lives throughout the war. The cost of the Normandy Invasion was being counted. Five destroyers, one destroyer escort, three frigates, one trawler, one auxiliary, one transport, one mine sweeper and one fleet tug were lost.

At Lancing I was belted, gaitered and on night sentry at the top of a cliff path – facing France across the channel. I wore my cap secured by the chin strap. There were rounds in the magazine, the bayonet scabbarded at my side. I stood high above the sea. The dark, dark sea below with bushes and blackness in between. I was not far from the college but out of sight and sound. I had not seen this part of the grounds in daylight. There appeared to be nothing other than the little footpath to the shore. Some distance away to my left there were rumbles, flashes and pyrotechnics with malicious intent. Tracer rounds and flares glowed and then died. Our troops would be advancing through France, Belgium or even Holland. My concern was much more immediate and indeed closer. I was guarding the cliff path.

A muffled cough and scuff alerted me. I fixed the bayonet and waited. Then heard another indistinct movement. In one single motion I leaned forward, put a round in the breech and pointed the rifle at the head of the path. No sound. "Halt, who goes there" I enunciated loudly and clearly such that any German would have clearly understood my meaning. Still no sound. After a pause there was another quiet scuff. "Advance one and be recognised." I moved the safety catch forward. "Halt or I fire." There was a belch, an unmistakable bovine belch. It was a vagrant Jersey cow.

A memory of Lancing which survives clearly and above all else is the chapel. It is unreal. The stonework, dimensions, slim columns and elegant manner in which the arches reach upward are awesome. I should like one day to revisit it.

PANIC STATIONS

We returned to our warren on the sea front at Brighton. The conveyor belt had been thrown in reverse. Where we had previously been encouraged by praise we were now damned for the slightest and most meagre failing. There was no march past practice. I felt that there was not that much that could be held against me. A gunner on the training staff – (a gunner is a sort of half way commission from the ranks. He wears a thin gold braid on his sleeve) – asked me why I signed my name with a full Christian name. He said that he thought I had too high an opinion of myself; that I came from a privileged background. I had not the wit then to reply defensively that my brother and I both had first names that started with 'M'. It was necessary that we should know which one of us was being addressed. I was one day to become very grateful that I had "failed". We were no longer just the type *they* wanted.

But I would soon find someone who did want us.

HAPPY MEMORIES

It seems strange that we could do anything at all on 17/6 per week. A bed for the night in the Seamens Rest was 1/6d. A pie and beans and a cup of tea must have been about a shilling.

Never before nor since have I, or would I ever in the future sleep with another man in the bed. Not any man. Not any bed. Certainly not a two foot six inch bed! Victor had not booked a bed in the Seamens Rest (near the dock in Chatham). It was too late for him to return to barracks. He pleaded. I can sleep anywhere; holes in rocks, in the bracken, on dry river bed gravel, on the floors of railway carriages – but on that night sleep was impossible – even head to tail, as they say, rest became a negative value. Please feel indebted Victor.

In London I knew my way about only a little. I found the street in which there had been a restaurant called "Beguinots" where grandmother once treated us and I had escargot. I didn't think much of snails but it is good that I had once tried them. There were black painted boards nailed over the front of the building. It had closed. I could find my way to the Commonwealth Club – brightly lit and packed with uniformed men who were quite noisy. The rooms were vast and a wide staircase led up inside the wide front doors. It was very brightly lit. I was not sufficiently worldly to stay there comfortably. I knew some other quieter places where I could get a cup of tea for a penny or two.

There was a wooden hut in Piccadilly Circus where WVS ladies issued tickets to service men for theatres. She said that there was not much left – but a performance by an unknown fiddler called Grapelli. The motherly woman was not sure if I would enjoy it. I didn't particularly. The theatre was less than a quarter filled. I am proud now to have been an audience for the great violinist. He was good!

A kind gesture, the memory of which, has remained fresh with me all my life. I broke my journey (rail warrant made out to Isle of Gigha) at Penrith. I made my way to Windermere, then caught a bus to Ambleside. My intention was to call to see my sister who was there at boarding school. Many forces families were dispersed and children's fees must have been paid by government.

Following a polite interrogation by the head teacher and an assistant member of staff, I was permitted to take my sister to lunch in the hotel close by. In days that were uncertain and emotionally bereft it became a fond memory of mine. I cannot imagine how I had enough money to pay for two lunches, but then it was not long after this that it became illegal to charge more than 5/- for any meal.

On the return bus journey from Ambleside to Windermere a darling English Mrs Tiggiewinkle, of at least thirty-eight years, stood to offer me her seat. A war brings out gallantry and all that is best in us. Unfortunately there was also much that was not too enjoyable. I declined her offer of course.

Ticket collectors at stations sometimes looked twice at the destination on my travel warrant. One never knows, there might have been an Isle of Gigha at the end of Lake Windermere. I was never seriously challenged.

I travelled several times by devious indirect routes. The Home Guard should have been called. I might have been an escaped POW with forged papers. Or, I might have landed by parachute, a spy or saboteur. Perhaps I just looked too young and innocent for that.

It was near Christmas. I was in Edinburgh. The streets were dark; some traffic was about with their hooded headlamps dimmed. I could not see Tolcross from the Kings Theatre but I did see vehicles disappearing in both directions; to Lothian Road and to The Meadows. There were excited little coveys of parents with children making their way into the theatre. I was peering at the black and white photographs taped to the bevelled glass panes in the theatre front doors – scenes on stage that could hearten and dispel the drabness of wartime. It was a variety show or a pantomime. I was about to turn away (I was in my seaman's uniform) when a mother with a young daughter asked me if I would like to use their spare ticket. There was a fraction of a second's hesitation before she made it clear that I was being treated, that I was not expected to pay for it. The tickets were numbered seats so, of course, I sat with them. The daughter sat between her mother and me. In the interval a tea tray was passed along. I regret that I did not maintain contact with them. I have always hoped that the missing person was not absent through the misfortunes of war. I should like them to know that I was truly grateful.

AT A LOOSE END

The navy was moving east – to the Pacific. The navy became embarrassed by the number of spare bods it had. There was hardly room in their barracks to accommodate everyone. There were certainly not enough ships.

A batch of us were sent off by train to Portsmouth Barracks. We arrived walking through the gates. There was an air of uncertainty if not of some chaos. It was very quiet. The weather was fair. They had nowhere to put us – a bomb had demolished a whole block during the night. Eventually we were taken in hand by a Petty Officer who gave us 10/- each and asked us to dump our kit and find somewhere to stay in the town.

After fruitless wandering we arrived in Southsea where nearly every house was a boarding or guest house, or would have been in peace time. We found a considerate landlady who permitted us to use the corridor. Head to foot we lay along the corridor floor, without bedding, where doors led off both sides to bedrooms. Their occupants stepped over us without comment; not even noticed. We just lay down and slept. They gave us some breakfast in the morning. It cannot have been easy for we carried no ration books with us. We may have had cornflakes, tea and toast, or more likely it was bread. We stayed there two nights and then walked back to the barracks.

Out, anchored in mid harbour off Whale Island was the Foudroyant, a French sailing ship captured from them several wars previously. The ancient timbers were large and heavy. The deck heads low – no wasted space – her gun deck lengthy. I supposed she carried at least twenty guns. I slung my hammock where real matelots had once lived. They had made silhouettes of their hands and paper cut-outs on the deck head timbers with smoky candles.

Somebody somewhere must have known who we were. The ex King Alfred squad. Our ploy here was really an exciting adventure – for a little while. We were collected off the Foudroyant daily by a fast triple screw air sea rescue craft that was employed in an unusual role.

Once on board, the three throttles were edged forward and the three Rolls Royce engines really lived. This was probably the fastest boat in the Royal Navy, designed for saving pilots who had ditched in the sea. The navy forbad slang words. Clarity of meaning was paramount, "Ditch" was not a permitted word. Verbal commands easily blow away in strong winds. Where a command is required to be obeyed immediately or simultaneously by a number of hands, it is uttered sharply. If a more gentle response is required then it is drawled.

The boat was built of plywood. It was intended to move fast and not carry much more than its three long sleek engines. Manoeuvring was by the throttle levers. Forward port, astern starboard, leave the centre idling and she turned almost in her own length. All three throttles full ahead and she took off.

We proceeded through the narrows, out of the harbour, turned to starboard and stood off Stokes Bay near Gosport. Above and not far from the little jetty were one or two huts. The place seemed to be "manned" by wrens. Our task was to retrieve spent torpedoes from the end of the practice run. Fleet Air Arm pilots were in training with torpedo dropping aircraft.

On a bridge rigged over some pontoons was a man who monitored the flights, measured, photographed and somehow marked the hits and misses; the flights, drops and runs. I was told that he had been doing this all the years of the war and that he had some serious disability – he had lost both his legs or something.

After an "attack" – the torpedo ran until it had exhausted its compressed air. It then up ended, water entered the head and a smoke plume developed. We drew alongside; hooked it on to our davit and hauled it partially on board. We then made quick time to Stokes Bay where the wrens took over.

It was still 1944. There was indecision. Or, rather there was nothing on which to form policy. Our land troops were working their way eastward on mainland Europe. It is amazing that we were kept well fed. They always managed to hold pay parades. We marched forward, saluted, off caps – then placed the cap on the table, flat side up, and our money was placed on it. There was never a chink in the British administration. Apart from two nights on the floor in Southsea I always had somewhere to sling my hammock. I believe I had risen to 27/6 per week by then, and I was sending 7/6 per week home. My mother put my money in a savings bank and added birthday money to it for several years. It was £23 when I arrived home. I found the bank book years later. Thinking that it must now be worth hundreds of pounds with compound interest, I took it to the bank to discover that interest was payable only on balances over £25!

I was just barely nineteen years old and still enjoying all the ploys. There were exceptions of course.

Because there were more bods than work it became ridiculous. A sub standard Petty Officer took a squad of us one day; and just to keep us out of the way made us sweep up leaves. This was back in our home port – Chatham. When there were no more leaves left he could think of nothing better to do than spread them out again so that we could be seen to be busy.

I started service life with "You're just the type we're looking for." That status had gone up and down of late depending on the market. We were rated zero by now.

From Collingwood block there were hundreds of steps. Stairways led down into the bowels of the hillside into vast caverns and tunnels which ran into the hillside from the lower barrack level. We were supposed to rush for the depths every time the air raid sirens went. It became so monotonous that one night I turned over in my hammock and went back to sleep. In the morning the sun shone on to the floor which had become covered with smashed glass from the broken windows. I had to ask someone to bring me my boots before I could descend from my hammock.

We were still well fed. Someone of my constitution and experience enjoyed the food. When three trays of tripe and onions were delivered to our mess of about eighteen ratings, I must have had a dozen portions. It was delicious.

An unhappy memory was the time there was a power failure. There was only cold water for washing our single plate and cutlery. It was unpleasant having ones pudding served on a plate that held remnants of stew. When it happened at sea, it was marginally worse – sea water is even less effective for cleaning off fat. Washing up liquid had not been invented.

We took greatcoats, gas masks and ditty boxes for short shore leave. We were searched at the top exit gate at Collingwood. Open the ditty box for examination. One contraband substance was tickler. Along with rum and kai the navy also did well for tobacco supplies. One bought proprietary cigarettes easily. More readily available in the navy than in Civvy Street. I remember Players – was it "No 1" with the "sailor" on the packet and Gold Flake. There was Capstan . They were 6d for twenty. Wills Whiffs and Woodbines were 4d for twenty (but perhaps that was at sea). "6d". Six pennies was half a shilling – five "p" today. We could buy a tin of best tobacco, a half pound probably, for two shillings and sixpence. It was tickler – pipe or excellent cigarette tobacco. One could also buy leaf – but there was a great deal of work with it. The leaves had to be formed firmly into a vast sausage laid individually one over the other – and mixed sparingly with perhaps rum, treacle (molasses) and then bound carefully with a great length of fine rope or heavy twine. There was an art, and probably myths too, and superstitions as well, with such practice. The final product, cut with a sharp knife, looked excellent.

The Petty Officers' mess had a machine which fed the tickler into the continuous paper from a reel – rolled it – moistened it – stuck it and cut it into cigarette lengths. It was hand operated and made a very presentable, firm cigarette.

When going ashore, several times, I put a half pound tin of tickler in the sleeve of my greatcoat. At the gate check I opened my ditty box, had the overcoat pockets frisked and walked out with a 2/6 tin of quality tobacco, enough to make more than 300 first class cigarettes. There was someone ashore that I knew who would appreciate it, but I cannot now remember who it was.

The NAAFI canteen decided to let its hair down. The manager had been told that scrumpy is an innocuous product made from pear juice. Several casks turned up in the canteen in the main barracks. It was possibly 6d per pint. The place was wrecked within a few hours.

Somewhat cooling one's ardour was to be drafted to work in the dockyard. I was. For several cold November days we sat in pairs on a stage (plank) hauled up the side of a destroyer's funnel. With chipping hammers we removed very thick layered paint in minute chips at the rate of about two and a half blows per second! In a full day this meant a great deal of resonant loud clanging only a foot in front of one's face. A destroyer's funnel, in such circumstances, feels like a couple of acres. There were breaks mid morning and mid afternoon. It was most unlikely that one would be lowered otherwise, even for the loo. That, and heaving 1 cwt. (112 lbs. or about 50 kilos) bags of coal around the barrack galleys, and there were many of them, were the two tasks that I have liked least in my armed forces careers. But, then, I was one of the lucky ones.

Somehow I was able to escape work some days. A clipboard and pencil were the only necessary "props" to get me through the gate between Collingwood and the main barracks. I was not once challenged. The guard presumed that I was on a legitimate errand. Unfortunately a roll call was held one day when I was absent. I was marched in front of the duty officer, a Lieutenant Commander, who examined my service record and pass book. He noticed that my next of kin held the same rank as himself. Looking up at me he stated that the service expected better things of someone like me, and put me on ten days 8a. Jankers was the slang for jail.

An hour earlier out of my hammock. On parade before others were up. Middle of the square in Collingwood. About two dozen of us, for various reasons, were inspected minutely and then given nearly forty minutes of drill. I presume that the Petty Officer in charge was also there for some misdemeanour. He experimented; allowing each of us to drill the squad. Then he found that I was quite able. Before the week was up I drilled the squad and the PO retired to his mess.

A contemporary of mine called Eric arrived back in barracks greatly excited one day. He had been on a cushy job in the main barracks in the library. When asked what he was doing, he told us that he had been to London and was signed up for a transfer to the Indian Army. His uncle apparently was the recruiting officer for officer cadets to the Indian Army. If he can do it so can I, thought I. After all I was once "just the type we're looking for." "Officer material" – and so, I was, once more. Twelve more of us besides Eric did it.

In London almost everyone was in uniform, the obligatory gas mask slung over a shoulder. Traffic was busy but sparse. I was able to walk to the hub of an intersection of many roads. A policeman was on point duty, directing traffic – there were no traffic lights there. "Please," I said, "Could you direct me to the India Office." He was young enough to be in the armed forces so I deduced that "the police" must be a reserved occupation, or perhaps that he was colour blind.

"Well! Mr Stuart," he said with a broad smile. "Do I know you?" I faltered, thinking that perhaps he was from a lesser place than London; Edinburgh perhaps. He didn't elucidate but obviously enjoyed his private joke. "Yes! Over there, past the Houses of Parliament, round the corner and turn left." Embarrassed and a little discomfited I arrived at India Office wondering how it was that he had known my name.

I received the King's shilling for the second time. It may have been 5/ – or even 7/6 this time. The contract was made. The interview took less than half an hour.

We came well recommended in spite of our failure to receive our commissions in the RNVR. Burma and the Far East was consuming war material and men. "I *was* just the type" someone was looking for. On my return to Chatham I hung my respirator over the post of the kit bag racks. In two inch bright white lettering on the strap was M. M. Stuart.

FAREWELL – HELLO

On the day of my departure from the navy I reported at central stores in the main barracks. "Leave your hammock outside on the ground." I must have kept my service respirator. No one went anywhere without one. Papers were ticked and signed and I was free to go. I picked up the hammock on the way out. All my kit went home with me. It was December. I was granted one week's leave. I went home to Edinburgh.

There was snow. Ann and I tobogganed at Barnton. Sally, her dog, sported endlessly down and back up the hill. She raced us on the way down, then inevitably beat us on the way up. Ann was an appreciable weight lying on top of me. Of all people I have known she had most zest. She was a bundle of fun. Somehow I forgot my camera – left it in the wash house at the back of her house. There was still none of my family at home.

A few miles only, over Blue Bell Hill, from Chatham to Maidstone. There I reported for duty in a brick built barracks. There were practically no similarities between the two services. Wartime life was never "looking back". All was forwards – to battle one supposed. As I was soon to learn in the Gurkhas it was "foravance". Their eager pronouncement to move on, usually hastily and almost impatiently, "forward advance".

Here Follows a Complete Collection of the Letters From the Wren.

It is preceded by a glossary and explanation of words and expressions that were then in common use. It may help you.

NOTE. Seamen were often referred to as "matelots". Amongst themselves but especially by girls.

1.   VMT. "Very many thanks". Communications during the 1939–1945 war were conducted for the most part by signallers who used Morse and semaphore. Messages had to be kept to a meaningful minimum Radios (wireless) were heavy and batteries were exceedingly heavy. Both Morse and semaphore could be transmitted by flag; and Morse by lamp and radio. Twelve words per minute was a reasonable starting speed. Americans who used the horizontal key with the dot to the left and the dash to the right reached incredible speeds.

2.   The Royal Navy organised its crews in "watches".
There was the Starboard Watch and the Port Watch. (Sometimes a Division might be divided into three watches — called "Red", "White" and "Blue"). Duties of the day were split into watches too:

Middle watch   – 0000 to 0400
Morning watch   – 0400 to 0800
Forenoon watch   – 0800 to 1200
Afternoon watch   – 1200 to 1600
First Dog watch   – 1600 to 1800
Last dog watch   – 1800 to 2000
First watch   – 2000 to 0000

3.   Duties of the day are spread more easily if shared by more watches – so four watches means fewer demands on the "hands". A "hand" is a "rating".

4.   All Royal Navy personnel "go ashore" when they leave the ship, even if their establishment is shore based.

5.   Hammocks were all that ratings had to sleep in anywhere – barracks or ship. There were no bunks except for officers and sometimes for Petty Officers. The reference to biscuits means "palliasses" – straw filled hessian "bags" which were used by soldiers when in barracks.

6. VMT U signal. Abbreviated form of "thanks for your letter"

7. A "48" meant two days. More than 36 and 24 hours was given in days.

8. "below". RN personnel went "below" even on shore. Signifies down stairs! Or, "between decks

9. "gash". Originally gash was rubbish – something to be thrown overboard. Usually it was unusable. The word became corrupted during the war to mean "spare", "give away" or "surplus to establishment".

10. PO. Petty Officer. Promotion from seaman went first to "Leading Hand" who had an anchor on his sleeve. The anchor was the type called a killick, so inevitably a leading hand might be called "Killick" by his seamen. There were many levels and designations of petty officers. Above them and forming the most formidable backbone of the navy were the Chief Petty Officers

11. "oppo". My opposite number who came on when I went off. Usually the rating from the opposite watch.

12. 2/O. Presumably the second in command.

13. Morse for "V".

14. VS Presumably voluntary service. Sometimes HO meaning Hostilities Only.

15. W/T. Communication. Wireless Telegraphy.

16. Kai. Something quite peculiar to the Royal Navy. Commonly known as cocoa. The navy had its own make in block form. Resembled cooking chocolate but was, almost, edible. Probably did much more good than coffee! Ships took on supplies around the world, like rum and tobacco, and kai must have been loaded in some foreign port.

PART 2

Letters from the Wren

Dockyard Signal Station,
H. M. Dockyard
Rosyth,
Fife
2342-31-1-45

Dear Mickey,

May I call you Mickey 'cos
I never can remember if it is one or two
F's – Moncrief(f). Never expected to
hear from you so soon what with
shaking down to a new routine, so was
most surprised on arriving down to
breakfast this morning to find a
letter to me. V.II.T.

Let me warn you. I don't know
what sort of a letter this will turn
out to be, or what length, but I have
the First, and half the Middle to
do, and nothing at all to do except
writing letters so they are usually
rather longer than they would be
otherwise, and any way, I am a rather
letter writer. But I enjoy it.

H. M. Dockyard Signal Station
Rosyth

2342 - 31 - 1 - 45

Dear Micky

May I call you Micky 'cos I never can remember if it is one or two Fs in Moncrieff. Never expected to hear from you so soon what with shaking down to a new routine, so was most surprised on arriving down to breakfast this morning to find a letter to me VMT. 1

Let me warn you I don't know what sort of a letter this will turn out to be or what length, but I have the first and half the middle to do and nothing 2 at all to do except writing letters so they are usually rather longer than they would be otherwise, and anyway, I am a rotten letter writer, but I enjoy it

Re your camera — at the present moment it is sitting in my bedroom, rescued from the laundry and I shall take it back to Duke Street the very next time I am that way We are back in four watches again which is a joy, but somehow I 3 don't think for long So I can get home every other night and last night was the first that I had spent at home since before my leave Did me the world of good and Daddy was a lamb as he saw I was out of sorts and fixed me with a drink before

39

dinner which recovered me completely. Now I feel equal to anything. Marvellous feeling.

I had two more goes at tobogganing after you left, but somehow it wasn't nearly so much fun. The first time, Ian was much too long to go on top of me, so I had to always be tops and anyway hadn't recovered from some dreadful bruises which must have been inflicted by you, only I didn't notice them at the time. The other time I went with a wren but she wasn't very large and we kept coming adrift. There were about six inches of snow on Monday night, the right sort of snow for tobogganing when at 0400 on Tuesday morning it began to thaw and has done so ever since. Most slushy. All evening it has done nothing but sleet most unpleasant and I want to go ashore tomorrow. 4

I see I have automatically put my service address on, but please ignore it and if you should write again to write home, 'cos I like it better that way.

To go home after all this and find a nice letter waiting for me is heaven.

Sally is as full of beans as ever. Terrific battle of will the other night. Having been told not to sit in the chair – she still did. We stared at each other for ages, then she had the impudence to slowly close her left eye then to open it. It was so funny, but she didn't gain her point so she evacuated the chair very quietly, she is a little devil though.

Have you ever watched cats in snow? Tiddles the other morning insisted on going out. Not at all pleased at finding snow, she tried to swim through. Finding that failed, for it was well above her little tummy, she then hopped like a kangaroo, or rather Little Roo in Winnie the Pooh, 'cos she does look like Little Roo.

Earlier on watch, I re-read the Just So Stories I adore them, don't you? I found a lot more to them than when I last heard them which was when Daddy read them to me, oh, years ago when I had measles Don't know which one I like best.

What sort of leave is it you get on March 8th? Do you arrive on the 7th or 8th?

The least said about this Poly photo the better, but I brought the whole bunch back here for candid criticism (I got it too) and this is the one which most people agreed about. If you think the same about it as I do I won't be at all offended if you send it back

Your late ship has been in de-oiling and de-ammunitioning and has now paid off and gone away again, so I don't know what has happened to her now. The other two are still with us

Do you manage to sleep all night on your biscuits, or still pining for your hammock? You won't have sheets anyway. Have you exchanged the frozen north for the sunny south It must be rather lovely round Maidstone Aren't you near Canterbury?

5

A most dreadful thing is just going to happen to me My voice is deserting me Everybody most rude. A most uncomfortable situation, but because of watches being switched round, I am getting the weekend off so

41

I hope to go and find it then

Just must give this letter a break as I've a few routine jobs to do

Back later Hurrah, it is almost time to go off watch That is what I like doing best: shaking my relief.

I do hope that you get on at Maidstone alright and if you should ever have a moment I should love to hear from you, but I 'spect you are pretty tired in the evening and don't really feel like writing

And please, any ruderies you might feel about this effort, —————— it is now 0130!

Much love
Ann

PS: How did you manage to spell my name correctly? Not many people do first shot.

Dear Mickey

Let me warn you, as I am writing on the train, I can't promise that the result won't be slightly incoherent But I feel if I don't write tonight, I don't know when I shall as I have no idea as to my future movements beyond this weekend, and there is the possibility that there won't be much time for letters apart from routine B & Bs

This is the Eve of my Fling scheduled to last about a fortnight, or so Spent a very busy day packing and to my immense surprise, found I fit into far smaller (and easier to carry) bags than I had dared hope. I have achieved two small bags which I consider ideal, as compared with (to?) lugging a large suitcase around: kind of distributing the weight equally I'm done if I buy anything at all as bags are strained to bursting and only just do up

I have a sleeper Not such an achievement now, for the Government no longer have the right to reserve 3rd class ones at all and there are more of them There is a vast change travelling now. Trains are about half empty The days of travelling like a sardine in the corridor are practically over. More trains too, and not nearly so late in arriving unless of course there is fog or snow. In fact, life on trains is fast returning to normal.

I plan to spend tomorrow morning in London, and arrive in Surrey for lunch, where I propose to spend the weekend with an ex-wren friend. After that, well, the Gods will provide.

At home, life has been jogging along in the same old rut. My flu family is now fit and thank goodness failed to pass it on to me. I believe in simple masses of fresh air, windows wide open and all that, negative draughts and extreme conditions, of course; – the belief that that kind of atmosphere will kill any likely bug before it begins, so to speak. Whether or not, it remains that I did not catch the Jones' flu, which was all that worried me, as then I couldn't have made this journey.

My sister has just been drafted from Berkshire to Arbroath last weekend, and as she wasn't needed at Arbroath then spent the weekend with us which was all very nice. Sally was overjoyed ——————— a homely little soul who loves nothing better than to have her family around.

Two highlights this week. Last night I went to a play based on Greig. Wonderful, taken just as a musical play, but simply dreadful and creating quite the wrong impression about the man and his life and music. I enjoyed it very much. Thought what they did – very well done, but such a fabrication about the man. A pity.

Went to a Nobs concert, in other words a concert to which everyone who is anyone in Edinburgh's musical world goes. They are exceptional concerts, quite remarkable, simply first rate. I enjoy them awfully. For the music, and it is a joy to meet everyone in the intervals downstairs and see old friends and exchange views Alas there is only one more Only four are given each winter.

I'm sorry Mickey this is such a dull letter —————— has turned out that way but my thoughts are with three hundred and sixty three and three quarter miles away, (the train having gone thirty!) There was a lot to tell anyone but somehow, news all disappeared Oh yes, it is such a joy to have a mother again, in more ways than one, but one in particular

—————————————————————— cooking Dinner at night I no longer have to cope with recalcitrant eggs, trying to make them appear poached, or anything like that Mummy does all that

But I'm not let off Oh no, I am the Table Maid, which means laying and washing everything and reminding Mummy everything that sometimes I think it would be far easier if I did it myself! But Mummy is the whale of a cook, does the most delicious dishes, so perhaps it really is better that way The other night we had pre-war sardines in olive oil, an unheard of thing now. O dear, sooner or later one invariably comes to food A bad thing Mind just isn't concentrating Must turn in now.

Best love
Ann   PS: Hope things are going alright
                        with you

45

Dear Micky

V.M.T.U signal! or have you already   6
forgotten naval language? This is not going to be one of my best efforts 'cos I
was very naughty last night and went out on the spree instead of going to bed
early You see, an old professor friend of mine and his wife asked me to go to
the Reid concert with them, so I went It was a very good concert Being very
kind hearted people they kept their supper back so that I could have it with them
after it was over, a thing I had not allowed for.

Then of course, the train back was late and no transport of any kind back to
the dockyard, so in the pouring rain I had to walk My own fault, I know, but
it was well worth it and I should do it again every time! So barely had I hopped,
or rather climbed into my bunk than I had to get out again Today is going to be
a very busy day, as our new Wren officer is coming to see our quarters so they
must be spick and span, and then I am walking Sally this afternoon and doing
Daddy's dinner later. I would rather have a busy life than otherwise.

I intended to go to a Chamber concert on Thursday evening but one of the
performers fell ill, which really was just as well for me, as they cancelled the
concert As Leary, our "dearly beloved" Signal Officer suddenly found out that we
were not reading our flashing exercises and came down on us like a ton of bricks
- so I had to return to read one.

Can't remember, are you a high brow or not? Me, I am every sort of brow. Just bought two new records, a terrible extravagance really Sur le Pont D'Avignon, Jean Sablon, and the Haiawaiian War Chant, only not the recording I wanted as it is obsolete. It should have been by Felix Mendlesohn, and sung in the native lingo, and sounds like a pig being sick, but I could only get it played by some Canadian band I don't think Daddy quite approves

Another thing I have just bought is a small reproduction of a picture by a modern named Marc. I had one already by him, some Red Horses This one is his Blue Horses Do you know them? They are rather odd, but have tremendous power, and the Red ones are extremely elegant. D.S.S. doesn't approve We are very candid at the D.S.S. I also found a very amusing paint book for children with Fougasse drawings which I certainly shan't give away

I took your camera around on Thursday, only your parents were away I only made the doorbell ring once So I gave it Mr Whats his name who was just recovering from cleaning the boiler, so had a long talk all about them

Have been asking everyone and the position now is that if I work a 48 for someone they will work a 48 for me, so I can get off to spend your 48 with you ? What would be ideal would be if I had Wednesday and Friday off anyway, and someone worked my Thursday, but that will have to wait Anyway I am sure I can have Thursday and Friday if things remain as they are just now. We seem to be remaining in four watches for quite a bit as a relief has turned up

The other day there was voluntary PT. Lord knows why, but we all trooped along It all seemed very easy and rather fun A Chief P.T.I. took us Next morning Oh boy, none of us could move, and it even hurt us to laugh, a very serious state of affairs But I am getting most awfully thin! Do you know, the other day I had four whole inches taken out of my bell bottoms?!

They still fit me

Glad you like the poly I think it is too Mrs Moffish for words, and very dreadful

Is army life very strenuous? I see you have got into the way of putting 0600 hrs where I would write 0600. A very military habit that

Sally is very well and much more under control, though we still have words over the chair We do a lot of walks to gether Last Sunday afternoon we walked for miles over fields and railways until we landed up at Hopetoun

Luckily I had remembered to take some money with me so Sally and I treated ourselves to a bus ride home It was the sort of day for walking A sun, and not too much mud It keeps both of us fit, I hope

I have a pair of socks made from sea boot stocking wool Would they be of any use to you, or don't you wear that sort of thing in the I.A. or do you need them for training over here? I think they are rather nice ones, so if you would like them, just let me know.

Do you ever indulge in Spending Orgies?

I had one the other day, but it was the first since Christmas The outcome was one or two new bits of clothes

At last I have found some thing for Daddy to give me for my last birthday, so gradually I am acquiring more clothes, but the situation is not as good as it might be, but improving vastly I have grown out of most things belonging to Pre Wren life ———————— I mean grown up out of not grown out of

What about yourself. This all seems to be all about my self which is all wrong 'cos this week nothing really interesting has happened to tell you I am dreadfully bad at writing letters 'cos I put down what I am thinking and forget to look them over to see if they are interesting

Did you enjoy that dance? Is there much social life in the evenings, or is it as dull as the dockyard?

When do you sport your white tabs and have dinner at night instead of high tea? That is what amuses Sister Maureen To bring them into the ways of high life the wren cadets are given dinner

If I didn't have night watches I don't know if I would ever write letters Somehow I don't seem to have time during the day, and anyway, it makes the watch fly Are you glad to have left watch keeping? I would rather watch keep and do days It is nice to be off when everyone else is working!

I now have to go below and feed Mrs Sam who is our kitchen range   8
The coal is frightful, all stones and doesn't last long

Gosh love to you Micky   9
                    From Ann

Dear Mickey

How difficult it is to start writing letters again I shall make a start and get my hand in on you! I suppose I'd letter put Cdt on the envelope, or do you mind dreadfully? For I'm sure you are an acting Second Loot by now; only letters take such a time!

Have just returned to roost for a short time before I set off on a final gad The purpose behind all this dashing about is to have a dress made. You see, it is being made in London and for each fitting I make the excuse to go to London An excellent idea, don't you think? The nose is being put to the grindstone very soon, though

I had an extremely nice trip round England visiting five different places in all. Very hectic going in all. While in London, was taken to an Old Vic production for Henry IV Part II. My third Shakespeare ever. Have come to the conclusion that it is a mistake to go to one of his plays without reading it beforehand I went with my cousin and we both experienced much difficulty during the first act Trying to sort out the various people, and find out on whose side they were fighting   All the king's sons seemed alike and so did all the Noble Lords that it was most confusing   Having straightened out everything during the first interval we then found that we enjoyed the play very much   It was as first rate as it could be Laurence Olivier hadn't a very large part but Ralph Richardson was Falstaff, the best ever, so I've heard

In fact well worth seeing Not an enthralling period though, or is that blaspheming?

Otherwise I did the odd cinema There are some quite good films at the moment, and at least one can get in, which you can't to any play

Went for a weekend to a garden city They have their points but I certainly shouldn't like to live in this one as it is a very dead hole. Has no initiative But very pleasant trees, fields, commons, large gardens to houses and municipal ones, galore; but then that is not everything Inadequate shops which I think is bad for a planned town Essential shops, I mean Being built on a rise so a very windy place

Travelled up through the midlands just after all this flooding but I didn't have to swim Just as well as I didn't have my rubber wings There was still much water but mere ponds to what there had been

While I was away, both my parents at different times, met your father in the dentist's waiting room What a place to meet

This morning we are having March winds and

April showers

Next time I hope to write to 2nd Loot

Love Ann

Good Morning to you Mickey,

I think that it is only fair to warn you, this is not going to be a whale of a letter. No, I am not going to drip or any thing like that

A very dull week really Sally and I started out on a walk last weekend, but it became so very cold that we cheated and took a bus back, and shortly after, it began to snow. Daddy wasn't too well and wanted a poached egg for his supper. Have you ever poached an egg? I had once before and it wasn't a success. However, always game, I had a second shot but no sooner than the egg was dropped into the not too vigorously boiling water, the white came away from the yellow and floated about on the top, and had to be scooped out at the end. Have since learned that you do the beastly things in a cup or put vinegar in the water. Have you any theories or does the same thing happen to you. The main thing is that Daddy now feels quite alright.

Couldn't go ashore as early as I wanted to on Monday 'cos we had a com pul sor ary lecture in the educational scheme.   A very Scots parson came to tell us about New Zealand, but he talked to us as if we were all dashing off or had a view to colonise the place. Also he was all for South Island and Mummy is North Island He wasn't too bad really and I managed to sit in the back row and get on very well with some darning and knitting which badly needed seeing to.

When at last I did get ashore and Aunt, Daddy's sister had arrived from Yorkshire They have a farm Very nice 'cos she brought up the etcetera to go with one's pudding and coffee When Family gets together it invariably listens to the Puzzle Corner on Monday Night at 8 on the wireless Between us we managed quite well, the Aunt spotting the DM (deliberate mistake).

Wednesday meant this voluntary PT stunt, so I tootled along again
This time it was not nearly so bad It didn't seem as long and though we were much more energetic, I haven't been a jot stiff since The P T I is rather a dear ——————————— one of the typical navy types all muscle; but makes us do things he knows perfectly well we can't The relay races are best and last time he let us do O'Grady I like O'Grady

As a belated Christmas present from the Aunt, I now have some gramophone records Do you know the Swan Lake ballet music? I haven't for long but am very fond of it and think it is very lovely As a complete contrast, the Façade suite by William Walton That I am not serious about, but think that the orchestration is superb very satirical or so it seems to me One record I must have before I die, and I am going in search of it as soon as I can, is Slaughter on Tenth Avenue, or some such title Ballet music of a kind but rather different It's one of these bits of music that just "gets me".

Went to the Scottish orchestra concert Apart from the Reid last week, which

54

can't really be called a full symphony orchestra; I hadn't been to a proper symphony concert for ages and was looking forward to it Perhaps I expected too much The main work was Dvorak's 4th symphony which is full of folk tune-like themes The 'cellos have much to do and they were rotten Never together and the technique was bad; and the wind was shocking I had thought that they were a fairly good orchestra but now I'm not so sure

The audience wasn't a nice one either The place was packed Always is for a Scottish Orchestra do Utter snobs they were, 'cos they weren't really very interested in the music, only concerned with being seen in the right place at the right time At the end, before the last note had died away, they had all jumped up and were fighting to get away It wasn't late either, only eight thirty So rude Sorry, have I bored you with my views, but I feel rather strongly about it all

Maureen turned up yesterday, a PO. Apparently not reliable enough, or some   10
such phrase However, she has 14 days leave out of it Daddy most awfully pleased to have her back, for we haven't seen much of her for ages and it was her birthday, so they were going to celebrate last night She is getting to be quite an old hag now 22!

David's address is: T, W, H. but we are all agreed that writing letters to him is a waste of time as he never opens them His room is full of our unopened letters Maureen wrote to him saying she would like to go down to see him Never had a reply Sent a postcard When she did arrive he had just remembered having a letter from her, was in too much hurry, and shoved it in his pocket So we have decided, she and I, not to write any more letters to him He himself has said he doesn't appreciate them The only way to establish communication with him is by postcard which he cannot help reading or else by telegram Over something Daddy got so desperate that he sent off one telegram an hour until he had his reply Expensive but effective!.

INT socks —————————   (sorry about the blot)

The lights in the quarters have fused so it won't be very easy cleaning this morning after we come off watch Daylight isn't light enough at 0800. Doing the breakfast by torchlight is no fun either, and for the wrens who sleep in curlers! —————————

According to a wren who has just come from Tees, your late ship has gone there to be broken up How true this is I don't know. There are all sorts of buzzes just now about the remaining two.

If and when you do get your 48, surely you won't feel like doing anything energetic after travelling all night, or will you? How did you come to strain your leg? Are you sure that you're not overdoing it?

I find that I write all my letters only every eight days Somehow, at no other time is there so much peace and anyway it is an excellent way of keeping awake Actually I do this watch every fourth day, but we take it in turns to get our heads down so it works out to every eighth, which isn't too bad Only another hour to go until I shake my relief for breakfast

Hurrah.

Love from Ann   PS: I never say anything I shouldn't

Dear Mickey

These are the socks I hope they are alright I have my doubts though They may be too long in the foot If so, don't hes it ate to return them, and I can chop the required off and put in an other toe They may of course be a trifle harsh, but I know from experience that that wool washes quite soft

This is not a letter writing watch but I am so sleepy that I must keep awake somehow. Only another fifty minutes, then my bunk for five hours I am in a sort of letter writing mood 'cos I've just written a long one to Mummy who hasn't been at all well I am sure she's been over doing things, but her CO has taken a strong line, and put her to bed!

Did some sea time today from the basin to Burntisland I can't really tell you much about it in a letter 'cos of security, but it wasn't in a very common type of BOAT. Not being British, they let us do the signalling It didn't last very long and fortified with a cup of coffee in a famous destroyer we had to dash for the bus to take us back, as one or two had to return to duty I think that is why I'm so sleepy, a morning spent in the open We have a new Wren Officer, and she seems to have her head screwed on the right way, 'cos she broke a time honoured rule, and let us go aboard in bell bottoms Usually we just have to wear skirts which are most inconvenient for climbing these beastly perpendicular ladders.

Maureen is still hanging around. She is on something or other leave which means she is marking time at home until they find a billet for her

We are all sixes and sevens just now. Various people are ill, or on compassionate leave and were just on the verge of dreaded three watches when two leave reliefs were fished out from somewhere, so we breath again. After doing various odd jobs and dashing down to shake my oppo, it is almost time 11 for me to turn in So if there is anything else I'll finish this when I do up the socks.

I've been insulted I've sent nine 13½ collars to the laundry. Admittedly I got nine back, but into my fold of 13½ there has been let loose a black sheep Someone at the laundry thinks my neck is 14½! What on earth can I do with a 14½ Tomorrow I must beard the laundry to give it back and to try and regain my own, which I think will be a fruitless quest unless the 14½ on realising after a frantic fifteen minutes of trying to make my collar meet round his neck that he has not increased in girth, or that his collar has shrunk, returns mine to the laundry Mine is named His is not.

    Well Good Night   Here is my Oppo

Friday afternoon watch

Sorry, they were still damp yesterday when I went ashore. Had a tremendous bit of luck As I passed the local fish monger I spotted some fresh herring roe Just adore it, hadn't had it for ages, and as the little man was surprisingly

58

generous, there was enough for Maureen and me to have for supper before going to a concert My leading hand and I are finishing them off tonight Lemons are around too, so for a week I am living in luxury and sticking them in my tea

The concert was extremely good, our old choir, and the strings of the Reid I had never heard the choir from an audience before, and was amazed to hear how good they were. Met many old friends whom I hadn't seen for almost two years   Must fly now.   Will write a proper letter later This is not one — only an enclosure written at odd times

Love Ann

3rd March 1945

Dear Mickey

Just a note to confirm Thursday What I think is best is this You say you arrive very early and may go to bed With luck I can get home about 0900, and shall I ring you then to find out what and when is happening If I don't hear to the contrary then that is what I shall do Will you be up by 0900, or shall I make it later

Have had a hectic and quite mad week Someone I trained with at Cabbala came up on leave and together we climbed the Pentlands, up a very steep bit There was a terrific gale blowing on top that we couldn't possibly stand up Another time, we went up Arthur's Seat Have you ever been up I have always felt that one day I should, and now I've accomplished it There was a gale blowing that day too

Maureen is still at home awaiting a draft Officially her leave ended yesterday, but she hasn't yet been told to where she is to report

Did you get the parcel

This is not a proper letter as I feel all-in Am taking French Leave this morning and going home to spend the morning in bed You see, not supposed to leave the place until 1200, but I see no point in hanging around here till then, when I could be in bed, so off I'm going

We have a new 2/O and RPO. They are dreadful

R

60

Masses of new orders of lists Efficiency with a capital E. Quite unnecessary as we were most well behaved before This will change the atmosphere of the place, and not for the better Please, I'm not dripping.

Since last night we now possess six cats One of ours has just had four kittens We were all very dubious about the whole affair, as last time, she made a mess of the proceedings, but this time she has managed very well It means a funeral though, as we can't keep them all Tiddles, the other cat is amazed with the kittens, and spends hours watching them She, or as we now strongly suspect, he, has never seen kittens before and is intrigued with the smallness of them

Later Sorry, didn't manage to finish this on watch My French leave was most successful Spring is here We can even boast two rhododendrons in flower and the violets are doing well My utility pen is making a nuisance of itself as usual It isn't entirely its fault as it has been dropped once or twice on its nib Sally sends her love.

See you on Thursday then

Love Ann

Dear Mickey,

This is a great day for us Though it was my day ashore, owing to a tennis match, I was spending the night here at DSS. About midnight, awakened by the most terrific din

Was definitely not amused Then I heard V's on various ships sirens,   13
and I knew.   13 Everyone went completely mad Flashing every available light, and sounding every hooter they could get hold of

<u>Aug 22 - 0430</u> I'm glad I was over in DSS. when it happened, for they didn't know at home until the following morning Edinburgh was very noisy I believe But it was fun here Everyone so happy, presumably at the thought of not having the Japs to fight, if and when they do go East Does the end of the war make any difference to you, or do you still have to finish your training and serve for so long Will Malcolm see India at all We've had no further word about our releases, except in VS groups one   14
to forty nine are going out in a month or two. I alas am far further than forty nine. However as long as they leave me here, I shall be quite content Life goes on much the same as usual Expect to depart on leave to Argyll within a day or two

It's very dreadful of us, but we are almost praying for rain, so as there will be plenty of water in the river for us There will need to be quite a bit for time.

David is due back from his school harvest camp any day now Poor lamb, he only gets half a holiday, but it should have been extremely nice in Hampshire during August

Did you enjoy your trip out or were the monsoons most unpleasant? Still, you will be up in the hills, won't you? How much longer do you remain a cadet?

This is not a frightfully interesting letter, I'm afraid, but honestly my life has just ambled on – there is nothing at all to tell you Dawn is breaking and I see the most unpleasant morning I've seen for ages Normally I don't mind the rain, but this morning I have to go to Edinburgh for a family lunch, and it is most unpleasant to arrive damp and unable to change

By the way, is it alright if I send these 1½d affairs to this address, as I believe they go much quicker Do let me know I hate letters to take time, longer than is necessary I expect you've noticed, this letter has been slightly held up So sorry and all that That "V" night instead of remaining in to do odd jobs, we went out round the yard to see what was what All rather dull really, except that we ended up in W/T office of a destroyer 15 with extremely naval cups of tea, and you know what that's like Then I've had Thank you Letters to write, and as you know, they take priority! However, as usual, I'm getting squared up on my morning watch, hence the dreadful scrawl and spelling Our watches have been changed and we do solidly from

63

2000 until 0800, which is a bit of a strain. One gets one's head down for an odd hour or so. Our Signal Lieutenant is going and the new one arrives today. For better or worse? It could hardly be worse, in fact it would be almost impossible, but then, these things do happen.

Best love
Ann

at Lodge, Argyll   4 - 9 - 45

Dear Mickey,

Many thanks for your air letter I received it the day I unofficially began my leave, and there not being a post office for miles, I cannot reply on one So I hope this doesn't take much longer It has been a glorious leave right from the start We motored over Daddy driving one car and Mummy the other We raced and Mummy and I beat Daddy and David who were in a very much smaller car, but we gave them a very large start from Edinburgh Maureen joined us the very next day Conditions were ideal for fishing but somehow the fish just weren't having any You remember the netting We had a day of it on a very much larger scale up the Loch, and did quite well It is a very much bigger net Over one draw we tore it practically in two, but someone had some string so we were able to patch it up again

I went through to Edinburgh for the weekend to see a friend of mine on leave The weather was as hot as the day we went to Roslyn, so we were not frightfully energetic One day we spent in the Rumbling Bridge area Have you ever been there? I love it and the villages have such lovely names, such as Crook of Devon Devon being the name of the river Somehow it doesn't sound very Scottish, does it We covered miles on foot, but took the train to Kinross and back

Another trip we did was to Dryborough Abbey Though I've passed through the

Borders heaps of times by car and by train, I've never actually been there. It was heavenly there.

It is the only abbey in Scotland, so the guide said, with Lebanon Cedars, planted about six or more hundred years ago. Sir Walter Scott and Earl Haig are buried there. It was all most interesting and we had a picnic lunch almost where the monks used to feed. Edinburgh was just unbearable that weekend, so I'm glad we were of one mind to escape to the country. I must say, I'm not awfully fond of towns, I do so like being here much better.

The sail over from Gourock last night was delightful and today couldn't be better, except all our water has been cut off ————————
a monthly nuisance while the pipe is cleaned. Most inconvenient. Frantic dashes to the burn for a drink!

Alas, there just is no fishing just now, no water in the river, so we are having an extraordinarily lazy time.

Family is on the loch at the moment sailing yachts and I am having an attempt at catching up on my correspondence which falls into abeyance during leave.

Am going through to Edinburgh tomorrow for a concert as the Liverpool Philharmonic Orchestra is coming up. But only for the one concert as the other two don't interest me very much. Then I shall return first thing the following morning. My leave will soon be over. I have been very lucky and have had seventeen days, how the first watch at D.S.S. will irk, then I'll be again in the ruts, and this glorious leave will be a dream – a lovely dream in the past

You seem to be having a reasonably pleasant time Does the end of hostilities mean anything to you, or do you dash off and occupy Japan
Demobilisation is being quickened up VS wrens up to group 49 are going out now and according to buzz other wrens will soon follow. Whether that means me I have not the slightest idea I think they want to replace us with men to alleviate the over-crowding in Depot, but then they just change our category to something more useful

"Havelock" is still around, but I don't see anything of anyone on board her. Do you remember the argument we had about a cruiser East of Bridge I was right It was neither of the training cruisers, but a sister ship

Love Ann

Dockyard Signal Station   19 - 9 - 45

Dear Mickey,

Here am I, back to the Navy, and oh what a difference to when I went away. I told you we had a new Signal Officer? Naturally he has instituted several changes. Also several people have left under the release scheme and there was a host of new bods. Very nice, came back to find myself as a watch keeping day man, a peach of a job. All night in and twenty four on and off. Alas, as with all jobs of that nature it did not last very long as still another wren was released and for the moment I have taken over her watch. But the Sig Lt has very definite ideas and is changing the watches around, so I don't know how long I'll hold it down.

Terrific tragedy. My garden has died on me. I don't know what caused it, but while I was on leave, everything had turned black and died. I don't suppose I'll be here next year to give it another try. And my michaelmas daisies were doing so well, I was going to have a lovely Autumn show. been looking forward to it all summer in fact. While at lodge came through for the Liverpool Philharmonic Orchestra's concert, but was rather disappointed by it. The Usher Hall, as usual when there is a fairly good (by repute) orchestra, was packed and there was a good crit next morning in The Scotsman. Notwithstanding it was not a very good concert. Adequate though, and in spite of what I've said, it was worth the journey.

I've been to Roslin again and have come to the shattering conclusion that the dungeons are not dungeons, 'cos if they are, then they are pretty comfortable ones for these days. I'm sure they would not have supported prisoners and the like so near to the kitchens. Any way, that is my theory, so I shan't be at all surprised if you disagree. Linlithgow Palace had a horrible system. You were lined up. When you had worked up from number six to number one, you were popped down a dark hole beneath the floor and just left. Number two then became number one, and he going down when starvation and rats had done you in. Most unpleasant I should think.

Are you so busy training that you never have time to write, for I'm beginning to find this correspondence a trifle one sided. What happens to you when you are fully trained? Do you sit out there until your release is due, or do you just serve so many years?

I have a cousin somewhere in the wilds of India, British Army, who is doing jungle training and how very stiff it seems to be. To me, one drawback about India is the snakes. Does one get acclimatised to them, I wonder.

David goes back to school this week. I have seen quite a lot of him this time, for usually I am doing three watches or something like that when he is around; but this time I had my very long leave, and every other day besides. The harvest camp he was at seems to have been fun, but very hard work. Argylls, who is usually so behind everyone else, was at most a month ahead this year. The Lothians are very late. The weather wasn't too sunny to speed things up Then there was a gorgeous period which speeded everything until a terrific thunder plump one day.

Now, dawn having broken I must "Away" and clean all the R - - - - windows of the tower. As this has not been done for some time it will take longer than usual which is a nuisance.

Much love

Ann

Sent to me via Grindlays Bank. Thence to Bangalore.

(?) October 45)

270103 (?)

Dear Mickey,

Since I wrote last, letters have been pouring in fast and furious from India
Many thanks. That was a lovely long letter which arrived during a very
letterless period of mine I think I must have been a little bit in the dumps when
I last wrote. Tell me before I forget, 'cos I've been meaning to ask you — Do I
still write to your bank address, or now to Bangalore?

The first thing that struck me when I saw that menu you sent was, how odd to
be able to have the whole lot if you want to, and not "either/or" as it still is
here. The other day when I was having a meal out, they would not let me have a
double ices, so that my supper would come to five bob Shame I thought, so did CD.
who also wanted a double one That is a dodge we learnt at The Aperitif one evening

Do you have newspapers with home news? We've been having the most terrible
gales Lifting haystacks and the like. In Ireland, houses were lifted around
So at home we were really very lucky to lose only part of a tree, though we had
the telephone wires blown down Most inconvenient

People say, just give me a ring about this and that, forgetting you can't
The telephone people are being very slow about restoring them I almost miss

my buses too, do I rely too much on "Tim" the clock, 952 The harvest also was blown about It certainly is not nearly all led The weather has been all against the farmer There was a lovely spell, and they went full ahead, but since then has been much rain, that they cannot get the stooks properly dried Leaves are falling now too I don't know if the swallows have left As I write, there should be a lovely harvest moon, but it is cloudy tonight, and very black

Fearful humiliation the other morning As usual I caught my naval ferry from Hawes Pier Went below to the cabin Two minutes out the boat gave a frightful lurch Had driven on to a sandbank Everyone dashed for'd Propeller buzzed madly round and nothing happened Dashed aft Still no movement Leant to Port, then Starboard but could not shift her We were sitting in two feet of water when the boat takes eight There we were a few yards from the pier and completely marooned The civilian ferry was plying backwards and forwards, and still we were in the same position I bet the civilians laughed when they saw the redoubtable Royal Navy stuck for a few feet of water It would have taken ages to have floated her, but luckily a motor launch came by and took us off But I was extremely late back and not missed at all!

This is a silly pad, isn't it, 'cos I daren't write on the reverse side, as it shows through, but as I was somehow donated it, I thought I might as well use it up

I faced the camera the other day, so if the result is a success I may send you one, but I shan't know for some time, as they take ages to develop, and if it is not a success, shan't send one at all

Your training seems to me to be under the expression Top Hole It must be rather fun, really, though it is tough going Do you pig stick?

Sally, silly dog is loosing her coat, fast and furious – all over the house and all of us With the cold weather imminent, you'd think she'd make all haste to grow her winter one Not a bit of it, and I am afraid that soon I shall have to lead a completely bald dog around, which I shan't enjoy a bit

David has gone back to school again, so the house is a bit quieter But not for so very long as we are expecting my Mama back daily It will be nice to have an ordered household again

The Navy has brought out a new kind of Kai which is in block form, but perfectly pleasant to eat raw. Not being too sweetened one eats masses, far too much really

Most probably will write next 2 – 8 watch

Love

Ann

Dockyard Signal Station 0300 - 9 - 11 - 45

Dear Mickey,

Is it an age since I last wrote, I cannot remember. As my entire correspondence has been held up, I rather think it must be. One piece of news which for me dominates all the rest is Mummy's demobilisation. She came out just when our Jenny left to be married, so ever since, for the past weeks my life has been one round of housework. I must say after a bit, I found it most wearing to do twenty four hours duty here, then twenty four at home. Daddy was a perfect lamb and did all the heavy work with the boiler. He developed a craze for porridge and I am now a porridge maker? To my eternal joy it never went lumpy on me, nor did I forget the salt. But it was an effort to get up early enough each morning to prepare the beastly stuff. Our combined housekeeping was really great fun, and we had a vast amount of amusement from it, but thank God it has ended now, and my life has more or less returned to normal, therefore giving me time to do everything I should do such as; well, writing letters.

My Navy has come all over Peace Time. They have the cracked idea that there is no longer any fighting and have settled to Peace Time Routine, the great point being one weekend a month, known as a Friday While. A delightful term don't you think! So I was able to go with family to the lodge for the last weekend of the fishing season. One heavenly Saturday morning Mummy and I drove out. It was a real joy to be alive. I have never seen Loch Lomondside in Autumn before. One of these cases where only seeing is believing. The sun shining on the coppery tints and all reflected in the water. There was every conceivable brown and gold, and a heavenly blue sky. The Lodge was looking marvellous. Spent a delightful afternoon on the river but as usual, alas no fish! Of course it got dark very early, such a bore. As if to spite us, Sunday was terrible. It poured and poured. Sally was disgusted, and rightly so. There was no pleasure in going for a walk. Mummy and I recovering from our household exertions stayed indoors all day, and found most wonderful stations on the wireless, all decent music. We came back on Monday, another glorious day. Loch Fyne was unbelievable, so still and lovely. Have you ever been to the Highlands in Autumn. It is all rather like chocolate box pictures but oh so much nicer.

Mummy and I spent two nights at the ballet. Now a confirmed ballet fan! I don't see how anyone couldn't be, it was so absolutely first rate and beautifully done that even if ballet itself is not liked, the whole thing was first class. You know it is lovely having a mother again to do all those things with permanently. Have been concert going madly. There have been some excellent ones recently. At some concerts, I met many people who, if it wasn't for these gatherings I would lose trace of completely.

It is the most perfect morning still, with masses of stars. Do you see stars at all? Somehow one doesn't, at least I don't associate stars with India; or should it be India with stars? G.M.T. is a bore as it gets dark so early It really has been a wonderful autumn Many trees still have a vast amount of leaves If you remember, usually by this time there has been such a succession of gales, that the country is quite desolate Not a bit of it this year I adore my sea trip from Queensferry to the Dockyard all the more on days like these. Farmers have got well ahead with their ploughing but not so lucky with the potato lifting as there have been a few damp days, so they have to wait until they dry for fear of rotting in the pits I don't quite get your reference re birthdays I had mine months ago.

Do you mind if I keep those stamps that you sent, as I collect them too, and you know, we collectors are a most unscrupulous lot Thank you very much for sending them It was awfully good of you to think of it and to take the trouble I haven't yet come across your friend Jim B , but I know he is still around as we know his signalman rather well on the telephone.

Things seem to be happening now, so I must stop Much love

Ann

Dear Mickey,

Thanks very much for your long letters. Before I forget must ask you to cancel my 19 - 9 - 45. I remember now I was in what you call a very bad mood when I wrote it which I shouldn't have done then

I have decided to take a spot of leave next week, as it will be my last before I am demobbed Hope to sting the Government for a warrant to Winchester, 'cos I want to go to see David I love Winchester Old things fascinate me Mummy and I are alike in that respect among many others

Life continues to be much the same except that it is much colder But not as cold as last year Trees are still tenaciously clinging to their leaves Dreadful fog the last two days Yesterday the Home Fleet sailed out and no one the wiser Then East of the Bridge a dreadful noise was heard The H.F. all letting down their anchors They had changed their minds It is grim working in a fog 'cos we can do nothing and never know where the ships are and have to keep refusing signals

My placid, almost cow like life is almost at an end After my leave I depart on an E.V.T. course I wanted to do one on horticulture, only there is no such thing so they are sending me on an agricultural one instead! Though how much can be learnt on two pigs and a hen with chicks I can't imagine That is the full extent of the Navy's livestock The camp is just north of the M.T.E, so I shan't be billeted anywhere dreadful It will be a change to have every night in, and complete weekends off

The only things I seem to have had time for recently, have been odd concerts. There have been some excellent ones. I go to as many as I can, but often I can't get over – they seem to be on the wrong day, but people are very good about working for me so as to let me away.

They are increasing the rations for Christmas I suppose it all seems very trivial to you, but it means an awful lot to us Even the Nutty ration is to be increased Otherwise restrictions still go on There is one relaxation, you may now lawfully go into a shop and come out with your purchase, whatever it is, all wrapped up in nice clean new brown paper! The dining car has returned on long distance trains but I'm told they rook you terribly for meals It is a break in the journey to trot along and look at fresh faces I think

Something sure was wrong with you if you fail to eat whatever it was, I hope you've lost it by now.

I expect I'll be going to badminton next holidays, David is very keen that I should I suppose I'll see Heda there

Had a letter today addressed to Ordinary Wren A.   am not amused (Don't you dare).

My gramophone record has grown by leaps and bounds Months ago for my birthday Daddy ordered some and they've arrived just about three months late But I'm awfully pleased with them

All the best Mickey and have a good time
A———————————————

the lodge,   Argyll   3 - 1 - 46

Dear Mickey,

I feel it is some time since I wrote. Life is so hectic at the moment, and one has just come to an end – the only one I know. Thank you for all your letters. I don't think there was any point to answer, I hope not, as I haven't them with me.

A very happy Christmas to you, and all the best to you in the New Year. I am afraid this will arrive a trifle late.

Maureen has achieved Christmas leave and the whole family is out here for New Year, – the first time we ever have been together for it over here. We came out on Friday to find sun, and it as mild as possible. A delightful sail over the Clyde, met over here by Daddy with the car and driven up.   It was warm enough on Saturday morning to sit in the sun, but the wretched thing sets just after two o'clock. Sunday was not a like day, terrific frost, and extremely cold, so different to the last two days, roads very icy, and I believe there were many accidents through the country and today, terrific reports of fog though there is none in our valley. It is so wonderfully isolated, and lovely log fires on in the house. We spent Christmas in Edinburgh, where it was incredibly mild. Alas I cannot go to badminton this year. There are very few courts, and the players split into two groups. But there are still the

MacVitie feasts. McV's still do us pretty well

For the three weeks before Christmas I was on an E.V.T. course in agriculture and the fortnight before that on leave. I went south, looked up old friends, and joined the whole family at Winchester. It was simply glorious in Hampshire, though a slight nip in the air.

Visual signalling is now a thing of the past for wrens, so if it hadn't been for Christmas I would be a civilian by now. As it is, I have to go to Rosyth tomorrow to be demobbed unless at the eleventh hour they will let me stay on. My fate will then be sealed and I shall tell you all about it next letter.

I hope you have had a wonderful Christmas. I started a letter to you in time, but with so much happening I don't believe it was ever finished. This past month has been simply hectic, and I 've appreciated very much the rest out here. Sally is loving being here, her paradise.

My agriculture course was the best thing I have ever done. Extremely interesting and the rest of the class were an extremely nice lot. All matelots! One nice part was that we were not confined all the time to the classroom.

David and Maureen are trying to play piano duets, but every now and again fearful hiatus' while they sort themselves out. It is most painful. There they are, each playing away, completely different parts of the same symphony, and Mummy busy typing on my right. We are a noisy family when all together.

I do hope it snows when we go back. There has been snow on the hilltops here, but that is no good to anyone.

Everyone becoming very gay, with this, the first peacetime Hogmanay. I wonder are you keeping it. Quite frankly we are not.

At the moment I have been pushed out on leave, as owing to my course I was not demobbed with the rest of the station. Life at D.S.S. had its moments, and we did have fun together. Also there were various perks.

David has shot up, grown absolute inches since last winter.

Don't be in too much hurry to return, even though the war has been over for some time, things are almost still as they were and with not much hope of improvement in the near future. In spite of various things, India must be quite fun. You do seem to be getting about and having quite a gay time. Will Malcolm be going out soon to join you. It is rather dreadful, but I haven't seen anything of your family since you left. I may see something of Heda these holidays, though.

My future is extremely vague, I just don't quite know at the moment what it is to be, definitely in the horticultural world, that I think is certain. But anything may happen. Are you still booked for the family office, or will you be able to busy somewhere, with an odd animal or so? Or become a tea planter for, as I said, you won't find this country the same, if you have been away. Oh I know the thought of green fields is wonderful, but one cannot live on sentiment. Must away to bed, the hour being 2300. Best wishes to you Mickey ————————

with love from Ann

Dear Mickey,

You can have no idea how busy a civilian's life is I hope you remarked the large X by the crest I was, after much humming and hawing finally discharged on Wednesday 9th and am now on my 56 days leave — an Acting Unpaid civilian I returned from Argyll to a week's stooging in Wrens Reg while they found out details of E.V.T., but at the end of it all, demobilisation for one Wren A.   I'm neither sorry nor glad It had to come some time anyway During that week I had to live here and it was a dreadful rush to get over there in time each morning and worse still, finding transport back at night But life still is pretty chaotic. Running round after family Went to an excellent ball on Friday in aid of the Lothians and Border Horse in the Freemasons Hall The buffet was superb Quite dream like All sorts of visions to remind us of pre-war times Let us hope they have come here to stay Things are still very restricted, though I did have a bar of chocolate wrapped up in silver paper the other day

We got up a party, and went to the Ice show at the Empire Really it was as all other ice shows, some very good skating there was An excellent bit off ice there was in the middle, some very good clowns Jack Hulbert has been here with Bobby Howe.

Is this boring for has your family told you of the current shows? I haven't seen them at all David can't have been in the same badminton lot as Heda It went well the night we went, and we enjoyed it very much, but many people have not A topical kind of show.

What sort of New Year did you have? Ours at the lodge was very quiet I travelled back on New Years Day, but there was not much doing thank goodness When I arrived here, I found Esse, boiler and cook all out, and had to set to, clean the flues of the beastly things, do the ashes and relight _____ and was I amazed when they both went first time?!

Sally and I went for the usual up the Almond walk this afternoon Everything is much the same as ever It was one of those lovely afternoons, sun, and sharpness in the air It is really comparatively mild still, for January, Jasmine doing very well, and we have some snow drops out Better still the Pullets have started to lay

It all seems very final, on Thursday I collected my ration card and Identity Card That has made my demob seem all very definite, ———

most of all it certainly is not all milk and honey being at home all the time, oddly enough. Soon I am going away, most probably to the south for a short time. To stay here and there with different friends and after that will stick my toes in and settle down to hard work.

David wants me to make up a four baller at golf next Tuesday. Am undecided as I have not played for simply years. And he and his pals have, still it will be rather fun. There is some hope if I'm allowed to play with Michael Pentland.

At the moment am very busy trying to find some clothes. A grateful Government gives me ample coupons but £12 . 10/-! Clothes finding isn't too easy either and shoes is still the end.

What a difference it does make and how one does notice the lengthening of the days. It is so depressing when the curtains are drawn before tea time. I'm very conservative about that. Don't like curtains drawn ever. So shutting in.

I am trying to go to more concerts now. Went to one last night in the Usher Hall, but I am rather ashamed to say, was reduced to a dreadful state by finding a complete group of gum-chewers in the organ gallery opposite. What is more, they chewed in time.

One snag about leaving D.S.S. is that I now have many of the D.S.Sites to write to. My letter list has grown so considerably, in fact in leaps and bounds recently, and I do try to keep it to a minimum so as to be able to write to everyone fairly often

Hope your course is going alright. Best of luck to you in all exams and, do Pass. Let me know, won't you?

Love Ann

Barnton
20 - 1 - 46

Dear Mickey

What on earth possessed me to buy this paper I cannot think but I regret that having it, I shall have to use it. Anyway, it's most distinctive except that I've used up all the envelopes!

How very nice to have had such a terrific leave. How many miles did you cover? Not unlike a cousin of mine in Washington who had ten days leave. She took four days to get to wherever she was going had two days there, then took the other four to return.

You are lucky to have some friends around That makes all the difference I think, to have somewhere to go where you can be civilised Do you know anyone in Bangalore, or is life there far too busy I suppose just now, while I write, things will be beginning to get hectic.

This winter is going all wrong It has been as cold as it could, but no

88

snow. Then there was a fall of snow but by that time there was a thaw on Now it is freezing hard but alas no snow!

The life of a civilian is most uneventful I shall be glad when I start to do something definitely Not that I am idle by any manner of means, oh dear me no. The days have far too few hours I find This week has been taken up solely with repairs to my civilian wardrobe. A most boring task but one which must be dealt with Two years accumulation there was but things are normal now, thank goodness

I sincerely hope that David is safely back at Winchester Do you remember last years last night party? This time we intended to go to the Cramond Inn, but at the last moment it was discovered that they Always close on a Thursday, so it ended up in the downstairs Grill at the N.B, at the usual table. I rather think that it was your ex-nurse who was our waitress

Only one High Spot this week Went to the Reid Concert last night It was a Tchaikovsky night, and the orchestra acquitted themselves very well

_____ for the Reid Afterwards went to have a meal at The St Giles but most unfortunate night Everything was "off" except for some rather nice fish Being an international day it was extremely difficult to move in Edinburgh at all, so really we were very lucky We even had to forego our lunch at the N.B, an ancient institution, why bless me, Men and Boys we (family) have always had this lunch every Saturday, without fail But family went to the match, the best they've seen for ages It was the Kiwis v. Scotland, and we won By what, I'm not sure, but I expect someone who understands these things will tell you

Sally has now decided to sit on my knee which makes things most awkward, as I always write on my knee, so I have to balance this on her back and it wobbles At the moment I'm in the warmest spot in the house Sitting on a small stool with the hot water pipes to support my back And listening to my nicest records on the gramophone I've had to come off getting new ones for some time while I hit myself up David has decided to start, so we are having great fun finding ones which he wants The T.T.R. train has been going hard all holidays. He and Michael worked out a most complicated system

Are you managing to take any photographs and can you now get over the paper difficulty? Things are still much the same, except that silver paper has reappeared

It seems to have developed into a very dull letter So sorry, but there, you know civilian life is My trip south is scheduled to start in ten days time. Whether it will ever materialise, I just don't know, but I hope it will as it will be my last trip for simply ages

Ha, lunch time at last

Much love

Ann

(Was this meant to be 1946 too?) 25 - 1 - 45

Dear Micky,

You are a pet to write twice so quickly I fully appreciate that from your end there will be a slight stoppage Reversing the tables in fact, like me last December, when I was deep in cows and pigs and things and just had no moments So I hope there will be a steady stream from this side This time next week I shall be journeying southward for a final fling

before settling down for good and all

How on earth do you know I have a mania about stamps Thanks awfully for sending that Victory one. I take turns in collecting stamps and records Now both most expensive hobbies I find

I can't believe what you say about those socks. Between you and me and the G.P. I am very surprised that they ever were wearable as they were the first ones I had ever tried I'm glad they are doing you so well

The other morning to my joy I woke up to find a white world Everything seemed perfect Quite three inches   Foresaw fun on the toboggan. Alas, the thermometer refused to cooperate. 32 - 33 degrees there were, and so it was no good Only froze late at night, with a complete thaw the following day How I wished for a day like the ones we had last year They were fun It may come later, but I wonder. Very much milder just now, especially after all this frost

Everyone is going down with flu, and Sally and I spent a very busy day doing shopping for different households. It was rather fun, and my bicycle resembled very much that of an errand boy's. It has a large basket which was completely filled. What terrified me were some eggs, but thank goodness I was able to hand them over unbroken, though there had been some very nasty near misses!

I can't think why that letter was postmarked January 3 as I posted it on Monday 31st. A very good idea is yours about numbering our letters. I think I have received them all. You told me next to nothing about your monkey. What do you call it and will you be able to hang on to it? I wonder what Sally would say to one. She is in great form, though we still have words over differences of opinion. Today I knew she would be miserable if I left her in the house even though for ten minutes but she wasn't so pleased to come when she discovered it was raining and defied me by not going faster than a trot which was maddening as I didn't want to get unnecessarily wet. I was on my bike and it is the usual thing for her to canter. She is so sweet when she is determined.

Practically all my week has been taken up with repairs, in fact I seem to have done nothing else since my liberation. Yes, next Friday I catch the night train, and spend the weekend with an ex-wren friend in Surrey. Then I'm not very sure what I shall do, but I shall be away for about a fortnight I think. See everyone I haven't seen for simply donkey's years.

To entertain a wren took her to see Valley of Decision - a new film I didn't want to go in the slightest. It was one of those lovely clear, frosty and sunny days – just ripe for a walk, but she wasn't that kind, so we went, me in a not-too-good mood for filmgoing. That I thoroughly enjoyed it shows you how good it was. A really excellent film, yankee admittedly, but one of their best. If it should ever be your way, do go.

I hope that by now you've had an odd letter or so from me. I've been writing fairly frequently this year. I shall understand silence on your part, but one thing do let me know what happens to you, where you are, and your rank.

Love   Ann

PS: Best of luck in all exams

24 - 1 - 46

Dear Mickey

For goodness sake; don't think that I shall always write weekly! It is just that I have an odd moment in which to write to someone and I don't know when I'll next have a chance of writing

I met your father last Tuesday, who told me more about Hopes It sounds really delightful

I'm not going back to college just now, maybe not for the whole term That settles itself later, but I shall definitely go back next summer

I don't know why I am writing I really have no news. Haven't done a thing last week 'cos I was tied to a sofa Me! To tell the truth it nearly killed me but I celebrated my freedom this morning by going around the Botanic Gardens The sun was shining and one or two lovely little rock plants were in flower and I felt that Spring is not so very far away We are having an anticyclone at the moment One moment mild, then it is so cold and ice everywhere I'm glad I'm not at college as I think it would be very damp But think of the lecture notes I'll have to write up! An appalling thought.

Little Sally is the same as ever   Oh yes, I know, do you know, I wasn't allowed to go to the rugger trial or for the walk? As it happed, the team won 24-0 and it was all rather boring whereas I listened to a most exciting match on the wireless between England and Wales 9-6. Quite the most thrilling for a long time Hope to have last week's walk this Sunday instead One of those perfect days, tho cold the sun is shining and it is very pleasant

I don't suppose I'll feel like writing next week, or the week after but may have to out of sheer boredom. You won't mind a letter under these circumstances? Ann

PS: Have found the missing letter, so thought I would send it, if only to complete the series. Am still in bed, though may get up soon. Hey me. Still deep snow everywhere. A.

Dear Mickey

How time seems to fly No sooner do I write, so it seems, than there is a letter from you and it is weeks later, and I find you are now a Second Loot Congratulations and my very best wishes to you How well you remember my line of scarves Thank you very, very much, for sending me such a gay one It now takes Pride of Place over all others And for the stamps I haven't found anyone else with them yet

The wild oats are sown and germinating (I hope). Meanwhile, I have started my training to be a gardener This entails going every morning 9-12, to the library of the R.B.G. to read, the idea being to know many weird and wonderful ideas I hate the mornings as the library is a stuffy hole, the librarian being an old maid —————————— he is a man? And it is never less than 65° which gives me an awful head But the afternoons more than make up for the mornings I join a squad and do whatever the men are doing There are no other girls at the moment They are all perfectly sweet, many of them ex service and we deal famously together So, for the moment, anyway, I like it very much indeed

Was about to have my nightly hot bath, which warms me up before bed, when I find the water is cold as the fire has been let out in anticipation of the sweep first thing tomorrow. So it is a rather cold Ann, sitting in a huddle in bed, trying to warm up before I go to sleep, who is writing to you I do most of my writing in bed now, as it appears to be the only time which I have to myself when I am left to myself. At the moment my Mama is away, so I have all the housekeeping and shopping to do, so as a rule, I don't get finished until late at night. The maids are always wanting something usually when I'm late in the morning or else when I am doing something else, so nothing ever is finished Such is life

———————————————   !

Winter is technically over now, for who can say that it is winter when the buds begin to move, and the Spring Flowers are out? Croci have been out for ages, and today I picked quite a bunch of daffodils Can find no one else what has I think these ones are exceptionally early Came upon some Scillas unexpectable and they were lovely I adore their. blue so they were picked and bowl arranged for them containing every available spring flower Our violets are out, but oh, what a tedious job picking them Worth it, though, for all their small size for they can be smelt far away Alas, for besides these things growing so are the weeds, and the grass One or two rhododendrons and primulas are out Are you in their country at all?

I went to Culross yesterday It is the most fascinating village; do you know it at all? Rarely a house more modern than 1671, and just full of James VI. Houses he stayed in Places he visited Things he did Mercifully most of it now is controlled by the National Trust, and they are saving many of the old buildings.

Saw a most handsome blackbird the other day, at least I took him to be a blackbird. He had a yellow beak and feet, and his feathers seemed predominantly green, with a bluey tinge, at least the tips were, in fact, he was a very handsome fellow.

Tell me, are you keeping up with your drawing. India must be full of things to sketch and paint.

Mickey, I am beautifully warm now, and just about dropping –

Good night   Love Ann

Dear Micky,

Have acquired some leave, so here I am, with family at lodge Usual April weather, and one daren't stir without a waterproof wherever one goes You know!

The valley is grand at the moment All spring flowers out, and others beginning I think that next week is going to be a busmans holiday for me as there is an immense amount to be done in the gardens across the road No fishing yet, not for another month or two. Mummy and I drove out and Loch Lomondside was perfect

Life has been very full recently Now I only have evenings to do anything in, and there never seems to be enough Various American ships are visiting our ports, and I went over the one which went to Rosyth Very interesting and my, oh, ice cream! But the British N.O.'s accommodation is better Ninety officers seems to be an awful lot for one cruiser It was the first time that I had been at Rosyth since I left in January

There was a Rugby International between England and Scotland last weekend at Murrayfield Not a very thrilling one as England played with one, and sometimes a second player off the field

The result being 27-0 to Scotland Some very fine passes, though

That Monday being the spring holiday was given the day off and went with family to Musselburgh Races A most successful day

Won 14/9! — Vast sum

Took a trip to Callander the other day Quite new to me, and quite enchanting Though a trifle tame to this part of the world In fact, life has been quite energetic just lately Have again climbed the Pentlands, but didn't see very far as it was misty and dusk It didn't seem to take at all long

By the way do you like Mabel Lucy Atwell's postcards, 'cos if you do I'll send you one but not unless! Thanks awfully for the stamps and the photographs You haven't changed a scrap

I know I'm bad enough but you don't seem to give me much news of yourself when you write

I love being at the Botanic each day There is a new plant out and the squad I'm in is most awfully nice, and most helpful At the present moment I hoe, prune, weed, whatever they do, from nine to five, with an hour off for lunch It doesn't exactly give me much time to myself of late, my evenings seem to have been taken up with walks, the theatre, and an occasional party

Maureen arrived on leave on Tuesday She is having a grand time at Arbroath These Fleet Air Arm stations certainly organise themselves

If you are a sportsman, then you'll be shocked by this piece of news We shot a fox last week and a vixen at that But it had to be, because of the hens. When we took to keeping hens, never dreamed that they would be so near to Edinburgh.

Went to The Dansant in the city chambers last week and from the marvellous buffet, incredible to believe ones eyes, but that is as with you now, is it not. We are now told, rationing for two more years, and a possibility of more shortages. The world is in a bad way, except America! Gramophone records are cheaper since the last budget, which to me is a good thing.

I am a very rich girl now – after six weeks overdue, my gratuity at last has arrived. But I somehow don't think it will last all that long. Some of it blued already, on books chiefly.

Has Malcolm weighed in on his training yet? Haven't seen your family around at all. Well Mickey, a hundred and one equally long letters are waiting to be written, and I must, or there will be such blasts that there won't be any of me left to write again!

Much love
Ann

Dear Mickey

Alas, all good things come to an end and we return to Edinburgh tomorrow, so I thought that I would seize the opportunity to write before I am caught up in the whirl again _____ a whirl which leaves me little time for writing.

We've had a marvellous time, everything has been perfect - including the weather which has made up quite for its bad start The latest job which the family has had to tackle has been painting boats By this time the sunny weather has arrived, so it was a very jolly occupation Very finicky work though, one just doesn't slap on paint, oh dear me no, the sand has to be brushed down, and paint put in the most awkward of places The fo'scle was such a place, the trouble being that our arms were only half the requisite length! But it was great fun lying full length in the boat, with the sun pouring down, wielding the paint brush

What with painting and one thing and another, I'm in a terrible mess The one thing and another refers to various scars and stains, honourably gained while hacking away at some of the undergrowth suffocating various rhododendrons at "the gardens". Brambles are the very devil to clear They produce roots as often as possible along the stem and then prick you violently when you try to remove them completely, and erase them forever from the face of the earth

We've been having great sessions on stamps, and the rest of the family were interested to see the victory ones which you sent me It is rather a bore as we all collect British Empire ones to the almost exclusion of every other country, so there are not the masses of swops floating around that there might be

Do you like Spike Jones or hasn't he come to your ken yet? At this moment there is a record of one of his barmy things on the wireless. I rather like some of them but the family doesn't care for them at all. They are all out at the moment, but being Sunday morning I wanted to sit out in the sun, and, anyway I shall be having all the garden I can cope with from tomorrow onwards. I love being at the Botanic and I'm quite looking forward to returning tomorrow. Most distracting I'm listening to a George Formby record now. I like George Formby
Something drastic seems to have happened to my spelling so before I make any more frightful errors.
Much love

Ann

Dear Mickey

Many thanks for the further batch of stamps. They are terrific in more ways than one, cos as well as increasing my collection, the duplicates are invaluable as swaps

That week at lodge passed like a seven day leave, and now that I'm back, seems rather like a dream

A very hectic week was last week, though nothing seems to have happened Perhaps it is because it was the last few days before David went back to school

At the moment am defying all elements by sitting outside on a cushion listening to a Haydn symphony. The chief element being the North Wind, which is effectively broken by the house when it is not driving a cloud over the sun, it is very warm In fact it is very jolly All kinds of birds rushing about finding food for their families, and others chirping I saw a nest of baby robins yesterday ———— very ugly they were too. Only a slight shower in the night, (we are needing rain, agriculturally, very badly) but what a difference it has made. Odd vegetables now popping up all over the place. It has been a good blossom year, so we are keeping our fingers crossed, as a frost would be disastrous Some farmers have their neaps in; this is thought to be a mistake as it is still early, and always this risk of frost

Played my first game of tennis yesterday A great treat — it was at a tennis club, and we were given six completely new balls. What a difference they do make. After six years of old ones, we kept hitting far too hard. I am hoping to have far more than I have had these last two years. These courts are practically next door to the Botanics, which is most convenient, as I can go there immediately after five o'clock.

Must fly Love Ann

The Lodge   12 - 5 - 46

Dear Mickey,

This is too good to last! But somehow, there has always been time these last Sundays to slip in a letter to you. I think your Charlie seems adorable. How old is he? Are you out of civilization now, and is it army life proper? I hope your truck journey went off alright.

Life is heaven at the moment, but not from the horticultural point of view. A serious drought is in force, holding everything back, but from the other point of view, to have had SUN, non stop for three weeks is almost a world record for these parts. All being well it looks like a good fruit harvest, if only the frost will hold off until it is set. Life still very pleasant in the gardens. The Botanic gave a smashing dance last week in the Walpole Hall, which has rather a good floor. Not unlike a Service one, but not nearly such a crush. Also most people knew each other.

Most leisure time at the moment, I try to spend sitting out in front of the house. It really is delightful, 'cos the walls break the wind a bit.
  Do you see any wonderful rhododendrons?

  Hope to put in a fortnight's yachting next month, off the West Coast. Sounds too good to be true, so I hope that it does come off. Not a very large one, just big enough for four I know quite well what will happen till just four and four, and four Don't you agree?

Unless I post this today, it probably won't be attended to for another week, and 'cos the postie collects any moment now.
Much love
Ann

The Lodge   Argyll   19 - 5 - 46

Dear Mickey,

Have been let out on bail again as tomorrow is Victoria Day, meaning that all Scotland closes down We motored out after lunch yesterday, family very gloomy, as there were bound to be hikers, bikers and chary bangs, especial on Loch Lomondside, and driving would be hell To their amazement, we didn't meet a soul, and it was the best and clearest journey we had made for ages There has been no rain and every thing bone dry, even the river ——— almost There have been various fires up on the hills, but we've been spared, so far.

Lodge is a riot of colour Primulas, azaleas, rhodies, blue bells and hosts of other plants all out Woke up really early this morning and ever since, heard nothing but a blinking cuckoo Don't like them

At Barnton we have been touch and go for frosts, but, touch wood, the fruit is still alright, and there has been a slight shower which should help it to set Hope so, as there was none last year But the danger is not yet quite over.

The gardens are still absenting most of my time, 'cos after a day in the open I find that I'm pleasantly tired, and don't feel up to doing much

Last night we had a wiz meal, better than you can do in India, strawberries, sugar, cream and Ice cream How's that?

Love

Ann

Argyll   9 - 6 - 46
Dear Mickey,
Thank you very much for your letter. Is it because you are further inland that they are taking longer, quite five days to come?

At last we have had our Victory Day. It rained in London, which rather finished the air part of the business.

The only thing we Scots achieved from the whole show was Saturday morning off. So in my usual style, came out on Friday afternoon. You see, no one officially cares a damn whether I turn up or not, they (the gardens) having nothing to lose. Most convenient. The bluebells were just about over on Loch Lomondside but everything is a very fresh green. Each time we pass Loch Fyne, we look out for a farm which has some highland cattle, 'cos they have some calves. Look more like shaggy dogs than anything else, and are quite adorable. Everything else unchanged. A west wind which means occasional cloud, but very warm, all the same. It seems to have been a very good spring for the farmers as their corn is good, not patchy as usual, and the milk so creamy it has to be tasted to be believed.

Went off fishing yesterday morning; it was really too bright, and I didn't get very far down the river, chiefly because it was so warm, and I was flower spotting. It is a joy in more ways than one, that the fish season is on again.

A busman's holiday on Thursday. Went all over the submarine, Scotsman. Wasn't really thrilled as I have been on one before, and one is very like another, but the girl I was with hadn't and was thrilled, and anyway, I was her guest
Five weeks today and I'll be afloat
Hurray. Love   Ann

Barnton

19 - 6 - 46

Dear Mickey,

I do hope you'll be able to read this I have a feeling that my writing is going from bad to worse, that is why I took to typing only it is in use at the moment You see, I have written a fair amount tonight on my knee in rotten light with a biro.

Many thanks for your last letter For me, the last week has been the usual grind, only that isn't quite the right word It has been rather showery, which makes weeding rather a messy business But so good for the setting of the fruit Alas weeds enjoy it too! But the gardens are quite lovely just now, and so very fresh.

Spent the weekend in Culross, —————— a very charming village Do you know it? Scarcely a house later than 1611!

Two main families, brothers, seem to run the entire village The Scottish National Trust has taken many houses in hand, and are redoing them properly, and taking the dreadful plaster off the stonework I think that as far as situation goes I prefer the North Bank of the Forth One has then both the sun and the river

Oh Mickey, must go to bed now. My apologies in case you couldn't decipher, but you should be able by now!!!

Love   Ann

30 - 6 - 46

Dear Mickey

Aren't train journeys boring?   At the present moment am travelling North to Edinburgh after spending two days with David We came down on Thursday night Friday being a London leave-out day. The morning seems to have been spent downing ices and drinking chocolate On these occasions food would appear to take first priority The second being either a show or a cinema This time a cinema

—————   The Lost Chance, which I had already seen No day in London being complete without it, we paid a visit to a Lyons Corner House for tea We had a small cousin to feed as well The high spot of the day was a visit to the studios at Alexandra Palace, as television is operating again, and then we watched the evening programme. We came back in the bus with the Javanese Dancers who had been televised, and they were perfectly sweet

Mercifully Saturday was a glorious day, as it was the day of the Eton Winchester cricket match at Eton It is a great day for Wykamists, and we did it full justice.

And so back for 0900 Monday morning

An excellent concert in Edinburgh last week by the Hallé Orchestra They were up for a week Simply packed

The King and Queen were up this weekend, so by being South have missed one or

112

two things, but we hope to go to the Garden Party on Tuesday So it is bound to rain

To show us some nice gardens, the Botanic took us a lovely trip about ten days ago. We went by Kincardine up to Perth Saw a heavenly garden, on to Braco, near Gleneagles for tea, then to another garden at Rumbling Bridge, then home by 2230. The country was really glorious, specially near Gleneagles Masses of whin and purple rhododendrons I was lucky and in a car, which was a joy Don't know the part between Perth and Glen Devon, and travelled for the first time over the Kincardine Bridge When I'm in that part of the world, feel I love it best but I'm fickle 'cos I feel the same way about the West, in fact about it all Have no desire (at the moment) to emigrate. They've done a certain amount of tree felling in that part.
All being well, join the yachting party on 15th July, somewhere in Scotland Depending on the wind, they just don't know where they will be I do hope it all goes off alright

Much love

Ann

113

Dear Mickey

Aren't I relieved to be safe? in harbour after a most exhausting sale from Tobermory round Mull arriving in time for tea during an appalling squall But it is fun for all that

I think the last time I wrote was 30th June

Right? That week was a very busy one Maureen's demob week and the Garden Party at Holyrood Also a play, if I remember rightly It is fun having my sister around 'cos then we can do many things together It does become rather boring when you are eternally on your own tot

Then approached the Great Day I thought I had told you all about it hence my remark — in five weeks, I'll be afloat The next door neighbours asked me if I'd join them for a fortnight on their yacht which they were taking for a month to the West Highlands Like a shot, I said yes, so all preparations made for me to leave for Skye on Monday morning The idea being to catch the 0425 train for Mallaig An excellent idea, which only failed in that as I never heard the dammmmmm at 0300! By the time we, Maureen as she was coming for the train journey, had come to, the train had left, so there was nothing to do but to turn over and wait until the following morning There being only the one steamer to Skye from Mallaig Success the following morning and we biked in for that train A lovely train journey right to Mallaig There Maureen returned and I embarked on a MacBrayne for Portree

There I caught the bus for Dunvegan on the opposite side of the island where I was to join ship. It was delightful. Dreadful roads, and everyone jabbering the Gaelic. The bus, typical, took its own time and made the usual unnecessary stops for ages.

A frightful storm caught us the next day off Mcleods Maidens and we had to heave to to reef the mainsail. It really was terrible, then died down, and we had the indignity of entering our anchorage at Rum under engine. Thursday a comparatively easy trip to Loch Aline(?) opposite. There were white sands there, which are supposed to sing when you walk on them. We tried and they didn't but perhaps it is because they were wet. Lovely dear green water. Irresistible, so we swam the length of the yacht. A long trip next day round Ardnamurchan point to Tobermory where we went ashore to have a bath at the Mishnish Hotel. A very good bath, but the kind of hotel which charges its residents a bob for a bath which makes you not want one, and which I think is scandalous. Next night we anchored south of Oban at a place which sounds like Puldoran, tho' spelt rather differently. Early start on Sunday in order to make your Gigha. What a day. The wind was against us and a dreadful mist, we sighted the island early in the afternoon but didn't reach it until 2230. Then a wind arose, and as the navigation with rocks is hell, we anchored thankfully in Drumeon Bay in the dusk at 2330 in an almost gale. As we left at 0600 in order to round the Mull on the right tides, there was no time to land, which I should have liked, as I had hoped to see your parents if they were there. A dreadful journey round the Mull. The tide race was terrific and there was the fear we had missed the tides. But all was well and so to Campbeltown. Just as well as a violent squall arose

23 - 7 - 46 Lamlash
Didn't have time to finish this yesterday. A calm day ending in a force 7 gale and just as we elected to lunch, sailed into another tide race. However ——————   here we are at Lamlash, hoping to make Sandbank tomorrow. ———— last port, as she belongs there. There are four of us in an eleven ton Bermudan rigged yacht. Great fun on the whole, tho the weather has been foul, but I wouldn't have missed if for worlds.
  Much love
                    Ann
PS: We have made Sandbank all right

116

Mickey, please don't think too badly of me, but letter writing is one of the many things which I shouldn't, but did, drop You see, I'm in a frantic whirl I loved your long letter What a time you are having How I envy you Hopes A year passed, I did much fishing in Hopes water A dammed up stream making a reservoir: and you won't be regretting Duke Street, will you

Does it make any difference to you being a
Loot? Congratulations

These last two months have been most uneventful I've been forced to have a quiet time as my left hand was U.S. Consequently it took twice as long to do anything but I am slowly returning to normal, but keeping clear of such unpleasant things as digging and carrying heavy loads So useful!

Working like a black in this garden, trying to bring a little law and order before I go away in October to start training properly In fact, I'm the complete rustic Since July, have been in a different department at the Botanic learning the ins and outs of propagating plants, only to rush home and try out all I've learned in order to try to stock the garden   Have had a crashing success with my seed sowing As it was home gathered stuff, I put in plenty, to find to my horror that they have all germinated, and I am left with several hundred lupins and several hundred delphiniums! As it is light until dinner

117

time I don't get in until then, completely deadbeat Fit for nowt That is why things have slid, but this weekend I have a cold, and so I'm catching up with everything.

Have only had one weekend off, and that was to go to Argyll for my 21st birthday Contrary to expectations it did not rain, so we went up the Loch on a netting trip I didn't have a celebration of any kind That is to come Before that I was, for a fortnight alone, utterly, in the house, except for Sally It had its points 'cos I could choose what I wanted for each meal, but somehow I didn't feel at all hungry, and far too tired to bother about cooking so existed solely on cold fish, and fry for breakfast I am a dab of a fryer now. I developed terrific generalship as to strategy as there was only one electric ring so could do nothing which needed more than one pan!

As I suppose you know, the weather has been appalling I've even had to give up bicycling to the gardens As a rule I loath bicycling but when going by bus means leaving at eight twenty, and biking leaving at eight forty, you can quite see why I'm peeved at foregoing my daily ride

I'm not at all looking forward to the next two years, but when I get settled in, I'll write to tell you just what sort of a place it is

My sister Maureen is now home for good, so once again for a short spell, we are a united family Life has been kind of dull ———— socially, just lately I suppose it is because I've been far too busy pottering Flicks have been definitely "out", but not so, concerts They are so very far and few between that I always try to go when I can There was the ballet and an odd play or two.

We've had the painters doing up the outside of the house Most uncomfortable, as we now live in a perpetual draft ——————— so that the windows won't stick They are left open and have to be tested each day, and it is very windy One of lifes minor trials tho' of course Autumn is not the time for it, but the windows would not stand the winter Even in these days we had to have a permit, and it was refused the first time It will scarcely seem possible to you but it is a fact that we are worse off than when you left Everything happens so gradually that one doesn't notice, but the countryside remains the same, and is taking on its usual winter look The harvest is very late and only half in but the trees are beginning to lose their leaves, and there is that nip in the air Chrysanthemums in full bloom, and we are all deep in next years bulb catalogues Dutch bulbs are back on the market, so this winter will be gayer with bowls of bulbs

Like you, I shall try to mend my ways ——————— my writing ones I mean letters seem to take longer just now, is it because you are further way?

(Oghi campaign in the hills)

I must pack up now for it is nearing eleven When I think of the old watch keeping days, this was the hour when I started my letters and felt very much alive Now it is quite the opposite I don't know myself – Im such an early bird!

Much love Mickey and I honestly will try to write again soon, but you do know at what sixes and sevens one gets from trying to pack to go off ——————— its like going back to school!

Ann

119

5 - 10 - 46

Dear Mickey,

Here I am, well in on my two years "Hard Labour". I arrived on Wednesday, and in many ways is reminiscent of the Service. Complete chaos No one bothered where I was to go, how I would find my way, and where I would get things, but a seasoned? campaigner such as myself, was not unduly disturbed Now, at times, feel like an old hand!

This is the nicer part of Leicestershire, is really Nottinghamshire, and not too flat The living standard is good Meals good and square at 8.15, 1.00, 4.30 and 7.15 and masses of hot water The day consists of taking voluminous notes at incredible speed at lectures, or else in doing practical gardening outside

Perhaps it'll seem funny to you but I can hardly stop myself calling my room mate, cabin mate and when I went out to Nottingham this afternoon thought of it as Going Ashore!

Hooray, tonight the clock is to be put back an hour

Read in an evening paper, local, tonight, that in spite of all, it is going to be a bumper harvest in this area

I was very sorry to leave the Botanic, loved my time there, really felt as tho' I'd gained much But it was getting me nowhere, and if I can cope, this place will

Rushed round Nottingham this afternoon trying to buy books, but, as usual, mostly out-of-print So useful Was amazed at the amount of toys in the shops, and bicycles of course, it is the centre of the industry, but it is a little hard that these things don't find their way into Scotland Also eating apples It was simply crammed Goose Fair was on, a yearly institution, but didn't get near the fairground with all the usual etceteras

This last week at home has been chaotic It is odd, but everything seems to be left until the final moment Do you find that At one stage, entire floor was covered with gear, which just had to fit into a trunk 3 X 2 X 1. Can't think how it did, and then just when I was getting organised, in walked the painters clothing all over the place.

The journey down was definitely good Through the borders, autumn had hardly touched Scotland a few leaves blowing around, but further south there is a barer feeling altogether and Harvest Festivals in full swing

I did notice in The Borders, Cumberland, I think grass being cut for hay, and it looks most awfully like a first crop Some fields with main crop spuds, just

121

shouting to be picked And here I am, pruning red currant bushes by the dozen I believe we go on to apples later

You simply must tell me if I now bore you in my letters with these constant references to Horticulture If you are of the many, then you won't be one jot interested and therefore bored

<u>Sunday</u> A most glorious day, just can't stay in, so I've commandeered a bike Loath biking but to walk would be too slow, so am going off to "Explore". Have every intention of going to Sherwood Forest, one day

Love

Ann

21 - 10 - 46

Dear Mickey,

Life grows more and more complicated You just wouldn't believe what we have to learn, and all so that a plant will grow! Am lost in a maze of notes of my own taking ————— am not very good at taking notes, the lectures are at such a speed As things are, this is not at all a bad place, tho' many civilians grumble I have known worse. We are part of Nottingham University We have a half holiday on Wednesdays and Saturdays, so I usually spend the weekend with my Grandfather It is a marvellous feeling of stepping out of one world into another Everything is so very different ————— ideas, manners and clothes.

They have a Saluki but a sheep chaser, so the poor animal never has any exercise, except for a crawl a day on a lead

Being a lovely day, (the odd part being it was far warmer out than in even with fires). I took him for a decent walk at a decent pace. Half way there he put up his tail, then took an interest in the hedgerow, and was overjoyed to find I meant a real walk, from his point of view. He was so surprised

Being England everything seems to last longer than up North, and the leaves are only just falling The hedges are rather gay with the red berries of the hips and haws and others Saw my first ploughed field on Saturday. It always seems odd to me to see people fishing on Sundays At least I don't call it fishing All they seem to do is to sit on their baskets, and fall asleep with their rods in their

123

hands: and they don't seem to have any fun in landing their fish. No. The other kind of fishing for me every time.

I think the crest is rather sweet! Very bovine as are the inmates!

What of yourself. Still at the back of beyond? Time you rejoined civilisation for a bit, or don't you want to. Had any more jobs to do besides being the O/C's that you appear to be. Signals and the like. Me, I'm falling asleep, a thing I do at a horribly early hour here.

Love
Ann

2 - 12 - 46

Mickey,

I've neglected everyone shamefully If only I could write with both hands, then I could be writing letters while taking notes

This place will be the death of me Tho' not exactly overworked, there is always plenty to do Do you remember the Goofy pictures you gave me I had them framed, and they are hanging on my wall — much admired by everyone They do cheer me up These walls otherwise would be most depressing

Have sown two wild oats so far One was a weekend trip to London to see my Mama and David, who is taller than ever Did nothing startling except to view the King's Pictures, which are on exhibition, and to go to Mme Tussauds, being Sunday, terrific crush in both

The second wild oat much more fun I went to spend long weekend (a wangle) with an ex-wren friend Ascot way Sunday went to a marvellous concert at Henley, and rode on the Monday Also had tea at Gunters, and bumped into an old Barntonite in Piccadilly Truly a most successful weekend Otherwise all other weekends are much about the same

I repair to the ancestral home, where I help my step grandmother to make cakes play backgammon with my grandfather who has been in bed Take the saluki for a 4 mile walk at 3½ MPH, and generally make myself useful! Tho' it is alright here, it is grand to get away at weekends.

Life here goes on just the same Notes, lectures, and practical work, day in, day out One is sent down if one fails to keep the head above water, so you must not be at all surprised if I leave suddenly

I've become very behind with everything so please do not be too cross with me for not writing before I do feel that Horti has first priority you see.

And what else have I to tell you? I have a one-track mind these days It is veg veg veg the whole time ——————— not very exhilarating for anyone else!

This part of the country is rather prone to flooding Had never seen anything like it, when all of a sudden it goes, for they then allow the water into the Trent

We have just over a fortnight to go, then Home James ——————— all very like school days! A decent holiday ——————— a good 3 — 4 weeks
Hope to play badminton A new club has been formed by Ronald Gill The qualifying thing is that one must be too old for the other one! So we should have some fun, 'cos it should be the same crowd
I don't know what else, if anything is brewing All I do know is that I'm in

for a very busy time, in the garden, and possibly in the kitchen as well.

How I miss my watch keeping for letter writing I knew where I was Every eight days (there was nothing else to do!) and no untidy ends Tonight I have written 7 which leaves me 4. Having picked up the threads again, will do my hardest to write soon.

   Much love,

          Ann

5 - 12 - 46

Dear Mickey,   A happy Christmas to you

You see, I don't know how long mail takes so I hope this will arrive in time.
I wonder how you will spend it. I suppose if you are at your base you'll have a
corking time ——————————— in more ways than one

Having had the mildest autumn – ever rain ————— ever rain ————— and rain
There was a sharp frost this morning and ice on the puddles. We were digging and
were beautifully warm. England has had a little snow, but Scotland had some ages
ago, between Perth and Aberdeen. I know that if I was at home, and looking out
of my bedroom window over The Forth, the hills would be white.

At home it will be the usual(ly) austerity Christmas, only Mummy bought in
Ireland at fabulous price a box of crackers, so at least we'll have a few bangs
with the turkey ——————— if it arrives. At least it is ordered.

Don't know the family plans, but do know that we are going to Argyll at the
New Year. It is fun there. Gets dark very quickly, and a huge log fire (rather an
exaggeration 'cos the grate is very wee, but huge comparatively). There won't be
much to do, but when the whole family is there, it is more than enough
——————————— and I promised to teach David Backgammon

A very happy and prosperous (that can mean anything) New Year to you
Much love

Ann

128

31 - 12 - 46

Dear Mickey,

My last letter to you this year, how final that might sound if it were not for the date! I trust you had a good Christmas. Are there many Scots amongst you so that you can Hogmanay properly, or are you all far too busy for that?

Since I last wrote, life has been hectic. There were exams and things at first, then since I came home there has been much doing and brewing. The inevitable Christmas shopping for one thing. Not quite as bad as usual. A few more things about, which was a help. You see, we Father Christmas each other! Also family is trying to organise a cocktail party, and everyone gets very excited and then nothing is achieved.

Edinburgh is very gay, lots of cocktail parties and the odd dance. Arrived home in time to go to the Highland Ball. It was a terrific success. They do many of the proper Scots dances, not the Petronella and Strip the Willow, but Duke of Perth, Speed the Plough (usually call it Follow the Plough by mistake) and Scottish Reform which are far, far nicer. Do you know them? It was a marvellous ball, 10 - 4.

As well as being my last letter to you, this is my first, and I wish you a prosperous New Year. It is now the 5 – 1 – 47, and since my writing worsened, I've been writing in the night train

Thank you very much for your two cables. Yes, I guessed you were busy. You must just not think of writing to me when you are busy. I am in the same position too you may have noticed! Writing where and when I can

We now possess a donkey, and much of my time has been taken up in exercising the animal. He is a darling. Four years, and is from Ireland. We have had him for three weeks, and his name is Luke. Not for a pet, but to work in the garden

Mickey, bad writing or not I must persevere or I shall never finish. Please forgive.

I know you'll think I'm quite mad 'cos I'm only going South for one night, this is Sunday returning Tuesday by day, but it is for a friends 21st. Have to return as am going to a concert in Edinburgh (This train is jolting I think I'm quite clever to be able to write at all whatever you are thinking!)

Am disappointed. No snow at all. A Russian anti cyclone at the moment and all at home are hugging fires. Slight frost in the mornings, but it always thaws, which makes the cars dirty, which, in turn annoys my Papa

Almost went with family to lodge, but at the last moment had two minutes, so stayed behind. It would only have been for the Sunday – all the time any of us could spare for our beloved lodge. It has been lovely there. Always is when it is damp and beastly in Edinburgh

I wonder if I'll ever reach London as the train has stopped six times, left late, been just on two hours, and we are not at Berwick yet

---

A horrid little man has got me up under false pretences. He says we are two hours late (only it is far more) but apparently he doesn't like people lying in bed until the last possible moment.

Hope this will reach you 'cos I'm not sure if I've remembered your address properly.

The next letter from me will, I expect, be from my institution. I think that I return for a further twelve weeks.

This wretched train is about 2½ – 3 hours late and doesn't do breakfast! Was given a biscuit with my tea, but that does not allay the pangs, and yet at home never eat breakfast. Hey me, be lucky if I have anything before 10 at this rate.

Sorry, I can't stop writing drivel, so I shall wish you everything you wish yourself for 1947.

Much love

Ann

Barnton   15 - 1 - 47

Dear Mickey,

Please agree with me and say you don't mind me writing to you on this paper, only I'm far too tired to trot downstairs for some proper paper.

Isn't it marvellous I'm A.W.O.L, only by this time a letter should have arrived at college explaining why I am late in returning I extended my leave myself, and for how long I don't know. For about a week, I suppose It has all been done in collaboration with my M.O, and therefore perfectly puccar ⸺ if you remember your naval talk Already have done very well out of it ⸺ this being the day I should have travelled back Had my young cousin to a fried onion lunch This is positively a ritual Poor lamb, he loves them so, but never has any in his own house, so he eats onion with us

Such a waste, had to sleep in the afternoon 'cos I got none last night ⸺ there was such a gale which positively moaned down my chimney Went to the theatre tonight to see Yvonne Arnaud She really is wonderful David went to London tonight, and the house seems very quiet

Family gave a cocktail party last week to which 150 came People say it was great fun I don't I consider that it was a dead loss Never had a moment to talk to anyone, let alone eat and drink!

Badminton alas has ended This venture was a success and I loved it, though I must say that the standard isn't very high ⸺ mercifully!

Do you know, on reaching London last week, it snowed A couple of inches at Hampton Court Marvellous dreams of tobogganing I had However, on coming

132

North next day, saw no snow North of Newcastle. Swizz. And for the past four days it has simply poured.

Hope I'm here next Sunday, 'cos then I'll be going for a walk. The usual ———————— up the Almond. It is all exactly the same. Sally and I went quite often until I went to college, but we've only been once these holidays. Nothing has changed a bit.

Have high hopes of going to see the Scotland Rugger Trial at Murrayfield, but it will depend on a great many things. Chiefly the weather and neither of us wish to stay if it is boring but the last Trial, before they went to Paris was terrific.

Edinburgh has been having a temperature of 53°, which you must admit is pretty good. We almost seriously thought of wearing cotton frocks and of having iced drinks! only there was a more than 60 mph gale at the same time.

Looked for the first snow drop this morning but did not see one in flower. The daffodils are about one inch high. They will get a nasty shock when the frost comes, unless the snow arrives first!

Mickey, I must stop now and post this, or else I just don't know when I will
    Love
        Ann

Dear Mickey,

I've done a terrible thing to you About a fortnight ago I wrote to you, but alas never posted the letter! If I find it when I go home next week I think I'll send it, if only to prove that I wrote it! And it will save me repeating all I put in it

Actually I haven't any news whatsoever as I haven't done a thing since 12th January.

As you see I haven't gone back to college yet, and don't suppose I will this term No I have not been sent down! You see, last week I was laid out flat, while someone stuck a knife into me and removed my appendix.

There have been terrific snows and frosts, and my sister has been out every day on her skis on the Pentlands All I've seen of it has been on the roofs of the houses across the street, and on the bus roof as it passes my window. No one can remember blizzards and storms such as the country is having at the present Yet there is none North of Inverness, they've even seen the sun We haven't for twenty days.

As I said in my letter to you (the one I haven't yet posted) I met your Father the other day He told me a little about Hopes

From what I hear life is not much fun at the college at the moment. They've had snow for ages there, so I can't think what outside work the Hortis will be doing Just think of a whole terms work to be made up A delightful prospect!
Hope I've got your address correct

Love

Ann

Dear   Mickey

I thank you for your letter, such a long one too, but then it is such an age since I last heard from you! Seriously though, I do truly and really realize that you have been very busy and myself know that it is impossible to write when sterner things are afoot.

Nothing much has happened to me since I last wrote as I haven't been allowed to do much. But all that is over and done with now, thank goodness.

Left the Home after having been there for four weeks, then a week at home which was very trying as I was not allowed to do anything while my bed still saw much of me. The snow was still with us and family did much skiing on the Pentlands; and there was always an occasional blizzard to vary things. In the midst of one, I received a letter from Uganda ----- it had a very warming effect! It is odd how quickly one gets used to the cold, we were terribly warm one day and discovered that the temperature had risen to 32 degrees! Then I went off to Belhaven which is next door to Dunbar. It was simply marvellous to be able to go down to the sea, and to sniff the breeze with the sun and the East wind with the usual tang blowing through my hair. You can have no idea. The snow continued and there was a day when we were cut off from Edinburgh by the drifts. After a delightful two weeks I returned home ostensibly for a week, but somehow it became lengthened into two. There was so much to do somehow. Edinburgh went gay and organised a charity ball to which we took a party of eight. My first spree for positively months and I couldn't have enjoyed it more. In Stripping the Willow with my usual vigour, I am still black and blue as a result ---- no, I wasn't at all rough, hadn't the strength! As a concession sat out one reel and had supper instead. It didn't seem worth going to bed when we arrived home, so we waited for breakfast, and slept all day. Shades of Wren life. Sally was very bewildered and couldn't make it all out, why she had no sleep one night sent to bed all day and was very worried all evening to know if the miserable performance was going to be repeated. She was vastly relieved when she saw us revert to usual behaviour.

I arrived here two days ago, the rest of the family following in dribs and drabs. There is the usual domestic crisis at home. This generally happens from three to four times in the year. The snow only having just melted, (though there are still some patches on the hills) spring is nearly a month behind itself. The larches are not really showing green but I did see some Alder catkins by the river. The snowdrops are lovely and I have seen a few daffodils in flower. My greatest joy was to see a rhododendron trying to flower. Everything seems unchanged here ------ I haven't been here since July. It is the smell in the air which I like so much ------ there is nothing to beat a West coast smell, I think. It is a much nicer wood which we burn, too. There isn't any chance of fishing as it is too early. Another couple of months or so.

You want to know my views on life over here. I think that my only difficulty is to know when to stop! I hope that it won't depress you too much. I should think that the propaganda you read is probably true as all propaganda is. The thing is that as our standard has been so low for ages, we don't notice. Money appears to have no value. Wages are fantastic, and most people work (if it can be called that) a five day week of 44 hours. Clothes are available at a price, and we still queue for shoes and stockings. Our clothes coupons have to last longer 'cos of the fuel crisis, which has also helped to make things short. In every food shop you queue, and tho' the ration is pretty small there is very little to "Ring the changes" with. It is very difficult to enter or leave the country for long, and one needs permits for everything from building of every sort to feeding livestock. Millions ---- and I am not exaggerating --- are being spent on nationalizing everything when it perhaps could wait a year or two while our position is still so shaky. There was an American Loan, but it literally went on films and tobacco, and not until too late was this realised. Food is very short, and this awful winter has killed many sheep, and the floods ruined much arable land already sown in England. Drink is a little easier, but the beer is water. Luxury goods are there but not worth the price except to people of the munition makers wage. Pineapples from 15/ upwards. Some of us are not enough full of vitamins and are therefore spotty! Many children are deficient in calcium. And, as usual, all our best things are exported! At least, these are my views on life here, but I may be mistaken.

I was not able to enjoy the snow at all, and was I furious? It was at the time when I had to take life easily. I am sorry, I appear to have spelt propaganda wrong before.
While on the mend, I tried to fill in some gaps which have been bothering me for ages in my reading. So awful not to know what various references in various books meant. To rectify this, I read books at my Grandfather's I would not otherwise have read. Some R.L.S., Vanity Fair, Jayne Eyre; heaps of gardening and farming books as well as books on Scotland. And Shakespear(e). To make up the lack of concert I listened to the wireless. Did you know that anything using electricity made from coal, isn't allowed to be used between 0830 and 1130, as well as 1330 and 1530, so the BBC shuts down then?

The nutty ration was halved last month, and has only been partially restored. Shame I calls it! I can't think why I am dripping to you, 'cos I usually reserve that privilege (?) to my cousin.

Isn't it awful, I have over a dozen long letters to deal with. They are suffering from a month's shelving ------- a dangerous proceeding.

If I don't stop now I shan't have a thing to tell you about next time.

Much love

         Ann

PS: Have I repeated myself as it has suddenly dawned on me that I wrote in March!?
    A

This Is My India

CERTIFICATE OF REGISTRATION OF BIRTH.

Coonoor Municipal Council.

Place of Birth _____ "Blair gowrie"

Date of Birth _____ 29th November 1925.

Nationality or Caste of Child _____ British

Sex of Child _____ Male

Name of Child (if Christened) _____ Moncrieff Milward

Father's Name and Surname _____ Robert L. Stewart

Mother's Name and Surname _____ Barbara Milward

Profession or Occupation _____ Lieutenant. R.N. - present tea-planting

Date of Registration _____ 30th November 1925.

J. D. Solomon.
Registrar of Births and Deaths.

N. B.—Compulsory Vaccination being in force in the Coonoor Municipality, please note provisions of Act IV of 1884 relating thereto, overleaf.

This child should be brought to the Municipal Hospital for vaccination on expiry of six months from this date, i. e., on the _____ 30th May _____ 1926.

True Copy.

Chairman, C. 200/26

1. TOWARDS COMMISSIONING

Birth
Army
Train
Convoy To India
Fanys
Southwards
Transition
The Troop Train
I Dreamt I Dwelt in Marble Halls
Officers' Training School, Bangalore.
Hospital – Fluey Spell
Lachman
Recreation
Porno or Erotica
Wildlife
Charlie Loris
Letters Home
Scorpion
Chameleons
Urdu Munshi
Serious Training
Commissioning Parade
Mrs Stevenson Saw Me in the Bath
Rob Roy
Nilgiri Hills
To Mangalore
Aid and Employment
Reporting For Duty

BIRTH

I do not recall India the first time round. Never the less it undoubtedly impressed greatly on my small mind – with which I have had to live the rest of my life.

ARMY

On the second occasion, we arrived crowding the boat decks of a troop ship. It was warm and sunny and beautiful. Bombay harbour – the gateway – looked tidy, smart and colourful. I thought the large brown birds were marvellous – they looked like the too-little seen buzzards at home. It occurred to me that they were probably not Bombay ducks.

TRAIN

I wondered if I would ever see the attractive ship mate of those ship board weeks. She, with two dozen other FANY colleagues had been allocated separate coaches on the train out of Euston. Door windows on two coaches declared in large letters – F.A.N.Y.

There was, and probably still is, a wide platform serving the train on the extreme left of the station. I had humped my kit bag and hammock along it the year before on several occasions. That had been during particularly bad times with bombing and the start of doodlebugs. The windows so high up in the wall surprisingly still seemed to have glass in them! Now a little before dusk a few hundred khaki clad kit-bag-lugging males eyed the very special ladies as they passed along the platform to their labelled coaches. The drafts had gathered over several days – ours in a large Victorian dark red sandstone hotel in London's Marylebone Road. During the journey by truck to the railway station, at the junction between Marylebone Road and Baker Street, the semi blacked out traffic lights turned to red and the convoy halted briefly. An elderly city-suited gentleman seeing us coming rushed into a little tobacconist. He emerged in time to throw ten packets of cigarettes over the tail board of our truck. He must have witnessed thousands of young people on the first leg of their journey to battle fields across the world.

The train was full, dirty, windows all darkened with paper pasted to prevent splinters flying should a bomb land close enough to shatter them. At least we all had seats which was a relief after many crowded journeys during my time in the navy. The lights were very dim as we went into the night and we must surely all have been sleeping and it was quiet when there was an alarming screech of brakes. The communication cord had been pulled – and the steaming engine brought the train, which had not been travelling at great speed, to a halt in black cold featureless countryside.

145

There were shouts and the engine wheezed and pulsated on full steam – what took place I do not know. Someone suggested that a deserter had made a jump for it. It seemed the most likely explanation. I wondered if the deserter pulled the cord to slow the train or had it been pulled after he made his bid for freedom. Unlike us there were others on board who had not the slightest idea where in the world they were going. Perhaps some were on their way to a second bite at the Burma 'theatre' – and its undignified demanding ways.

Someone had calculated the survival rates for the drafts that preceded our small group – officers for the Indian Army. We were number 47 draft, I think, and the odds had improved in recent years. In very early batches, which had supplied young men for the Indian Army for all of the war theatres, the survival rates were between 3% and 10%! Such statistics seemed to do nothing to demoralise. The figures for more recent drafts were much more promising .

It took all night to reach the departure port. Some wag from another detachment moving down the corridor past our compartment said that if we were destined for Burma direct we would have been issued with arctic clothing to confuse the enemy. He joked that we might be on our way to Bloodyvostok! We, at least, knew that we were not.

As day dawned I was the only one in my little compartment who recognised the vast dockside cranes and the bombed burnt out blackened sugar refinery on the Clyde. I had seen it in flames the year before. This was Greenock. Kit bags humped once more, we snaked from the train at the dockside up the longest ever gang plank into a fairly large grey liner now become travel worn troopship.

Everything went so smoothly. War seemed to have simplified matters and concentrated minds – single minded purposefulness with someone at each turn to organise and direct. I think **that** may be the reason that we won the war. No doubts, no mistrust. We were so young, so excited, so fit, so expectant.

CONVOY TO INDIA

The ship made its gentle way down the smooth Clyde. I recognised the road my family had frequently used since the early thirties to-ing and fro-ing from Gigha. Only the year before with my father well wrapped up in the back seat I had driven our open Austin past Dumbarton Rock. Ann, who was a wren, was beside me and all three of us on leave at the same time from the Royal Navy. Ann was really more impressed by my father, Lieutenant Commander RN. I think she felt that she should salute him whenever he spoke to her. We had collected her at the lodge in Argyll on our way from the Isle of Gigha back to Edinburgh.

After that – Bute and the "Kyles of". My kit was stowed in the dormitory cabin about midships on the starboard side; probably the target spot 'for' a U-boat's periscope sights as we travelled south. Then a shallow sea fog set in and there were destroyers and frigates whooping and ships all over gathering and forming up to make a largish convoy. For a brief moment a massive, absolutely massive, figure loomed in the haze. It was a warm summery day and, although misty, it was light and moonstonely colourful, and this huge giant making us look so tiny came by, close, on its way into the Clyde. It was the Queen Elizabeth with probably thousands and thousands of Americans on board.

FANYS

I moved across afterwards to our port side and leant my forearms on the teak rail. A FANY was to my right. We were as millionaires on a peacetime cruise – perhaps. My previous naval experience meant that I was reading endless lamp Morse signals going between half a dozen ships. I glanced at the FANY – she was lovely of course and I mean not just lovely because she was woman and it was wartime, she was exceptionally good looking – then I saw her eyes, and her lips seemed to coordinate with the effort that her eyes made as she watched the Morse lamps. Surely a khaki clad member of the Field Ambulance Nursing Yeomanry would not be reading along with me the convoy's Morse communications. She was one of those exceptional ladies in SOE, trained far beyond all that I had ever achieved and reading the Morse with less effort than I – and I was not too slow!

"You're one of *them* aren't you?" She drew the correct meaning from my obscure question and just gave a small nod and a half smile. They were recruited to the ambulance service as a cover. It was never discussed again.

She came from Surrey, or Kent was it? She told me she had springer spaniels. There was a time when I could remember her name but it eludes me now. I wonder if I ever had her address, one did little in the way of recording information then and all letters were censored of course. Cameras were forbidden – security was paramount. Many years later I was to have several springer spaniels – liver and white – and bred a few too. Judy was my first and favourite. In her eyes I sometimes thought I saw my late mother's look. They both had brown eyes.

We put on a variety concert which served two very useful functions. The more extrovert or energetic among us were kept busy. Less control would be needed on the crowded deck space which became quite hot as we journeyed southward. And then it entertained the rest of the troops on a couple of evenings. I remember playing a small part in a sort of 'vice versa' play which some others had written. I wore a pretty flowered cotton frock and a large beribboned straw summer hat and 'entered right' smoking a small cigar. I think the outfit came from a large props and costume store for not one of us, including the lady troops, would have had a stitch of civvy clothing with us. That all went home the day we 'joined up'. I do not remember my lines.

SOUTHWARDS

The last I saw of Great Britain for a couple of years was the bluey grey cone of Ailsa Craig in the clearing mists as we made for warmer seas and the clime of the flying fish.

The sea became more blue. The bow waves rolled back more sharply. The bright white spray sparkled intensely and held my gaze hypnotically. Flying fish flew out of the crests and glided along in the troughs of the disturbed sea. If I did not look up I would not see twenty-two other ships all determinedly making their way towards SEAC, the South East Asia Command.

My arms rested on the teak rail now embellished with a thousand initials of those who had fuelled the theatres of war. "Springer spaniel" joined me. We wondered for how many these pen knife carvings might be all there was to record their passing.

The sea journey had been a period of comparative idleness and a welcome rest after my exertions in the navy. Now we were to prepare for Burma to put an end to Japanese ambitions in the east. I was still an officer cadet but in khaki this time and I had been learning Urdu and jungle warfare in Maidstone! And there, along with the grounding in the language, we had been subjected to endless painful endurance tests – yet once more in the relatively tender age of this thirteen of us who had been transferred from the navy! I was now a lithe nine and a half stone, most of the surplus having been shed whilst energetically serving in the navy.

TRANSITION

Geographically a short remove over the North Downs; from navy blue and grey destroyers in Chatham docks to khaki and brown earth survival skills. There was one, Lever, arrived confident straight from school. He donned primrose string gloves to walk into Maidstone. I used to wonder if he removed them to salute an officer! First morning, roused by loud shouts from the sergeant, he introduced an element of polite quieter talk. "Where is the power point for an electric shaver?" We had not heard of such a thing – nor had the sergeant who remained strangely undefiant.

Where did all those incredibly athletic men come from who made us march, run and dig fox holes to our exhaustion; but not quite, or we would have failed. Did the RAF do likewise? I wonder.

The sun shone pleasantly. I remember taking a punt on the river once. It was probably with Joan from the NAAFI. The bluebells covered all of bluebell hill and the woods around were filled with them. A nightingale sang. The popular song was "A nightingale sang in Berkeley Square."

Cadets were disciplined in every way. A 10 p.m. curfew return to camp was in force. Someone told me of a gap under the wire fence – out on the Maidstone side of camp, he said. I did not tell him of my ruse to get in after curfew.

We had been in the "Running Horse" at the junction of the camp's back road and the main road from Chatham. It was pennies for a half pint of beer but a gin, even, with "mother's orange" in it was 1/6. High social life was beyond our pay so friendship with the moneyed classes such as the NAAFI girls was a means of extending our social horizons. It was nearing 11 p.m. and early dark. Joan asked what would I do. The gate was timber with an excess of barbed wire, the sentry box dimly lit from overhead. She feared I would be court marshalled, dismissed the service, disgraced before I had hardly begun.

My penknife soon secured a short straight length of hazel from the roadside. "Right – your arm in mine." Straightening up we walked boldly to the sentry who snapped to attention, opened the gate, saluted and wished us "good night, sir."

The first lesson a recruit learns is to recognise rank and respect an officer and salute. In that poor light a sentry, a trained soldier, could be forgiven for not being able to see that there was no rank on the epaulets of my tunic. "Well done – goodnight" I said as I returned his salute, my "baton" tucked smartly under my left arm. Around the centre of camp where the two main roads crossed, Joan and I would part and a little stock of discarded hazel sticks began to develop.

Somewhere down the Medway river past the derelict vast buildings beside water filled disused quarries was a wild training area. Someone had said that I was a good swimmer so I was recruited to retrieve what they said was a pair of ducks. There was certainly something afloat in the middle of the vast quarry pond. They said I would be invited to a share of extra rations.

It was lonely in that huge expanse of water; deep, clear water – bottomless, land locked, unmoving and it seemed quite sterile. I kept my mouth shut and there is no memory of any taste. After what seemed like an incredibly foolhardy distance of unlaboured but not artistic breast stroke the bodies loomed closer. I could have chosen to go back or to continue. Visions of a suspended lifeless body in mid water – my body – occurred to me. I was not for dying yet! With the two necks in my mouth, a head out each side I retrieved the water fowl. By the time I reached the shore it was evident that I had a pair of great crested grebes. I declined the offer to the extra dinner that evening.

Apparently these old brick kilns had not functioned for many decades. Great idle cathedral like hulks of buildings, one with a tall brick chimney. A grey stooped man suffered our presence with patience. He was old even for a 1914 – 18 war veteran and his memory was unreliable. He could not remember how long it was since the factory had been working. As a tease several cadets acquired a smoke generator in an attempt to get the big chimney smoking again. I did not hear if the ruse worked or if the old man saw smoke issuing from the chimney.

It was a lonely unused area. The narrow road neared what I supposed must have been the Thames estuary. We saw them coming from quite some distance. The land was flat. Our bivouacs , green and hidden amongst low gorse bushes. We were "stood to" and operating a secure sentry system. My co-sentry, younger than I, for I had my naval experience behind me, said "What shall we do?" "Leave it to me" I reassured him. The younger soldier and his ATS girl approached oblivious of everything other than a rabbit scudding for cover.

I recalled another earlier sentry duty. Belted and gaitered I waited in the dark at the top of a cliff path. It overlooked the English channel. There was a stumble on the path below me, then silence. A breathing sound, "Halt who goes there" I enunciated loudly and distinctly such that a German would have understood. There was silence. "Advance one and be recognised" I added and cocked the bolt in my loaded rifle which was pointed directly at the source of the sound. I was about to take more positive action, even omitting the "Halt or I fire." When there was a belch and a low moo. It was a Jersey cow. So the young couple advanced to within about four paces before I challenged them loudly in the manner that I had done with the cow. The ATS girl leapt off the ground and into the arms of her muscular escort.

A mental shift of gigantic proportions. Perhaps I had never felt at home in the navy. It was an easy adjustment to come to the halt on the opposite foot and to pivot the wrist to convert the naval salute to that of the army.

I had become accustomed to sleeping in a hammock whether at sea or on shore. Now my first task was to take my hessian palliasse, remove the previous owner's straw and refill it with fresh. I suppose it was not barley straw for I did not get the impression that it was at all itchy. Beds had to be made up immaculately, folded blankets, edges precisely in line. There was no place for the slightest individuality. A photograph at the end of the barrack room showed the regulation manner of layout for inspections.

Bed boards went missing on cold evenings. They were sneaked out of one's bed to fuel the iron upright stove. The warmth was welcome but the practice led to thieving of too many boards and discomfort. Unlike hammocks which were fool proof.

We were instructed by some memorable warrant officers and officers. Some of them were war damaged. A younger officer set a marvellous example of ducking and weaving imaginatively as if under fire – using a tree trunk, a hollow, rolling behind a small mound. He was very young, a captain, he had experienced live fire probably in Burma.

On the grenade range, all went well. We lobbed after removing pins and ducked as earth and bits flew. All went well until one grenade failed to explode. The sergeant lost his nerve. We were not sure if we should stay down, wait, retreat, investigate or what. He must have been shell shocked in battle. He took us to a safe distance and called for help to detonate or remove the faulty grenade. It was said that a recruit had been killed by a "69" grenade. These were for training and made of Bakelite. A ball bearing detonated the charge when the grenade hit the ground. The ball bearing had struck someone on the temple.

Someone who later became a good friend of mine lost a leg from wounds sustained during live Bren gun fire on an assault course. It is essential to train infantry in the belief that they can run along a three inch wide beam; climb rope nets – crawl under barbed wire and through drain pipes with bullets and explosions around. Self belief, even pride in a strange demanding expertise, is necessary or we would not stand and fight, let alone attack an enemy position. The training in both the navy and the army was unbelievably thorough.

Around the camp were small boards mounted on posts. These had surfaces that would register gas. The whole war was conducted with an anticipation that gas might be used. Gas masks went everywhere with us. Poison gas smells like geraniums. The instructor had a geranium plant. We smelled the leaves. We donned gas masks and entered the brick ill-lit building. It was full of smoke and we knew that without the gas mask we could not have survived. It was a great relief to get out to the fresh air and the sun and blue sky.

My most thorough training so far had been six inch guns. One hundred pound shells; swab out between rounds to douse burning cordite before reloading. Eight crew; then the CPO instructor would remove one at a time. The remainder had to improvise and keep the gun firing. One seaman crushed his fingers when the shell rolled on the steel deck. He was an invalid for some time.

Then point five Vickers, and twin Vickers and Oerlikons and aiming off; for wind speed and direction of enemy aircraft. Torpedoes, depth charges and now a simpler set of weapons; rifle, (Mark IV?) Bren, mortars, Sten and .45 revolver, sometimes a .38, and grenades. We went by truck several times for range practice near Sittingbourne. My Mother had sent me the diminutive "Observers Book of Birds" and I recorded the dates and places of sedge warblers, reed bunting. Beside the river on a beautiful secluded path I watched a kingfisher. Whilst in Maidstone a tank transporter lost control and careered down the hill, smashing into buildings. I heard there were fatalities.

151

ARRIVAL IN INDIA

For several days we were holed up in a transit camp at a place called Kalyan on the western Ghats out of Bombay. I was intrigued by the similarity with our starlings of the mynah birds. They exactly filled an identical niche. Their flying and flocking and unruly behaviour seemed to differ hardly at all.

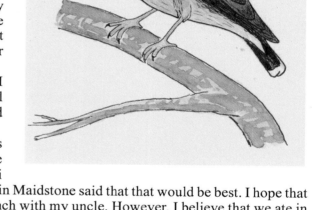

It was monsoonal! Nine inches of rain fell one day and my leather boots beneath the bed grew mould over night. There was no gutter along the eaves, not that it would have made any difference, and the water was shed like uneven panes of continuous glass outside the hut's windows. Mud was everywhere, not that we ventured far; there was really nowhere to go! During rare gaps between the torrents the mynahs spread out and fed on grubs, flies and seeds amongst the grass. At night a thousand fireflies illuminated their airborne wanderings advertising for mates.

One day I took the train to Bombay to visit an uncle. I used the ordinary local service and sat amongst colourful sari clad mothers and children with baskets of fish, hens and even a goat!

Not until this day had it occurred to me that perhaps I was less than good company for the burra sahib, my uncle, the manager of a large branch of the Hong Kong and Shanghai Bank. I banked with Grindlays only because someone back in Maidstone said that that would be best. I hope that I did not smell of fish or goat or child as I was treated to lunch with my uncle. However, I believe that we ate in the bank!

The red betal spittle on the roads, and on pavements where there were any, astonished me. It did not seem reasonable that there should be so much of it. It surprised me that people could and did freely foul every inch where one walked. Now, of course, our own streets around every cafe and sweetie shop are surrounded by a veritable minefield of discarded chewing gum. My sister prefers to think of it as pigeon droppings which I too am inclined to consider a lesser evil. At least chewing children could be persuaded to behave considerately but there is little we can do about the pigeons. I feel strongly that freedom is one thing but such antisocial behaviour should be curbed – a fine on the spot for anyone discarding chewing gum where we must walk. It would make our villages attractive once more.

Railway children intrigued me. They were so natural, uninhibited, the lowliest and the loveliest little children of unsurpassed friendliness once we had overcome the little act of "baksheesh sahib". The pathetic expression would break into a ready smile with that fleeting expression of guilt for having tried to con me. I have never aspired to being a burra anything. Once it was seen that I was not someone with whom to plead poverty we soon had an easy conversation. Their hair was sometimes matted and they were not particularly clean but then they didn't seem to be dirty either. Perhaps their rugged health showed through. They all had the most gorgeous smiles with lovely white teeth and clear complexions.

We could readily establish humour and behave as equals. They lived by the lines in sidings in nomadic shelters covered with palm and paper bags and mostly ate the discarded foods that would not survive in a fit state until sold in markets or shops. It was thrown out of railway wagons on to the ground and it was ripe and certainly nutritious. Some of my happiest memories are of railway children singing for me – songs they had learned from endless train-loads of service people moving through their territories – the popular songs of the forties.

THE TROOP TRAIN

The long troop train snaked across every kind of Indian landscape. I loved it all.

The sounds of parakeets, bee-eaters and bulbuls and so many other birds thrilled me. Perhaps I had absorbed the symphonies of some of them prenatally and as a swaddled infant on the tea estate where I was born.

Endless paddy fields were linked one with another by their watery life blood system. Dhoti clad men, heads swathed in white cloth pagris, maintained circulation – opening and closing little dams in the mud banks. A few water buffaloes added to the memorable picture as the colourful sunset shed shades of greens and browns, indigos and rainbows for miles around. At that time of year the rice was several inches tall and the figures moving gently about the flooded fields were mostly occupied with fishing. Arcs of net were thrown over the less well grown fields. These were the fish that I would have encountered on that train journey to Bombay.

Then gardens with palms and poinsettias, sweet jasmine and bougainvillea gave way to arid desert. The straight tracks stretched to oblivion on the horizon without a bend and the heat became considerable but drier.

I often sat with my feet on the running board in the cooler draught of the open doorway. We were going south to Bangalore. I do not remember how many days it took. Every dinner time the train would stop – not anywhere in particular, just somewhere, with not a dwelling or cultivation in sight. The engine's fire supplied hot water at least for the tea (cha) and it may have been that some parts of the meal were cooked somehow there up front. We went in pairs by rota to collect the large black hot pots and carried them back to our carriage. We ate beside the track and the only signs of life were the occasional laden camels passing in the distance or a large dragon-like lizard scurrying for cover. I think that it was here that I first enjoyed the cheerful chatter of bee-eaters but also encountered the atrocious behaviour of kite hawks. So they were not "Bombay ducks." Often, almost always, they would be referred to as shite-hawks.

I DREAMT I DWELT IN MARBLE HALLS

A few days out of Kalyan the engine suffered a serious fault. We limped into the railway station in Hyderabad in that princely state in southern central India.

Here was an example of a well run state with advanced social, medical and educational institutions. It was certainly clean, tidy and disciplined as we saw during our brief one night stop.

We were transported to a palace. There seemed to be no one about but I was aware that the minimal palace staff had conducted us to a marble hall which had a round central opening in the centre of the roof. Under this a fountain played into a surrounding moat holding ornamental fish. It was cooler, almost comfortable, and the marble floor was not too much of a deterrent for some sound sleep to the accompaniment of the watery sounds. The forty or so of us occupied only the lesser part of the hall. It was that vast!

OFFICERS' TRAINING SCHOOL, BANGALORE

It is strange to have no memory of arrival at the railway station in Bangalore, for I do remember saying farewell there some months later to a very young Anglo-Burmese girl who was returning to Burma. She had lodged at 6m Military Road where I was to stay myself post-commissioning for a celebratory night. She may have been sixteen, her age was difficult to determine. She was bubbly like an active child, all

Officer Training School magazine

154

smiles and laughter. She was often with an American and I once had a photograph she gave me which he had taken of her sitting on the bonnet of a jeep. I think that the American was not her father.

Not far from "6m" in Military Road was a Chinese restaurant which we used as much as our pay would permit. It was less than a one rupee rickshaw ride from camp into town. As it was likely that I would eat there fairly frequently I cultivated a conversational relationship with the waiter. Anticipating enlightening and interesting conversation about Manchuria or at least Hong Kong, I asked him where his home was – he was from Liverpool!

Hair had to be trim. We were going for a commission. Across the road from the Chinese restaurant was the hairdressers. Indian staffed, accomplished, providing quite an experience! I tipped, from my meagre pay, quite substantially and got a preferential service. I did not have to queue for long. My regular hairdresser would not readily relinquish me to one of his Indian colleagues. The cut or trim, a wash and the most tremendously relaxing and yet bracing massage to neck and shoulders – I emerged with spring in my tread and head held high.

Bangalore's maidan is tree lined. A superior town with stone built houses and shops surrounding it. There is even a large Episcopal (I think) church mid point on one side. Pavements were well made up.

The OTS Bangalore covering several acres at the edge of town gave way to gritty arid desert to the south which we used for field craft training.

Neat, colourful, lawned, as well as the dry season would allow, aligned and regular were white and terracotta mess halls and accommodation blocks. The halls were terraced by arched stone-paved walkways along both sides providing an architecturally pleasing design and relief from the rectangular. They cooled the interiors, protected the inside from the glare of the sun, and provided cover for punkah wallah boys who swung, with ropes tied to their toes, the mat fans back and forth across the ceilings of the rooms inside.

The first "billet" we were allocated was a long room divided by head high partitions. It contained perhaps twenty of these cubicles. Chicken wire filled the space above the partitions – to keep the tree rats out!

Timber rails surrounded the door and someone had swung on the overhead cross bar but had put his hand on a small black snake resting there which bit him. He died, they told me.

The monotony of sameness day by day was relieved by two activities but there was little time to indulge them except on Sundays.

One was tree rat hunts and the other was "tribal" warfare between billets in which a variety of weapons was used; the ultimate seemed to be flit guns firing methylated spirits – alight. Sunday mornings were punctuated by the dog diminishing tactics of the man with responsibility and expertise in getting rid of undesirable "pie" (pariah) dogs.

HOSPITAL – FLUEY SPELL

A strange nausea overcame me at some point in the six months course. The doctor in the hospital did not know of my previous service in the navy. It felt like 'flu to me but he deduced that it was the rigours of the training I was undergoing and although I have never seen the medical papers I feel certain that he wrote "psychiatric case" on my record. Little did he know that Bangalore was almost a holiday camp compared with much of my time with the navy.

There was one obstacle to overcome before I could be granted a commission. This was an eight foot high wall which we had to scale wearing full kit! Part of the assault course. Without the aid of someone from behind and another on the wall I was just never going to make it – on my own! The technique, which was relatively easy for someone even a few inches taller than I, was to run at it and allow the momentum to carry one upward with a boot a few feet up the wall's front. I always slipped and landed crumpled on the ground.

Hospital was a welcome break in an airy light ward, civilised, comfortable and comforted. Some new nurses arrived from "Blighty". Green they were, not used to the way of things in India. I asked one to accompany me to a meal in town, which she did. A short rickshaw ride to the other side of the maidan, down Military Road and halt on the left going down the hill at the Chinese restaurant. We dined. The waiter, from Liverpool, did us proud and it was a little oasis in an otherwise somewhat brutal regimen. We rickshaw-ed back to hospital and I was soon discharged in a day or so back to the resolutely unbeatable brick wall.

Somewhere over the next weeks with endless practice after each day's parades and training I did manage to scale the wall – in full kit. I felt I was now assured of my place in an Indian army regiment. There had been some correspondence with a copy to myself about my suitability for the 1st Gurkha Rifle Regiment. I had, as had everyone else, stated my preference of regiment – the order of the three I gave is now forgotten. I was to be commissioned, when the time came, into the 3rd Queen Alexandra's Own Gurkha Rifles. I could not have wished for better! It suited my temperament more than the "firsts" would have done, I thought.

After demobilisation I made some effort to maintain contact but survival in civilian life took precedence. My young wife and I did however attend tea at Buckingham Palace once and we met John Masters there, the great author of stories of life in India.

I went back to ask the nurse out but she had learned fast. Nothing under the rank of major. The scaling of an eight-foot wall was hardly the entree to the affections of an unattached lady in the huge sub continent of India. I have since thought, but consider it most unlikely, that the nurse dining with me was a psychiatrist's ploy to put me back on duty in my booted feet. But no, I doubt if he would have shared a newly arrived young lady with a mere cadet!

Wedding of Major T. M. LOWE and Miss CHERRIE JONES.
A group taken outside the Gymkhana Club after the wedding. From left to right—Rev. Father VANPEENE, Mrs. JONES, the Bridegroom and Bride, Brig. L. B. JONES, Miss NAOMI JONES (Bridesmaid) and Major A. R. H. DEE (Bestman).

Photo from the Bangalore Officers Training School magazine.

Major T. M. Lowe, staff of OTS Bangalore, married Cherrie Jones, the commandant's daughter. I was later to join Lowe's regiment and read his accounts of my battalion in our Officers' Association news letters.

LACHMAN

We were now in a block which permitted some comfort and privacy. Two shared a room and two rooms shared a bearer. The bearer's name was Lachman – a deeply dark-skinned dear of an elderly gentleman. A Tamil, he was white haired with kindly ways and the most polite and respectful manner. It was his responsibility to keep us smart; he would not allow me to tie the laces of my boots which he had polished to perfection. Belts and anklets were worn for most training and they too were always smartly kept by him. He was a perfectionist in every way and openly enjoyed his service and the responsibility for his charges.

Chota hazri is literally little breakfast. Every morning he wakened us with mugs of tea, two biscuits and a banana – one of those little local plantain flavoursome ones. He spoke enough English for his work and I sometimes talked with him about other matters. Reluctance or language limitations prevented too detailed a conversation. One morning I had been a little slow to arrive on parade so I asked him why he had not roused me a bit more vigorously. "No Sahib, no, all the spirit might not get back in." Oh that all the world should feel that the spirit is more important than punctuality.

RECREATION

A pleasant sound came from the main road which ran through the camp. Strains of "the Isle of Capri" in waltz time played on local wind and string instruments. There may have been an imported trumpet too which leaned a little more heavily and emphasised more the melody and the beat. A drum, two-ended I would think, made up quite an expensive group. A wedding at least I thought until I came nearer to the group of thirty white dhoti clad men. The coffin was carried on a barrow, the funeral to be held somewhere across town. Sometimes I wonder if the melody is an ancient Indian one that became "borrowed" for the song that we know.

There are so many ways of disposing of the dead. I remember being told that in Bombay suburbs it was not unknown for a hand or arm to be found in the garden following a Parsi funeral. They take their dead to the top of a high tower for the vultures and other birds to demolish. The Towers of Silence. Skeletons of all kinds of creatures used to find their way to loading bays by the docks, there to be transported to Europe for glue and fertilizer and bone meal. My father tried when I was young to shock me by suggesting that that was how dessert jellies were made! I have not yet witnessed a funeral pyre other than Rajiv Gandhi's on television. It takes quite a lot of ghee to make a certain job of it.

I had never excelled at running sports although I was, if anything, better equipped for "half miles" than "100 yard" sprints. It came as a surprise to me that I had stamina for "cross country". I entered, just for a lark, the training sessions for this voluntary pursuit and the results were so promising that I was included in our team for the annual SEAC eleven mile.

A great effort of will kept me going until that stage is reached which may be described as second wind. It still took effort but the pain seemed to diminish. Perhaps it was a numbness that sets in.

Dear Lachman always had a large glass of freshly squeezed limes ready for my return – nimbu pani. He just waited there ready with the glass in his wrinkled black hands for the very moment that I arrived back at my room. And the gusal water would be ready, heated by the bishti wallah and poured into the galvanised tub that Lachman would order as he saw that I had finished the cooling slaking drink. It is of such acts that make parts of one's short spell on earth so very special.

Life is dramatic without our assistance. We need not try to write a script to keep ourselves entertained –

life throws its little plots at us in remarkable ways. On the big race day, more than half way round the course, we were strung out with some of us in the lead over a stretch of a mile or so. There was no-one in sight as I hurtled through diminutive fields around small holdings and simple houses of mud bricks and thatch. The sun was very hot.

A sense of elation and achievement spurred me on. Gazelle like I floated over little bushes when something fleshy growing on them caught my eye. I was thirsty. The "farmer" wouldn't miss one surely. A bright shiny red one loomed at about hand height and I picked it and popped it into my mouth. I was ready to relish the refreshment that it would provide. It was a pepper, a red hot cayenne chilli pepper!

I was counted in at the tape among the first 35 out of about 250 that started the race. I think our team won. I may have been 16th.

There were dances in town. I went to one. I am no dancer unless it be Scottish country dancing. They seemed to be church run and the "talent" was Christian. The ladies were looking for husbands or a cash relationship? Confession would provide absolution which the two main religions most certainly would not. In any case the breath of the two "girls" that I danced with was overpowering and less attractive than fresh cardamom and cumin. I did not give it another try.

PORNO OR EROTICA

In that part, fairly far south in India, there were strange temples. There was not much spare time for sight seeing. A brief look at the carved stone of the outside walls made clear that woman and copulation was a worshipful part of life. What is one person's pornography is another's erotica. These scenes were dignified by comparison with the behaviour of some cadets who woke me in the early hours when we were still in the cubicled house. "Pass the Dettol" was the panic cry, as someone sought to save himself from syphilis. One could not go half a mile in town without being offered a "saf biwi"! Clean woman.

The children, boys, who hawked sex in the streets probably interpreted "saf" as "prostitute" and had no reason to understand the soldier's emphasis on clean. Their wages – of sin! – may have been little indeed, perhaps only to get to watch, well hidden, for free. It was to be several years yet before I would experience sex!

WILDLIFE

I have never accepted that the past should be called the days of the Raj. India was as much home as was Scotland. Requests would be made of my family in the days of Empire to help rid a village of troublesome wild animals. Uncle Dick is pictured with a leopard. Uncle Mike's floor cover was the skin of a troublesome tiger.

At the extreme edge of the training area was a greener small valley partially grown over with shrubs and grasses. We used it occasionally for field craft and other training.

One pleasantly warm day we rested on one side in the shade of a small tree. We were quiet. Others were still moving about somewhere else in the little valley and they flushed a leopard. It slunk down the opposite bank and disappeared into the scrub.

I met quite a few snakes. Perhaps eight or ten in two years. Some must have been harmless. I did not make a study of them, and usually my proximity to them was intentionally limited.

The briefest encounters were two incidents. One was just en passant, at speed. I was running fully kitted along a bund, which is the Indian name for "shut" or "closed" and often refers to a dam. It may have been a couple of hundred yards long – water in the reservoir on one side and a steepish bank on the other. There was only a narrow track formed by regular use by human and other creatures. Our combined speed, in opposing directions, must have exceeded thirty miles an hour. I suppose the snake saw me. It was over six feet long and I did not slow to take a better look. I was aware too that a group of monkeys were behaving strangely and capering about at the other end of the bund. They must also have seen the snake. I was soon clear of all the excitement and back on gravelly open dry land.

Dick died in 1933 of cholera and was buried in the Nilgiris in a cemetery near Kotagiri. Everything was so terribly British.

The second occasion never ceases to astound me. The speed with which adrenalin courses through the body is unbelievable. I was on my way down into a "nullah". This is the name of a gouged river or stream bed and signifies usually that it is dry, although sometimes it may fill with water in a storm. When I say that I was on my way down I mean that I was in mid air having launched from the edge towards the flat grassy floor some four feet below. Pack and pouches, ammunition and rifle and wearing army boots indicate quite a load. It was my crafty intention, learned as a child when stalking rabbits in the wilderness of my Hebridean home, to use the obviously dead ground and get ahead of the "enemy" and take them by surprise. The surprise was mine – launched into mid air and beginning to descend at the great speed which gravity compels – I saw a cobra below me.

Needless to say it saw me coming and scooted somewhere out of sight. I scooted too. Upwards with only one "knees bend" on the ground. I landed back up from where I had jumped – pack and all. This so surprised me that I went back that evening with a couple of friends to see what it was that I had done. Without pack or rifle, and without adrenalin, having checked that there was no sign of the snake, I could not possibly jump back out of the nullah. Nor could any of my friends.

We had an entertainment hall at the edge of camp where buildings gave way to open desert. I was making my way there to watch a film one evening when the projector operator came out with a long handled shovel in his hands. It held a dead cobra which he had bludgeoned in the projector room.

CHARLIE LORIS

I acquired, and should not have done so, a Slow Loris. A fellow cadet had purchased it in the bazaar. I think it had been Charlie, a large man who seemed well equipped for the rank of CSM in the British army. He was wise enough to dispose of his ownership of the creature before he moved on to an officers mess, if in fact he did.

The Loris came to be named Charlie, but bore no resemblance to the large man from whom it came. Later, with the Gurkhas, the Loris was to be called Banmanshee (wild or mad man). The Loris was slow, quiet and thoughtful and tailless. His coat was grey, short haired and soft and he had pleading round prominent dark eyes. He was small enough for a fabric watch strap around his waist to form the means by which he could be restrained with a leather boot lace through which he never chewed although I suspect he could have done! He was to stay with me wherever I went for the next eighteen months.

I gathered a reputation for being the animal lover which propelled me into unique situations for all the time I served in the Gurkhas.

LETTERS HOME

The photo on a glass plate, 1918 on promotion from Midshipman to Sub Lieutenant.

It was later that I acquired a camera so at this time I was sending home small water colour pictures of the colourful scenes around me. The tree rats, the multicolour flowered thorny bushes of the desert and the women carrying water to and from the well. How on earth can a shrub, and there was a tree that did it too, produce a whole range of colours in their flowers on the one plant. I had not experienced anything like it before. It seemed to break some natural law to do with genetics. The shrub which was thorny grew in spite of desert conditions and the predations of a few goats. Its habit was that of a gooseberry bush with flowers carried on the extremities. Pink and yellow and pale red, and less frequently almost bluish. The inflorescences were like heads of multicoloured forget-me-nots. I sent home pressed flowers too.

Of course my mother knew India – she had married there at the age of seventeen or eighteen, perhaps twenty. My father was "Geddes" axed from the navy in which he had served since the age of twelve and a half. At the age of twenty-two in 1922 with no trade or profession he "went tea planting". They had met in Cologne when he was a dashing naval Lieutenant in the Rhine Flotilla with his own command – a little patrol boat with a prominent gun on the foredeck.

My mother was staying with friends, the consul I think, and there had been dances, receptions and every condition to precipitate a romance for the two of them with the moon over the broad river.

An adolescent enquiry by me of my mother, when I was once doubting that I would ever have the courage to marry, led to the question "What did you find so attractive in Popey." She replied that it might have been the way he unbuttoned his elastic braces and let them flick over his shoulders. They had a troubled marriage probably because he had known no family life yet she had been nurtured in a very loving environment.

The trees with red and yellow "tissue paper" flowers reminded me of mulberry trees. It was in these trees that the tree rats often took refuge after being hounded from the "billets".

Havoc with foods, biscuits and sweets was reason enough to warrant tree rat hunts but to find ones socks in the drawer chewed into a nest-full of pink babies was the end.

SCORPION

My father was not devoid of humour. It was his own brand and did not amuse everyone and probably served to annoy quite a few. Something on his glue and jelly theme and more to surprise me than amuse me was his story of Indians buying stamps merely to lick the flavour of the glue off them. He seemed to enjoy my disbelief, or was it my discomfort?

On the way to buy some stamps at the little post office in the camp I came across a black and very lively scorpion. Caught in the open with nowhere to hide. It attracted my attention and a couple more cadets joined me. I was interested in its behaviour and made it raise its pincered tail in response to my gentle jabs with a small stick. I was fully aware of its capabilities and would not have risked being nipped by it. However as always in my life there was an angel on hand to protect me. A bishti wallah or sweeper who was passing intervened. In his tiny vocabulary he dissuaded us from staying near the creature and it went on its way. It was unhurt by us and the Tamil servant would certainly not have harmed it. There is a place for every creature in this world. I know some who would have stamped on it and gone their way without remorse.

CHAMELEONS

We had not been marched remorselessly in the navy. They had other forms of torture suitable for the confines of ships. The army made up for it both at Maidstone and now in the heat of the sun. Many of the roads around Bangalore were of stone. Some were made up with gravel and others merely tracks worn by use. Camels made little impression on the ground with their soft padded feet but bullock carts had iron rimmed wheels. We were stopped for a welcome breather beside one of these roads on a gentle hillside. Bushes and occasional small trees provided no shelter from the sun for our brief stay but there was enough greenery and grass to harbour wild creatures.

Packs and gear were on the ground with rifles "piled", their muzzles linked together to form pyramids. We took a quencher from our water bottles. Someone relieving himself in the shrubbery noticed a strange creature on a branch. An eight inch body, a long prehensile tail, and bulbous eyes acting independently. Its face was ugly by human standards but as chameleons go I would give it credit for being an excellent specimen! It was a lively green colour with dry crinkly skin. Then someone moved it to the road and it turned brown. On the rocks it went nearly white. We put it back to pursue its slow aerial perambulation of the branches. "Fall in." We had to scramble into our kit, collect our rifles and form threes in the road once more. We did not see it catching grubs with its long sticky tongue. For those of you for whom the first half of the twentieth century is only history remember that there had been few feature cinema films in colour. We were pre-television and almost all books had only monochrome illustrations. It was a richly colourful experience.

URDU MUNSHI

There was order in India although there had been a mutiny in the Indian Navy up by Karachi but I do not remember when, and it seemed to be over fairly quickly. Our minds were still focussed on survival against aggression by Germany and Japan. We were mobilised, we served, we still worked with a common aim. We were all loyal, Africans, Indians, Australians, Canadians, everyone, to a cause. The same cause.

We were the allies together bringing to an end the insurrection and we had won.

Field craft and formations. Hand signals, the crafty use of the terrain. Realistic exercises were supplemented with illustrations in AITMs "Army in India Training Manuals.

An event which marked the end of hostilities was when my close friend Speirs, close because we were alphabetically linked in everyday happenings, was allowed to meet his father. It was with Speirs that I shared the room. Four of us shared Lachman's services. We had also strangely been bracketed by our shooting prowess. We had shared "kitties" from our first shooting days in Kent and continued to do so in Bangalore too. With the only two maximum scores we would sometimes shoot it out for the kitty to go solely to the winner but

164

not all the others had the patience to see an end to it.

His father had spent the war in a Japanese prison camp and being repatriated via India, father and son were able to meet. What a poignant moment. Son such a big boy and about to become an officer. Father was emaciated but I believe that he might have been worse. Many were. They had probably not seen each other for about five years.

We took some chairs and sat in a comfortable corner outside our room for Urdu coaching. Our munshi was Muslim. He took us through the basics with a gentle manner. We asked him how many wives he had. He had two. Our interest stemmed from naivety. We were conditioned for strict monogamy with images of the devil and hell for what seemed to be perfectly normal to him. He politely satisfied our curiosity. Two houses both supported adequately by him. The two wives did not meet. He stayed with either as it suited all of them apparently. He needed his reasonably paid employment but made it clear that the prerequisite was the ability to support the second wife.

SERIOUS TRAINING

There must have been uncertainties about our training. Where would we go. Many aspects of infantry skills are common wherever one is.

Apart from field hand signals we saw nothing of communication systems. Radios were large heavy items. The "36" and "48" sets were both a full load for a man. The batteries were heavy. They were for close quarter use and within the Brigade. The Division wireless to HQ required a "22" set and was so large that it occupied the two sides of a mule's full load.

We could transmit over 200 miles with improvisation and choice of site and an extra long aerial. This wireless set went on one side with the accumulator (battery) on the other.

But we saw nothing of that during training. We shot, we mortared, we map-read, we field-crafted. We personnel-managed – a little. We climbed over, along and under 'assault' courses. We progressed only slowly with Urdu.

We exercised in 'the field', open desert areas with scrubby trees and little

cover from the ever present hot sun. Meals arrived on military wheels and, were for me, also palatable. Our breaks in training attracted the kite hawks, the opportunists in the food business. If one did not hold a free hand over the top of the plate a pair of talons would remove the prime protein portion leaving a hungry pang in the belly for the rest of the day. Two inch mortar flares were held aloft for their brief burning spell by a small fabric parachute offering some fun. One trick was to tie a morsel of food to the rolled up parachute. A hawk grabbed the food and made off. His efforts to fly were gradually overcome by the resistance of the now opened parachute. It had either to relinquish its food or land with it if there were not many people too near, then hilarity as someone was roused from his post lunch snooze as a hawk made off with some food tied to the slumberer's knife, fork and spoon – which were personal and not easily replaceable. They were always retrieved.

COMMISSIONING PARADE

General Christison

Selected, polished, prepared, groomed and drilled we were ready for the big day. The march past with the band. I had done it before – the eyes right was the same – the halt command now given on the other foot and I had learned to salute with the hand held differently. The pace was different of course; the navy had been quicker than the army. Little did I know then that the Gurkha pace was to outstrip anything I had ever known, even in the navy.

The Sunday morning prior to the parade day I was woken by a loud explosion somewhere not distant. It was the dog cull. The "expert" took the opportunity of low activity to lay baits for unwanted and scrounging "pie" dogs. The bait was meat but

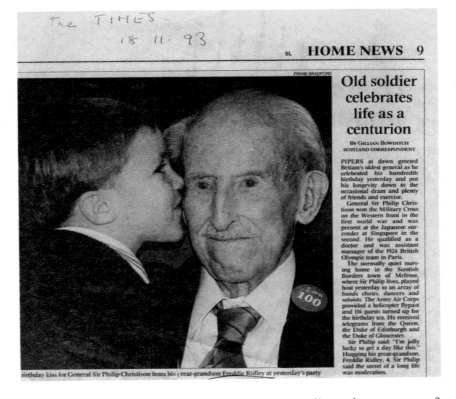

The TIMES 18.11.93

sL **HOME NEWS** 9

FRANK BRADFORD

Old soldier celebrates life as a centurion

By GILLIAN BOWDITCH
SCOTLAND CORRESPONDENT

PIPERS at dawn greeted Britain's oldest general as he celebrated his hundredth birthday yesterday and put his longevity down to the occasional dram and plenty of friends and exercise.

General Sir Philip Christison won the Military Cross on the Western front in the first world war and was present at the Japanese surrender at Singapore in the second. He qualified as a doctor and was assistant manager of the 1924 British Olympic team in Paris.

The normally quiet nursing home in the Scottish Borders town of Melrose, where Sir Philip lives, played host yesterday to an array of bands, choirs, dancers and soloists. The Army Air Corps provided a helicopter flypast and 116 guests turned up for the birthday tea. He received telegrams from the Queen, the Duke of Edinburgh and the Duke of Gloucester.

Sir Philip said: "I'm jolly lucky to get a day like this." Hugging his great-grandson, Freddie Ridley, 4, Sir Philip said the secret of a long life was moderation.

birthday kiss for General Sir Philip Christison from his great-grandson Freddie Ridley at yesterday's party

with a charge and detonator in it. Someone suggested that it was a shame for a dog to die at the moment of great expectation – rather should it be allowed to swallow the meat and the explosion to follow the fulfilment. That would be internal combustion! I saw dogs heaped on a cart go by an hour before church parade.

More than fifty years on I have a book called *The Admiral's Baby* written by Laurens Van der Post. It is the story of the part played by General Christison, and by the author and others in post war Java. It was this general who formally gave his approval to the body of men now to be commissioned into the Indian Army. He took the salute.

There was an aircraft factory at Bangalore. Much of the labour force was Italian prisoners of war. They made and sold, from chunks of aluminium, some excellent cigarette lighters. Most of us smoked. I had taken to small cigars and there were some fragrant ones made with greenish local leaf.

Donning single pip epaulets, with the rank of second lieutenant, we were granted two weeks leave starting that night in lodgings in town. It removed the noise and the responsibility for the inevitable celebrations from the camp. My upbringing had been staid but I enjoyed the others' unbridled enthusiasm and joined rather wild but harmless company. We drank more than was good in a club or hotel – pretty gardens, lawns, bougainvillea and cannas. It was dark but there were lights hung around the garden.

Someone was thrown into the swimming pool. I shared a rickshaw for the journey back to the digs with Charlie. He insisted that we stop on the way and then disappeared into a luxurious bungalow through open French windows. The last I saw of him he was standing beside a large bed which contained a voluminous woman in her nightie.

He didn't chastise me too severely next morning for driving home without him. On arrival at 6m Military Road, rather late and with the door locked, the landlady with a grab at my tunic front propelled me at speed across the courtyard. Somehow I negotiated the pond in the middle and made it to my room to land heavily on the bed. I do not remember anything more of Bangalore.

MRS STEVENSON SAW ME IN THE BATH

Thomson and I were paired for our leave. He and I had been together in the navy. Speirs and Gunn seemed to be together. The four of us elected for the Nilgiri Hills south of Bangalore. We had chosen from a list of hosts where we wished to stay although I had asked to go for the second week, with Thomson, to my father's cousin in Mangalore on the west coast. I was returning to the place of my birth.

The wedding photographs are dated 1924.

My birth certificate is Indian on rough

dull paper. The entries in black-scrawled "Indian" ink proclaim 29th November 1925. My mother is given in her maiden name.

The ratchet railway runs from Metapulliam up the steep track from the plains to emerge from intermediate jungle to cool eucalyptus-clad blue mountains.

At times the line crosses deep gorges spanned by slim scaffolding. The bridges are not visible to passengers through the carriage windows. This makes it an eerie and breathtakingly exciting journey. We were entering tea garden country. The towns in the Nilgiri Hills are Ootacamund, affectionately abbreviated to Ooty; where Indian Nawab and Maharajahs holidayed and honeymooned, Coonoor and Kotagiri. The tea estate, my first home, is beyond Kotagiri.

1924 My father demonstrates the quality leaves of the Nilgiri tea.

Nilgiri tea is distinct from all others. It is picked in the same way, but then it is fermented only partially before kilning. This puts it between a China and an ordinary Indian tea.

Our hosts lived in comfort with a full set of servants, as was common, in Ooty. There was a long table for dinner. I sat on my lady host's left, Mrs Stevenson. She asked me if this was my first time in India to which I proudly announced that I had been born here. On reminding her of my name she took only seconds to announce loudly so that all at the table should hear. "The last time I saw you I bathed you!"

After dinner in the evenings we walked by a small track through fields of tall crops to the club. After in the dark, one of the group started a nonsense panic about the possibility of there being leopards in the crops. Although it was unlikely it was not impossible. We chose the main road for our return in the dark behaving at times like giggly frightened children.

This was the time when such club establishments were seriously having to consider the membership of Indians. There was uncertainty on both sides. Not many Indians were prepared to break with tradition.

169

ROB ROY

We hired a car between the four of us and explored. It was an open long brown bath shaped car. It came with a driver without much English and apparently too little fuel.

One day we went to see "Rob Roy", my first home. In my sister's cloakroom loo today there is a water colour of this bungalow.

A pretty setting in hills with garden and tea bushes around. The road down to the bungalow is steep and the view vast, distant and almost mountainous. Green leafy tea bushes clothe the undulating land and shade trees punctuate its regularity. The painter would have been family or friend.

My father told me that he had so impressed the gardener of the need to keep the plants in the garden borders watered that he found him one day out there watering in the pouring rain.

It was from the deep valleys below that the elephants would come. When they did intrude the available workers were mobilised with tin cans and stones to make enough noise to deter them from entering the tea bushes and creating havoc. A tigress would sometimes frighten my mother with its incessant deep throated mating pleas in search of a male. I have had a fear of that sound ever since.

1926 In the garden at Rob Roy.

170

When we returned to Scotland we lived downwind of the Edinburgh Zoological park and we would hear wolves, tigers and lions. My childish nightmares were of tigers leaping onto the backs of horses as we rode. Elephants' trunks reached in through the window. I would cringe against the bedroom wall and my parents came to comfort me. My sister's cot was moved into a new corner of the bedroom and next morning father was concerned that perhaps there were "draughts there" – her comment in the morning was that she had not seen any "giraffes" in the corner. There are no giraffes in India, however!

Is this the way we learn. We sense the perils experienced by our parents and the impression stays with us. Equally it is interesting that fear may be overcome by the example shown by parents. With me here now in Islay is the third generation of chaffinches that have known me. Two young sisters still fluffy were brought by their mother some years ago to the kitchen door and she carried food to them which she took from me in the kitchen. Last spring some of the sister's offspring seemed not to need any tuition in approaching quite close to me. Intuition; example; education?

The driveway at Rob Roy descends fairly steeply to end beside the house. Mrs Stevenson told me of one of my father's tricks. He would partially apply the hand brake of the car and then let it run down the drive – with no driver in it. It always stopped short of the edge of the drive. Had it gone further it would not have been possible to retrieve it from among the tea bushes down the hill.

171

NILGIRI HILLS

Our drives about the hills were stimulating and dreamlike. The weather was always good. At four to six thousand feet on a latitude roughly level with Madras, which is hot, the climate is enjoyable – the days warm, the evenings cool. Eucalyptus trees cover much of the higher land giving it its blue cool look. In every direction it was hilly. Gently rounded ranges interspersed by deep valleys.

The car was old and bath shaped and the body a muddy brown colour. A thermometer on top of the radiator; the hood was always down; the upholstery of cracking leather. It could well have been the car my father had twenty years previously. Our driver had no English and the Urdu we had been learning would have been useless if he was a Tamil.

The car juddered to a halt on a high curving bend in the road. The land rose steeply above us and a porcupine had shed a quill which was lying amongst the stones, pine needles and rather short parched grass. On the lower side the land fell away and then continued hill beyond hill into the lazy horizon. All had varying degrees of tree covering, more dense in some places and sparse in others. The driver indicated that we had run out of petrol. So what is to be done now? There seemed to be no habitation nor sign of human life in sight. He produced a jerrycan and signified "money". We had a whip round and raised some rupees. Enough it seemed, for the driver walked off after tucking a siphon tube into his clothing. No traffic passed in the twenty or so minutes that passed before the driver returned with petrol.

We had been to Rob Roy – quite remote and further than the driver had anticipated. It was some way beyond Kotagiri. From the painting, and the fragmented stories I had been told, I recognised the steep drive down. The arrival at the side of the bungalow (orig. Indian Bangla), the garden and the veranda.

There was no one about. No occupants it seemed yet the house was obviously inhabited and doors and windows open. A chokidar appeared. Elderly, wizened, black chiselled face; that dark Tamil colouring that seems to reflect the blue of the sky. The hair was nearly white. He spoke no English nor Urdu. I mentioned my name – for him it would have been "Ishstooart". Not an instant response – but a flicker of half understanding.

I had broken my leg falling from the veranda into the flower border when I was about a year old. I demonstrated an infant in my arms and pointed to the veranda. Then the tumble and the breaking of my leg.

He had few teeth but his broad beaming smile exposed them. Hands held palms together, "Ah! Ishstooart?" was all he could say!

It must have been a long drive if we travelled to Madras by car for the X-ray. I would judge the journey by trains would be near impossible.

My mother held daily sick parades for the workers although she was young and untrained.

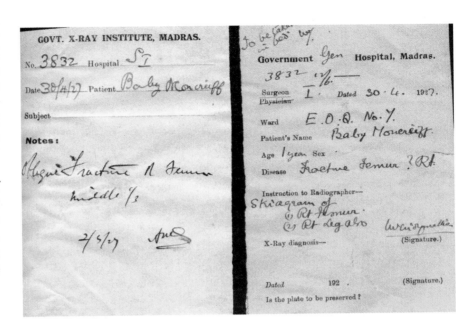

TO MANGALORE

How Thomson and I got to Mangalore is now vague. I remember arriving by train through forests and jungle terrain, and there was a part where villagers appeared to live an idyllic life among lush vegetation where food both vegetable crop and animal meat and milk seemed plentiful. The women there, in those days, wore nothing above the waist. All were a lovely bronzed colour. Such a contrast with the near ebony Tamils I had been with in Bangalore. The trees as we descended towards the coast provided a haven for a great variety of brightly coloured birds; scarlet, golden yellows, greens and often with black as well. A paradise except that it must often be drastically hot and sometimes very humid with it. The bird song was outstanding.

On that journey or on some other occasion I remember travelling northward off the Nilgiri Hills down towards Mysore. We passed large hardwood trees of mahogany and the like. At one point slightly lower down to one side of the road was a herd of wild elephants sporting in a large shallow lake in a broad clearing in the jungle.

My father's cousin was manager of a clay tile factory. He was sufficiently rewarded to afford a few servants and I think he did not drive the car himself from the station to the bungalow but I am uncertain. His was quite a lowly position and not too well compensated considering the rigours of the climate. Companies tended to provide perks such as pensions and education for children which would have been unaffordable with more modest employment in Britain. They never had children.

The factory produced roof tiles, and I suppose drainage tiles too, which sold in many distant parts of the subcontinent.

It was during a journey in the car, either then or on a subsequent occasion, that I had my first experience of rioting. Some of the crowd banged on the roof of the car. Slogan shouting and noisy responses were designed to intimidate or to make points, register grievances or further political aspirations. I imagine it was more electioneering in the van of independence than a gesture against the British. All was peaceful for the next week of our stay.

The highlight of my sojourn in India was a journey up the river in a clay boat. On the Malabar Coast there were interesting dugouts and outriggers, all made locally by hand with the minimum of tools; constructed with nine tenths skill and little in the way of tools. But then the tools were locally fashioned. All was sustainable; nothing consumed – except the fish which the outriggers sought in the dangerous surfs on this nearly endless unbroken shore.

Our boat was not a dug-out but a planked affair. Its foot wide timbers were perhaps an inch thick and maybe more. They were edge to edge and not lapped as in more advanced craft. Coir string bound them to each other by holes along the planks' edges. A tarry substance prevented the ingress of water but the boatman attended to the odd bead of water developing on the inside as we travelled. He also handled the tiller and the single rectangular sail, expertly seeking the lesser currents that suited our travel up the swirling deep water. The westerly wind alone, which for much of the year runs strongly inland and upstream, provided the power. The boat descended the river entirely by crafty steering in the fast current without the sail. By then it would be almost down to the gunnels with a full load of pink yellow clay for the factory. Our boatman spoke not one word of English!

Our hosts motored us through the hinterland. The native state of Coorg. More trees, more colour. Hills, quite rugged at times. Deep gorges and rivers. A wild country peopled by colourful characters going back without change for many millennia.

174

A tall figure stood proud on a hill. It could be seen from a whole day's walk away. The Gumpta is the god. His arms are long, fingers reaching to the knees, a sign of godliness in much of India. His stone effigy was cut from a single piece of stone and stood forty-five feet high. It is said that there is as much below the ground to secure it upright. Are we missing something.

My neighbours here would not today mix a batch of cement without a mechanical mixer yet these monuments were hauled and upended at a time when we imagine that the wheel had not been invented! Or had it?

The stone statue stood in an acre of grass surrounded by a substantial wall of black stone. Low internal walls and paved paths were symmetrically laid out. A little ornate stone hut served as "altar" and seemed to be the priest's shelter. I seem to remember that he was dhoti clad and acted as the chokidar, a caretaker.

Note the size of the man at the foot of Gumpta.

Offerings of food to the god lay in small brass bowls and plates and one supposes that the chokidar ate them after they had been displayed to the god for his consideration all day.

Somewhere not far from the factory, near the shore, my cousin showed us the yard where coffee and cashews were packed. The nuts had come by dhow from east Africa and squatting women shelled them expertly by bashing the outer shell with a stone whilst holding them with their toes. The coffee lay in conical heaps awaiting the removal of the beans for packing. Dogs and children seemed to have free range over all. My father used to tell me that tea from India was labelled "untouched by hand" but was packed by foot in the plywood tea chests.

A young man shinned up one of a group of tall palms; bare feet on the palm's trunk and a hand-held waistband round the tree. At the crown he seemed so far away and small against the clear blue sky. Two coconuts soon fell to the ground and were decapitated with accurate blows from a sharp machete. We drank the sweet refreshing aromatic coconut milk from the large heavy green spheres.

AID AND EMPLOYMENT

At the southern foot of the Nilgiri Hills is Coimbatore. (Bombs during electioneering on 2nd February 1998). It is the textile capital of India. Large factories housed endless looms and much of the material bought in bazaars across India was made here by a large workforce. I have been told that with American investment most of the workers were laid off. "Minders" turned out more cloth with automated looms with a substantial financial gain to the Indian owners.

I had always held that aid to India should not take the form of power tools. Not that there is electricity everywhere, but it still normally needs two to drill a hole in a piece of wood. One to hold the drill and the other to operate the leather thong driving the shaft which holds the bit.

My daughter and I travelled to India and Pakistan in 1986 and the door had not been fitted to my friends wash house by the time we arrived. The carpenters came while we were there and the whole door was assembled on the ground using feet and hands. The panels were slotted in and the stile and rails pinned together by wooden pegs in holes made by a "two man drill"! The iron bit being the only part which would have been made by someone outside the village. I am not sure if glue was used – that would have been a local product too – probably not bovine bones! Foreign debt, currency problems and unemployment follow some investment aid programmes.

REPORTING FOR DUTY

Mangalore and Dehra Dun, a hill station, are almost at opposite ends of the earth. I was far south on the sunny western shores of India. My regimental headquarters was in the north at Dehra Dun, roughly in the middle of India. Pakistan was not even a glimmer in someone's eye.

I know that I went to Madras, on the east coast in order to join a train that would take me north, well over another 1,000 miles. I

176

remember the location of the hotel where I stayed. It was blisteringly hot. I suppose that I was more than a little conscious of my new single pip status, and that I wore my peaked cap with some pride. We had been kitted out at a durzi in Bangalore; probably shoes, socks, a suit and a cap. It had not been quite a parallel of the experience of Gieves in Brighton in the Navy. It had taken a great deal of hard physical training and much learning over a period of three years to achieve my officer status. I could now skipper a landing craft – well almost! Read Morse and semaphore, interpret charts and maps, find my way by the stars and theodolites, handle an incredible array of weaponry from depth charges to torpedoes, weigh an anchor and even swing the lead – "deep nine"! I now knew the ways of "beehives", which blow neat holes in the ground, and could make Bangalore torpedoes out of drain pipes!

I had to wait a day or two in Madras before there was a train that would take me where I needed to go. Madras provided me with an experience of really roasting dry heat with sun for all the hours of daylight. I would certainly not have enjoyed a posting there. I frequented the (European) swimming pool. In its clear blue water I learned to swim a length and a bit under water. I had been called on to retrieve objects from the sea bed below the pier in the island where we spent the most formative years of my childhood. I prided myself on the length of time I could stay submerged. No snorkels or flippers then!

Then for a few days I suffered the confines of a rail carriage and remember nothing at all about the journey which must have taken several days. I cannot have been indifferent to the wildlife, the birds, the scenery and the activities of everyone en route. Perhaps I was just tired; relieved that after all this time my training was complete and I could look forward to work

I do remember being quite petrified once more of monkeys on railway stations and one nearly touched me with its filthy arm through the bars of the carriage window. I just drew away before its hand touched me. Perhaps it might have grabbed my ear. Perhaps the monkey was trying to be friendly and I am biased from yet another of my mother's fears that I had acquired. I noticed that a dominant male tended to lord a group or family which seemed to own a platform or the whole railway station. Females of all ages would present to the boss male if they had been distanced from him for a time and he would mount them with feet holding their hind legs to penetrate them for a few token thrusts of acknowledgement. Social bonding. The only other males that were tolerated in the group were juveniles.

2. TO THE HILLS

Dehra Dun
Integration
Frontier Warfare
Hill Station Luxury
Music
To the Hills
Saitbir Pun
Hindus
Camera
A Monstrous Amphibian
Albino
Jackals and Mohammed
Cards
Across the Rivers to Agra
Agra Revisited
Jangla Railway Station
Science
Flying Foxes and Jackals
Riding Dr By Pony
Corn, Grapes, Figs, Tomatoes and Gifts
Shoots
Trip to Div HQ
Village Hospitality
Water or the Absence of It

DEHRA DUN

Three Gurkha regiments were based in Dehra Dun at the time. The town was fresh, tree-ed, orderly. There were good shops and interesting eating places. It was a short run into town from the regiment's HQ. I think we used a taxi. With so many Gurkhas about it was a secure and tidy place to be enjoyed.

The officers' mess was a low building. It was attractively furnished. The dining table was long and items of mess silver adorned it. There were strict points of etiquette which had to be learned and were peculiar and individual to the mess. They could be acquired by stealth and observation. There was a parallel with the monkeys on the railway stations – boss males show juveniles that they are inferior in order to be tolerated. Eyeing over the top of spectacles is a gesture designed to intimidate. Absolute silence is observed at breakfast. Discomfort must have been experienced by many in this situation, but when one is a perfectly decent guy and stands one's ground yet respects elders and betters, then there is little more that the "superior" officer can do without becoming ridiculous.

One incident illustrates rivalry amongst males. A "pukkha sahib" major who had airs more appropriate to pre-war polo army life possessed miraculous handlebar moustaches! No different from many others he indulged too liberally one night and had to be seen to his bed in a stupor. I had nothing to do with it. I was newly arrived from that primitive cadet and other rank status and was not necessarily known to be equipped with any manners. I was therefore behaving impeccably. In the morning the pompous guy looked in his mirror to shave and discovered one side of his moustache had gone!

My accommodation comprised a large square tent with a thatched roof built over it. The thatch kept it cool although it may have harboured all sorts of creatures. In the hottest part of the afternoons I would rest in the relative cool of the tent but would be distracted by the call of the brain fever bird. It starts its set of trisyllabic calls at a comfortable pitch. It then raises each subsequent call by less than a semi tone. In every series one is convinced that the last call has finally been made – only to find that it would go one higher.

The annual sports day took place on the football pitch. Guests invited, pipe band playing, teams entered for all kinds of events. It was sunny, but then it seemed to be sunny all the time in Dehra Dun. I felt lonely and spare, knew no-one and was not being made welcome by anyone. I have always made myself responsible to see that newcomers are talked to and introduced to others. It is such a small effort for a great reward. I do remember the bishti wallahs' race. It was natural that I should wonder what was about to happen when a few bagfuls of full grown chickens were emptied, alive, onto the middle of the ground. Then a couple of dozen of the less well dressed camp staff lined four sides of the pitch. The chickens were concentrating on handfuls of grain. The starter's pistol rang out and the men raced for the chickens. All got something even if it was only a leg or a wing. The chickens were dispatched quickly and humanely although some gave their pursuers quite a chase. I looked at my printed programme to confirm that it was the bishti wallahs race, the water carriers.

INTEGRATION

I was moved from Regimental HQ to the second battalion. I was familiar with signals probably more than every other officer in all of the rifle regiments of the whole vast Indian army, this was not surprising after training with the Royal Navy. I moved from my thatched HQ tent to one a little smaller in the second battalion's lines. To its HQ Coy which included the Signal Platoon.

I was wondering what to do on the first evening when I heard a strange new sound. It was music with a steady beat and song. I did not have to go far to find the source. There was a semicircle of tents joined end to end each with one side lifted to form an auditorium. Tables were erected in a long row with lights strung overhead. Seated behind these were almost all of the King's and Viceroy commissioned officers. Entertaining them were dancers from the battalion. It was not seemly for the women of riflemen's families to entertain. Young soldiers dressed in long colourful dresses, donned jingling bangles on their ankles, and danced in rows. On their heads they wore tiara head dresses with long hair wigs. Voices and mandals produced rhythms and a beat and sound that I preferred to Indian music which is more sophisticated. Perhaps it had more in common with Scotland. We're both hills people.

I approached cautiously. I waited at a respectful distance in the darkness of the night. I did not know what occasion it was or whose party it might be. The man who was to become my closest friend and helper approached me and invited me to join them. It transpired that an officer was leaving and this was a farewell party. Many of these KCOs and VCOs had been through North Africa and Italy. Sicily, on the way too, and battled hard to gain Salerno from the Germans before ending up at Trieste. It was Subedar Budibhal who conducted me to a chair and placed a small tumbler in front of me. The glass was kaccha, distorted, locally made with bubbles and bumps in it. Then he poured a clear liquid and apologised for it not having the strength that he would have wished. He said, that at home, it would have been unwise to smoke near it for fear it would ignite. It was rakshi.

The songs ventured into the erotic, the heroic, the historic and back through suggestive and perhaps vulgar except that in this context it was perfectly acceptable. In parts of the Himalayas the effigies and drawings about a village are of an erect penis. The rakshi accelerated the conviviality and bonhomie. I was receiving the most perfect introduction to those with whom I was going to work for the next year or two. There is a process called "pagdening" in bee keeping. Pagden had discovered that it was possible to amalgamate two hives of bees without them killing each other if the introduction is made slowly. The secret was to put the two brood boxes together but with newspaper between. By the time the bees had chewed through the paper their "buzz" had become universal. When the party was over I was not sure in which direction I should go to my bed! Budibhal was at hand once more, took me to my tent, up-ended me on to my bed and probably tucked in my mosquito net. I slept well. I had thoroughly enjoyed the party. Subedar Budibhal never again spoke English to me. It was forbidden for English to be spoken except with the clerks. All documentation and "admin" was in English.

Although the Subedar was nearing retiral age, he had been a regular soldier since a boy, his face was smooth, round and boyish because Gurkhas do not shave. The Nepalese are fairly hairless and what hairs do grow are removed with tweezers weekly or as necessary. He had all his teeth but his hair was greying. I think it turned quite white during the time I knew him. He was described to me as a likeable rogue, who had contracted syphilis in Africa or Italy, but a more helpful and respectful man I could not have inherited. He was platoon commander of the Signals Platoon – and then I turned up.

FRONTIER WARFARE

The days were taken up with instruction on frontier warfare and gurkhali. I had "done" small ships with all it entailed, then jungle training and urdu. Now it was frontier warfare and gurkhali! Many of the words are different in Nepal. The first change is the verb "to be" which occurs in nearly every sentence and military command. It is "hai" in urdu but "ccha" in gurkhali. After all this I concluded that I had done everything, seen everything (including the Taj Mahal) except I have not yet flown an aeroplane. With one eye only now, and with time running out, I think I probably never shall.

The far north, when India was the whole subcontinent, ended in a point that squeezed between the Hindu Kush and the Himalayas with the Karokorum behind. At that time it was inhospitable and inaccessible and resembled the warring clan system of Scotland but they seemed to be more expert and very enthusiastic about war. There was no road through to China other than by yak caravan and in any case westerners were not permitted to enter most of the countries like Tibet, Mongolia, Nepal. Hunza was an isolated self governing province, almost a fictitious, Shangri-la? Hardly anyone had been to Hunza. It was said that men lived to be 100; that it was self contained, self supporting and the diet was fruit and vegetables and one supposes goats and their milk; that a man did not sleep with his wife for three years after a child was born; that the population was stable and health something taken for granted. I remember hearing later that the first domestic fowl had just arrived so eggs and chicken were not on the menu until quite recently.

A jeep had been dismantled and carried up the mountains in pieces for the use of the head man. He could only drive a few hundred yards apparently up and down the one village street – and petrol had to be carried in over passes and rough tracks for 150 miles. It was said that the single telephone line when it existed would disappear in mile lengths overnight. The copper could be used for so many purposes not least to bind shaky rifle barrels to prevent them exploding.

There was a 200 mile wide land of mountains, snow, lush summer valleys and violence between the administered borders on each side. Rifles were made locally and warring with neighbours was an accepted part of the calendar. It was the army's task to facilitate movement of traffic between major townships of the North West Frontier Province – the NWFP.

Twice weekly "ROD"s (road opening days) to Kabul and even to Nowshera and Peshawar meant that the army had to piquet all vantage points along the route and occupy them for the day to give safe passage to traffic. This was life in those parts and had been unchanged for several generations of British officers.

Shinkiari
13 July 46

Signal Officer

How is your 48 set battery position? Div Sigs haven't produced six they promised with new sets just delivered and if you have two or three over your requirements I'd like to borrow them. If not our 48 set link may pack up on the second day but that wouldn't be much of a loss!

Yours
Duncan Hawkes

"Enfilade" and "ambush" entered my vocabulary with serious meaning. Homemade bullets are sometimes large calibre and still moving fast enough to hurt. RTR with flag, heliograph or lamp meant "retreat" and was the signal for a piquet to leave its hill top as a column moved on through the lower ground below.

Morse with a flag was instant communication and "r t r" is so easy… dot dash dot – dash – dot dash dot. One can flag it as quickly as say it. I can imagine a modern army in those parts running out of batteries for their walky-talkies and no-one knowing morse or semaphore any more!

HILL STATION LUXURY

Between training sessions, on days off, we would go into Dehra Dun. Somehow I had acquired some poplin (synthetics were not to be for another ten or so years) and I asked a reputable durzi to make up four shirts for me. There were two pieces of material – pale blue and pale coffee and I have favoured these colours ever since. Perhaps they were already my colours. I was to call in the next day for a fitting! They did (fit) and were a few rupees each. These, and two hideous ties, were my first civvy clothing items in my possession since I joined the navy on that day when my clothes had been wrapped in brown paper and posted home.

It was 1946 now and Britain was still without good stockings. With the war only recently over, young ladies were still using paint-on seams. I could send silk stockings and silk scarves by air mail reasonably cheaply and I believe they were much appreciated. I remember sending them to one young lady but it is possible that there was a second! It is a long time ago – over fifty years and I was still not twenty one. That birthday was yet to be celebrated – in a tent in the snow and some thousands of feet high in the Himalayas.

A Laurel and Hardy film was on at the cinema. The title was "Lost in a Harem", Harem was a forbidden word so the posters and cinema front announced in large letters "Lost in a ….."

Marie was a Marilyn Munro of a lass. (It was in the days before Marilyn Munro). Marie expertly played works by Mahler for me on her little grand in their house in Edinburgh. She was always well chaperoned – mother and auntie in the next room. It was alright as long as they heard the piano. Mother used to bring a tray in when it was nearing time to pack up. They need not have worried. In all the time that I was acquainted with Marie the closest I came to her was a peck on the cheek one day as I left the house. She was the girl that I was going to marry. That was absolute!

An imposing jewellers shop in Dehra Dun's main street undertook to make a silver-gold brooch fashioned as the regimental badge with crossed kukris. It cost me all I could afford – about one fifth of a months pay. Most of our pay went on our mess bills anyway. She treasured the brooch, I think. Marie's letters were less frequent than those from the wren who kept me informed regularly of every happening in "Blighty". I sent the wren, of my days with the navy, some stockings and a silk scarf but she impressed me more as a thoroughly robust outdoor type who would have preferred hand knitted wellie boot socks. She kept me well informed of happenings back home.

Blighty is a corruption of the Hindi – "wilayat men". "In home" is the literal translation, I think. British soldiers have returned to dear old Blighty for some time now. We have brought so many Indian words to our language. In the navy we did our dhobying.

I could afford it only twice. A bistro run, owned and cheffed by a European. The semi open air dinner house where food was cooked centrally on a charcoal fire as we watched and supervised – "a little more please" and the steak was perfect. But meals in the mess were good.

There was a vast concrete swimming pool at the edge of the cantonement. I swam occasionally. I was more interested in observing the terrain, the wildlife, birds and the most stimulating day for me at the pool was when a water snake resisted removal. Around the pool was a shallow broad concrete channel. By the time the water had circled the pool it was pre-warmed by the sun. The pool was fed by the river which emerged from a gorge in the hills not far away. My colleagues were out walking the hills one day and found a man's body in a small pool.

A made-up road ran through our lines. A little traffic passed through. Charcoal burners brought donkey loads of their wares. They were licensed to use certain timber and trees were preciously guarded. The charcoal was prepared in earth and stone mounds very skilfully venting the pyre as required to prevent flame but allowing smouldering.

MUSIC

Some Gurkha families lived with us. The family lines were separate and one saw little of them. The children were schooled in camp and I enjoyed the drum practice by boys. Twenty or more behind a line of trestle tables wielded their sticks most expertly and took utmost pride in their skill. The rolls and rhythms pleased me and I still enjoy similar sounds. Was it an innate liking or have I acquired it? My favourite video now is River Dance whose music bears a strong resemblance in its simple primitive beats. Irish, Scots, Nepalese "hills" people. Soon I was to move to a remote part in the Himalayan foot hills but nearer the snow line. There I was to hear shepherding boys yodelling to each other across the valleys from conifer clad steep hills. Yodelling? Swiss? Hills! Communication. Are you still there? I'm here. Keeping in touch; where there are bears, jackals and a host of imaginary and mythical creatures – it is reassuring.

Our entertainment was usually a nautch. Groups of Gurkhas squatting on the ground with mandals on their knees drummed marvellous and complex rhythms. The ends of the mandal are tuned as bass and treble. When we moved into the hills I took some lessons in playing the instrument. There is a tarry lump in the centre of the parchment which aids resonance and facilitates expression by regulating vibration with deft strokes of the hand. A hit and then removal of the hand from the skin, hinging the heel of the hand on the mandal's rim, produces a fairly lengthy sustained note. If then the vibration is damped with a touch of the hand, or just a finger, on the tarry lump – all sorts of articulation may result.

Song accompanied the mandals, rather than vice versa. The repertoire was considerable; songs of home, of places and leave. Going home required time and effort. The normal leave was three months! One to get there, one to return and a month at home. I would receive letters on paper, hand made, from rice straw. Edges often were not cut straight, they just ended where the material ran out. Hindi script was something I was learning, but I already started on Urdu script, and Hindi is totally different.

Letters were usually appeals from families requesting their rifleman's leave to sort out a matrimonial problem. My clerk interpreted for me. Clerks were an underrated and inadequately acknowledged cog in the great wheels of Raj government in India. Modest men from lower ground, not at all Mongolian featured, and schooled really well, they would produce endless typed lists, balance sheets and indents for supplies.

I asked the clerk what would take place when one of the riflemen was at home. It was my responsibility to grant him leave on compassionate grounds. The letter stated that his wife was having an affair with another man. The clerk said that if he did return he would probably have killed the other man. Otherwise he would not return. One has to remember that places in the army were much sought after, and that no soldier ever wished to leave or desert. Families vied with each other to get sons into the army. It was a sad day that was to come soon when I would have the unenviable task of reducing my company by about a third!

TO THE HILLS

I suppose that intelligence reports had come through that trouble was expected in the North West Frontier Province – and more likely beyond that – in the unadministered 200 mile wide tribal territory that lay between India and China or Russia. It seemed so easy in those days to run all military and civilian provisions just like clockwork. After all, we had run a brilliant war machine for six years and still continued to behave in exactly the same manner. Orders were given and obeyed and not questioned. Great pride was taken in acting with precision and skill. There was a strong sense of team work, esprit de corps. Unexpected problems were met with extra effort and incredible improvisation. Ends were to be achieved which in themselves were reward enough. Never a word of complaint – that would have been an admission of weakness and inadequacy.

It seems that this was to be the last that we were to see of real belief in self – in Britain, in Empire, in leadership and as an example to the world. Too little has been said in commendation of the thousands of unsung heroes who sweated, toiled, and suffered deprivation, isolation, injury and sickness in all theatres over the seas. Some felt deprived of their early adulthood by the war years but many willingly and proudly carried out duties under conditions which the average citizen of today would not wear.

A convoy of trucks arrived spot on and lined up in exactly the order that our battalion needed. Presumably the extra transport came from Divisional Headquarters for we had only very few trucks; just a couple or so of "passion wagons" – 15 cwt "Chevs"; and perhaps some three tonners and three motor bikes. Our mules were there when we arrived in the hills.

Our mules made mostly comforting sounds.

Those glorious foothills of the Himalayas clad with conifers so like the Scots Pines of home. The hillocks and nullahs coated with thick quietening carpets of brown shed pine needles. After this we were to proceed to areas where no wheeled transport could go.

Now we had only two motor cycles, three ponies and forty-five ill-tempered, obstinate but hard working mules. However, there was no other form of transport that would take us where we were going.

I chose my own tent site. I was particular. A knoll like a landward peninsular cut about with deep gullies would give me exclusion and privacy and yet it was fairly near the entrance to the camp so that I would be aware of comings and goings. There was not room for anyone else to pitch a tent on the same little promontory but I had a chatti always filled with water and often fellow officers would come by to "borrow" a drink of cool water; cooled by the process of evaporation through the porous red pottery with its blue design. I managed to claim two tents, each about eight feet long. Saitbir erected them quickly precisely and exactly where I would have wanted them.

SAITBIR PUN

Rifleman Saitbir Pun had become my batman. All Nepalese are small. If it had not been for the Police Platoon who were chosen partly for their height, I would have been about the fourth tallest in the company. I am five foot six inches and a little bit! Saitbir was small. When he stood to attention with his rifle by his side, the muzzle levelled with his nose!

Saitbir was supportive and conscientious, and he was good with Charlie too. Sometimes he would take the little slow loris to his own lines in the Pioneer Platoon to show to his colleagues. He never once allowed the creature to escape and was responsible in everything else he did.

I do not remember discussing the exact siting of my tents with him. The Nepalese have an innate sense of aesthetics and common sense with which I can live most happily. The tents were end to end and positioned exactly so that the gable flaps could act as an entrance porch in the middle so that I had a doorway. To the left was my bath house and store – not that I had much gear beyond my bedding roll and clothes. I had now lived for almost five years in uniform, without any civvy clothes, with nothing personal, everything was "issue".

Eventually, in a few days when we were settled in, Saitbir dug out my dwelling end of the two tents. He left two pillars of soil for the tent poles but I had now a bed on which I could sit with a well for my feet. I could also stand up in the middle of the tent where previously the tent ridge was too low and my back was sorely bent. Much later he and I constructed a rockery outside my bed head end and I could open up the tent flaps to view the sunsets and watch the toad which made its home in the rockery amongst the ferns.

Our new home was almost in the peak of that wedge in the north among hills that were thinly conifer wooded. Through gaps between the hills were snow peaks bright in sunshine with a blue sky and China or Russia beyond. Somewhere to the west the River Indus ran broad and lively and further upstream it took a turn round the back of the Himalayas. My tent was nearest to the entrance to the camp. Beyond were the hills rising, range by range until they joined the snow covered Himalayas proper. A few yards towards the camp entrance was the slaughter shed.

Soft silent pine needles covered the ground, from trees so like Scots pine that one could be forgiven for imagining a return to Perthshire or perhaps Argyll.

Below the spur was a trickle of water which ran round and partly through the camp and eventually joined a river of medium size. The horse lines were not far from my little home and the mules made mostly comforting sounds. Mules are silent, mute creatures and unable to breed being a cross of two species – the horse and donkey.

The platoons of Headquarter Company were discreetly dotted about me although none overlooked me. My signals Platoon and the Pioneer Platoon were fairly close.

Our regiment was recruited from Gurungs and Thapas with some Puns and a few, very few, others. It made sense for, Nepal being so like Scotland with a strong "clan" system, it did not do to mix peoples indiscriminately. It did seem to me that there was a pride in what was undertaken, a belief that we were good and probably better than others. It was one big family that pulled very much together. There was little in the way of pretension. Openness between everyone regardless of rank was evident. The only exception to this showed a little with one, or perhaps two, senior KCOs who were career minded with post-war staff college on their minds. But we still always shone in performance in front of strangers; with any other battalion.

The latrine for other ranks was one long deep trench with canvas awning around. Gurkhas and many Indians too take a small water container with them. Loo paper is unknown as, indeed, it was in my childhood on Gigha where there were no loos. If I asked for someone I could not find, he might have gone "tatti phalne" which literally translated means "throw a turd (or log)". Not a hint of a smirk. Factual forthright statement.

HINDUS

A rifleman, or perhaps it was a naik (equivalent to a corporal) had gone missing. He was marked AWOL and faced procedures for punishment on his return. His absence was taken seriously but with an unbelievable open approach before a verdict was reached.

He was "tranced". He had been to the mountains where the snow was deep. That was further than he could have walked in the time that he was absent. He had been "transported". I was not party to the proceedings or even to the report. I can only say that he was released from the army to a monastery to train as a Buddhist monk.

The spirit has meaning amongst most of the people I came to know in India. Christianity talks about spirit but my closeness to Hindus particularly, and to some extent with Muslims too, proved that they believe spirit. My own "spirit" was considered by others, rather than was "I". So, if "I" had failings it would not have been held against "me", but was it considered rather the result of turmoil and difficulty within the system and circumstances. Strangely there was therefore a fundamental absolution that need not be sought by me. It was granted. What a dilemma.

CAMERA

During this time we were able occasionally to take leave in Lahore. It was 100 miles to the great Jhelum river and another fifty or more beyond that to Lahore. On one of those days I bought a camera. It was my first since a little wooden box camera that I had had when very young. This was an elaborate bellows Kodak job. It folded quite flat and was not too heavy.

Film was not easily obtainable so I bought a large roll of air reconnaissance film in a round cigarette tin and made up my own films with old discarded spools and backing paper. I became quite adept at cutting, elastoplasting and rolling with my hands under the bedclothes. I have no idea what speed of film it was but my photographs were acceptable and most were very good. The film was probably the best. I still had some left until I left India.

A MONSTROUS AMPHIBIAN

The little streams ran when it rained which was not often. They became static but not stagnant pools much of the time. The use of the latrines by troops was total so there was no fouling about the camp. It was natural for local inhabitants to relieve themselves wherever they were but they never came into the camp; they would not have dared. The army was virtually in opposition to the populace. After years of rule it had become a "them" and "us" situation. There was no fraternisation.

The streams gathered and joined a sizeable river with some large pools in it not far beyond the lower end of the camp. I could hear the children from the village sometimes as they swam and played and jumped into the water from a rocky overhang. I have always explored and rarely kept myself ignorant of my surroundings. It is surprising that I have not come to grief through my incessant wanderings and investigation. One sunny day as I walked down one of the streams, literally poking around the puddles and holes and examining the crevices I met the most unbelievable creature. Of course it ran for cover and my view of it was brief. It seemed to be the size of a fat badger and its sides were fat and flabby and bounced just like a badger does when it runs. There the similarity ceased for it had a leathery skin and no hair nor fur. It was dark if not mostly black or grey. It vanished. I was uncertain whether to be cautious and retreat or investigate further. As always my curiosity got the better of me but all I found was a hole hardly big enough as a refuge unless perhaps there was under water. Then I found four inch long tadpoles which were not at all developed so they were newly out of the spawn. I had happened on a large amphibian. I never saw it again and we moved before the tadpoles developed at all. I have no idea if it might have been a danger to me. At the natural science museum in London I was told what it was, but I have since forgotten.

If I had to choose somewhere to build a bungalow it would be where we had our Mess tent – a clearing in the pine trees, level and clean. Carpeted with pine needles and the only long view was westwards over the endless lower plains with not a sight of habitation. Actually, there is a dak bungalow further up the road in the hills which had a dramatic view northwards over great valleys and ridges covered with pine trees. My daughter and I were entertained there to lunch forty years later. It was very beautiful, very remote. Set in an area where the pine trees were more dense but the views through the gaps were to distant mountains some snow covered and to the Indus must lower in the foreground. The sun was pleasant on the day we lunched there. Butterflies dotted about the flowering plants that were planted around the perimeter of the drive. We were in our host's car, driven by his son in law. I thought "dak" meant "post", as in mail, but it is possible that it interprets more accurately as a travel lodge. Our D Coy Commander stayed there with his wife briefly. I favoured our spot for my house in heaven.was no fouling about the camp. It was natural for local inhabitants to relieve themselves wherever

(14) An Italian coast defence general had arrived at MALTA after capture by 51 (H) Div. He considered that we had been very unfair in coming in on a rough night and with no moon, since all his soldiers had gone to bed. His story would indicate that the use of rather unusual weather conditions pays.

Auchinleck

general

Commander-in-Chief in India.

The Auk used to come to stay with us. He said he enjoyed the peace and the simple unsophistication of our mess.

Note from an Army in India Training Manual. The Auk also stayed with my uncle and aunt in Chittagong where my Uncle was the District Commissioner.

We were only eight or nine at full strength. The Colonel, 2 i/c, Adjutant, QM, 4 rifle Company Commanders and myself i/c HQ company. The

Kings Commissioned Officer (KCO) strength had been run down pending Indianising which was soon to become complete. I more than doubled. My job was to run HQ Coy and be Signals Officer, Pioneer Officer and Intelligence Officer. Each of which posts would have been filled by a European KCO previously.

What with the high casualty rate in Burma where many Indian Army battalions served, and the losses in Europe too, then demobilisation beginning to show and the run down of the massive training programme in India as independence was being negotiated, there was a strange unreality for that year. Until the riots quite abruptly brought us into "action".

We had calculated, somehow, back in Maidstone where our Army training began, that there was only one officer left alive from draft No 1; two from No 2 and four from No 4 – until we came to draft No. (about) forty-three only half alive. We were draft No 47 and the Burma Campaign was then still going badly. And all this was after I had spent a year or more training for my commission in the Royal Navy Volunteer Reserve! So I had been about two weeks too young to go on the Normandy invasion and I was returned with no thanks to barracks in Chatham. Some bright spark had requested a transfer to the Indian Army. The Navy was capsizing with personnel and no ships, whilst Burma was still consuming bodies so, during that week in 1944, thirteen of us did a quick change to a different salute and the halt on the other foot.

Small ships would not have carried a signaller and we soft-faced "boys" would need to read commands and signals and make appropriate responses as we nosed landing craft into the beaches. My signals training for small ships service was a great asset in the new role. Now, in the hills, although we had those heavy "18" and "48" wireless sets, we relied a great deal on flagged morse. Every company or platoon would have a signaller from the Sig. PL, but in any case there was a short vocabulary which nearly everyone understood.

Ann, the wren, wrote to tell me about demobilisation. She says *"visual signalling is a thing of the past."* In the Royal Navy!

Mountain warfare was conducted in a set manner. Always – always – all high ground was piqueted before any unit moved in that type of country. No chances were ever taken – too many armies had been decimated and too many bodies picked off by sniping that it had become as instinctive as flicking a fly off ones face to piquet all the heights before moving on. Units would be instructed when to RTR (retire) back into the column with a quick flick of the flags.Much of longer distance signalling was done with heliograph. Hollywood made some films of the North West frontier – and whilst the average cinema goer could be forgiven for thinking that those flashes from the hills were some Heath Robinson job with a shaving mirror, this was not so. Setting up the heliograph and siting it onto the position of the receiver was a precise task at which our signallers were adept. One has to remember that we had veterans of the North African and Italian campaigns and there was great expertise with economy of effort – we worked marvellously and reliably.

We demonstrated to the rest of the brigade one day. We had to manhandle the 4" mortars to the top of a fair sized hill and deliver some shells – all much as a race to see how quickly we could establish

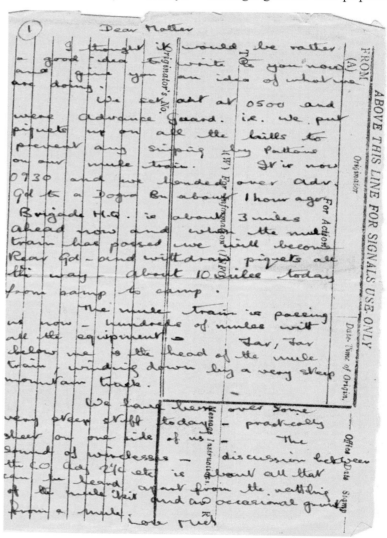

dominance in the area. I see from a letter sent to my mother that "we had our spitfires on call and they put in some very spectacular attacks – one was very low in the valley below us"; and, that I was acting brigade intelligence officer at the time.

"Pioneers" was another of my platoons, but I had an excellent Jemadar in charge. A plumpish man, middle aged and much darker than almost all the other Gurkhas, most of whom are honey coloured. He was one who actually had stubble on his chin; sometimes the others were shiny faced as they do not shave. They have little facial hair and spend perhaps a few minutes each week with tweezers. They were retiring at sixty and sixty-five with faces that looked so youthful – and they almost invariably had all their teeth. We only once sent a man to a dentist in a whole year!

The Pioneer Platoon. Saitbir is second from left in the rear row.

The Pioneer Jemadar once let his stubble grow a bit too much and he experimented with methylated spirits and a match; which no one ever tried again! He was quiet, had little sense of humour but was a good kindly soul.

I instituted an inter-section competition during the time we were in our lovely pine wooded camp. I think my pay was about Rs 250 per month – and I put 50 rupees towards a monthly binge for the section achieving the highest score.

Halcyon days indeed – everything running smoothly, peace, time for sitting round a fire – impromptu singing to the beat of mandals before bed time in the dark nights.

How I do wish that tape recorders had existed then, and that colour film had been available – not that my pay would have stretched to such luxuries. The colourful memories are so clear but only in my mind.

When walking about the camp at night there was often the 'whoosh' of a gliding flying fox over ones head, and then the not very loud crash as it landed on the next tree and then scrambled yet up again. Strangely I never actually saw one – except its outline occasionally against the sky when the moon was bright.

Jackals are a little like ill bred wolves. They howl at the moon – or at nothing in particular. It is a challenging male that howls when there is a moon. There was a knoll about 50 yards from my tent and over several nights around the full moon I could see this jackal sat there howling westwards to the setting moon.

Some nights the jackals would start their hysterical screaming. It seemed that they ran round and round my tent. It was amazing how close nature came to the human infiltration of its territory.

I was born in the Nilgiri Hills where wild elephants roamed in herds lower down and tigers and much other exciting life stalked about the hills. It was, in those days, uncommon to have a house which did not contain several ornamental trophies such as skins on the floor or heads on the walls.

I imagine that my mother, who was really no age at all, must have been petrified and I doubt if my father provided much real comfort or feeling of security. Of course there were plenty of servants and tea estate workers around, although only the house servants were ever near at hand when work was not proceeding in the bushes close to the house.

Boys would be sent with sticks and tin cans to bang when elephants threatened to come into the estate and cause damage. The bishti wallah would check under the bath tub, and around the wash house, that there was no cobra lying in wait at bath time. In fact the wild life did not really pose a great threat and yet its proximity must have been a worry to my mother from Surrey (Richmond, Surbiton, Kingston, Croydon, Cheam were her firmer terras).

We lived near Kotagiri and my mother travelled the miles to Coonoor for my birth. I believe all went well and I know she was a good mother who loved her children as infants and again as they grew up – myself, and brother and sister who were later to follow.

Shopping could not have been more different (further in style) from the present ASDA, Sainsbury, into the car boot, credit card system. The khansaman would see my mother and give her a list, probably weekly, of requirements which he could not obtain from villagers nearby.

I recall being told that one day cook asked for something which my mother just could not write down. "Just write 'starbree'", he said, so my mother put it on the list. Back came a bottle of strawberry essence.

One day now back in Scotland some quarter of a century later, and some years after my mother had died, my father opened a jar of cape gooseberry jam which she had made in the year following my birth. It was obviously an occasion of some import to my father and I can recall his expression now. A moment of better-than-normal relationship between myself and my father. The jam was delicious.

By the 1950s my father had already established himself as a considerable authority on matters food and health and in particular growing methods, the effects of processing and chemical additives in food. Not really in that connection, he did once say that in Kotagiri the only available supplement to my mothers milk was Cow & Gate. He would infer one supposes that such a "food" would not have greatly helped me and perhaps could be blamed for some of my developing complaints; mainly colic! He told me that I was a noisy infant and that he lost much sleep, for however attentive was my ayah, she would not normally sleep in the bungalow, and my mother and father would be left to do the night shift.

None of this was told unkindly. In fact it was at a time when I was being particularly favoured and respected during my university three years. Also my father was then covertly courting my step-mother-to-be.

Photographs are normally taken, or in those days certainly were, when everyone was posed, smiling, clean faced and probably best dressed. I was privileged, being well chronicled in Kodak (box camera) and later thoroughly identified by Cash. So it was later that I saw from photographs that my Ayah was bosomy and very black – being a Madrasi. I just know that her pores oozed cumin and coriander and for me I believe she became my security. Probably my earlier introduction to solids was with surreptitious treats resulting from the intrigue between the khansaman and ayah in the cookhouse. I have enjoyed curries ever since, not just as food – but as comfort too – and so I know that God is a big black woman!

I was watching some rugby replays on television – Barbarians versus England. What a game; great play with some lovely opportunist moves in the second half. They showed Steel Bodger in the stand and Princess Anne too. I remembered Steel Bodger playing in the days when I would consider it abnormal if I did not get to Murrayfield for an International match. Peter Kinninmonth must have played about that time too I would think.

Peter had been our QM (Second Bn. Third Queen Alexandra's own Gurkha Rifles).

The SCOTTISH TEAM *versus* WALES, at Murrayfield, 3rd February 1951.

Reading from Left to Right—(Back Row) D. M. Scott (Langholm), D. M. Rose (Jedforest), N. G. R. Mair (Edinburgh University), J. M. Inglis (Edinburgh Academicals), D. A. Sloan (Edinburgh Academicals), R. C. Taylor (Kelvinside-West), M. J. Dowling, *Referee* I.R.F.U.). *(Front Row)* R. L. Wilson (Gala), R. Gordon (Edinburgh Wanderers), R. Gemmill (Glasgow H.S. F.P.), A. Cameron (Glasgow H.S. F.P.), P. W. Kinninmonth, *Captain* (Richmond), W. I. D. Elliot (Edinburgh Academicals), J. C. Dawson (Glasgow Academicals), I. H. M. Thomson (Heriot's F.P.), I. A. Ross (Hillhead H.S. F.P.).

The photograph from the programme at Murrayfield the year that Peter was captain of the Scottish team.

I was HQ Coy Commander in those days and I had additionally taken over the QM's duties as well for a few weeks while Peter was away somewhere. It was then that I discovered that arithmetic was not so difficult after all.

I might have been a genius if it hadn't been for school which had left me with a self conscious grin and the general impression that academic subjects were difficult and probably beyond me. But when these great long lists of petrol and diesel issues came in, they had to be totalled.

I decided that I had much better things to do with my time than labour over them, and I had seen Peter add them quicker than I knew how. So I devised a way! I discovered that by making tens out of every combination of two figures and remembering what was left over it became quite simple. So eight and three is one more than ten! Five and six likewise, or that eight pinched two off seven leaving five. It was all new to me. I suppose all of you do something like that anyway. I no longer needed mental fingers and toes to count on. Or start with eight and go round four corners of a four counting from eight thus nine, ten, eleven, twelve! Or eight and add five the same way but with the dot in the middle too! Why hadn't someone told me before. Oh what a genius I could have been if it hadn't been for school.

ALBINO

A river which would be sizeable in wet weather ran around our beautiful camp. The children from the village were noisy, like any in the world who are happy. They were revelling in a spontaneous mood which came upon them when they decided to go daft in a large pool in the river which was otherwise partly dried up. A small cliff overhung one side and the clear soft pine-needled carpeted bank on the other formed the perfect picnic or leisure site. It was shaded in places by the spaced trees. There was an echo there which made music of the sounds of the children.

There was much splashing and jumping in and diving off the high rock on the cliff side – much blowing of spray and the deft wringing of noses with finger and thumb as each boy came up for air and rose head and shoulders out of the water; as we all do in these circumstances. There was one boy – remarkable because whilst all the others were uniformly golden brown skinned with mainly black hair – he had blond hair and his skin was pink with the sun. I assumed at a distance and without much thought that he must have been fathered by a European who had been in the army!

Forty years on – and of the age group that was right – I saw him. I'm convinced; in the middle of the main road in town. He was directing traffic about the buses which terminate there – whether official or self appointed I shall not know – but what I did discover on this closer contact was that he is an albino!

JACKALS AND MOHAMMED

I walked up the hill between the "scots" pine on sparse dried grass and aromatic pine needles. The smell was perfect, like mown hay. It was sunny and very warm but enjoyable. Parallel tracks ran with the contours of the ground and drew my attention. Sheep and goats perhaps but there were no sharp prints; pug marks. I was there intending to catch a couple of praying mantis to feed to Charlie Loris. I lent on a pink flaky pine tree trunk as my hand stalked upwards ready to pounce on a plump mantis when something caught my eye and I froze. Coming along the track was a pack of jackals. There were seven. I presume that it was a male leading them, but I could be mistaken. I was now flat against the tree. The jackals trotted past me not three paces from me and not one of them looked up or was even aware that I was there! Perhaps it was a female in the lead and the others were intent on keeping her well in sight!

I continued along the hill in the direction the jackals had gone. I did not see them again. Then I walked higher and the trees above me became more dense but still open enough for grass to grow. I was sitting looking down on the village when a smartly dressed proud young man came up to me. He wore pressed khaki shorts, three quarter stockings and looked almost a military man. He had that proud bearing of the local rulers and a fine prominent nose with it. He had some English and I asked him about the jackals I had seen. He had not much good to say of them. They carry disease (rabies) and they are sometimes killed and their skins sold in the village. Can one catch rabies from a hide? We agreed to meet again and he invited me to come shooting some day. I said I had no gun but he assured me that he had two; and ammunition as well.

Wherever I have gone and whatever are the conditions I have always made the best of them – better it seemed than many of those around me – my beer mug is always at least half full and never seems half empty. I had two tents, pitched end to end in a lovely level site which fell away to a small nullah at the rear. To the front the view from the end of my main living tent was unobstructed by other tents. It looked between those beautiful pine trees across ground covered with fallen pine needles and to the west. I had a grand view of the setting sun.

For extra comfort, my batman, Saitbir, dug out half of my main tent so that I could stand erect in comfort. This also meant that I could now sit on my bed with my feet in the dug out well. There had to be a soil pillar in the middle to take the centre ridge pole on which hung the hurricane batti – one per officer. My other tent housed my galvanised tub and served mostly as store and bathroom. I am fairly certain that there were dug latrines somewhere not too far away but I have forgotten where.

It was warm weather, and I remember at one point saying to myself that I could stand any amount of cold – but not this heat! I was soon to discover how wrong I was. To aid cooling and avoid heat stroke I had a saucer of red pepper and salt to dab at. I had bought an earthenware chatti – unglazed so that it sweated and cooled the water in it – which I kept in the wash house tent. There were not many who had the luxury of cool water to drink and I had the occasional visitor come in to cadge a glass off me. Water was piped from above the village which I was fortunate enough to visit again forty years later. Some days I took a walk; I'm an inveterate finder-outer and nosey-into. Sometimes I took a shot at a dove with my .38 revolver, but it was a stupid ploy for had I hit one it would have been almost irretrievable for dinner in the officers' Mess.

Life has been full of exciting confrontations and discoveries. There is always, everywhere, so much to see and never time enough to spend on investigation and observation whether it be something which really frightened me or just a harmless spider constructing this weeks web. It seems almost incredible that on the edge of our camp of some 450 men, this creature was living unnoticed and undisturbed, except apparently be me. Perhaps there are Loch Ness monsters after all.

CARDS

There was a newsagents at the bottom of the car park below Surbiton Station – on the corner of the main road which runs from Kingston – through Surbiton. The newsagents, at the station car park, was where I bought two packs of playing cards on my last leave before embarkation for India. My Grandmother lived across the railway line and up the hill a little way. A rough path between high chestnut paling fences ran eerily up between dark tall trees with mud and ivy about it. I do not think that it would be in use today unless it has been improved and lit more effectively. Perhaps it is a street now.

The two packs of cards were well used (one red and one blue) throughout the troop ship journey to Bombay and then after commissioning at Bangalore, again, in my Gurkha battalion as we sat around storm lanterns in tents on the heights at the west end of the Himalayas. The card containers came to grief – I know because the packs were transferred at that time to boxes which had held anti mosquito sparklet bulbs – the individual sort that you break the end off after you have tucked your mosquito net around your bed or bedding roll ready for sleep. Dear knows what insecticide they contained. It would at that time have been considered preferable to suffer a few upsets from chemicals with unknown side effects than to have malaria take a hold in an army unit.

We did have a problem with malaria one summer – about eight men (Gurkhas) caught it. There was an enquiry – or a bit of a witch hunt – and I was the one to be blamed first.

The colonel was not at all pleased although he did not quite accuse me outright. Later it was found that the cases of malaria all had one thing in common – they were all men who had been on short rest leave to somewhere in the foothills – was it Nainetal or one of those places where Gurkha soldiers went if they were not due to make the long trek home which took some of them a month each way on foot.

I had trained near Agra as the battalions antimalarial officer – identifying anopheline and culicine mosquitoes in puddles and learning the craft of covering all water courses in a film of oil/paraffin containing dichloro-diphenyl-trichloroethane – yes you've got it DDT! Then there was personal protection as well as spraying inside buildings and tents, proper use of mosquito nets, mepacrine tablets, and creams to be applied to face, neck, wrists and hands.

> Pure = P.P. D.D.T.
>
> Contact poison — nervous system — absorption takes place through chitin. .   Mosquitoes die 1 → 12 Hrs. depending on dose.
>
> Harmless to animals and humans in doses used.
>
> Can be handled dry , but is absorbed by the skin as an oil solt.

Extract from my notes at the anti malaria course near Agra. DDT is safe!

One night I was patrolling on my own amongst the "D" company tents to see that all personnel were indeed under their nets. I had developed a technique which was noiseless and did not disturb anyone bar the culprit. I carried a tin of water around and any heads sticking out – or feet for that matter – it was reasonably warm even at night in July – September, where we were – these exposed parts would get one or two drops of water on them from my tin. Sometimes the owner woke up but all of them knew what it was about and a signalled or whispered instruction soon put them back safely under their nets. Well as I was saying – one night when this was my ploy – D Coy Commander came by on his way back from the Officers Mess tent and upbraided me for being in his lines. He was the worse for a bit of drink so did not find it at all easy to accept that I was there for any good purpose. I heard no more about it however.

25. ANTI-MALARIAL TRAINING.

IF....

If you can use intelligence and reason,
 When listening hard to what the doctors say,
And realise that in the rainy season,
 You have GOT to fight mosquitoes every day ;

If you can bear to hear the fools who chatter,
 (Of course, you know, I NEVER use a net !)
And tell you that it really doesn't matter,
 Yet still obey the orders that you get ;

If you believing others may be slacking,
 Can go and watch the doings of your men,
And finding that some discipline is lacking,
 Can give a talk about it there and then ;

If you will try to minimise infection,
 By thinking what to do about the drains,
And then ensure by personal inspection,
 That everything is right before the rains ;

If you will rub the ointment with your finger
 On portions of the body that are bare,
And when the evening cometh never linger, —
 For then it's time for trousers everywhere ;

If you can chide the other silly buffer,
 Who sits about with shorts above the knees,
And tell him what you think he ought to suffer,
 For giving chances to anopheles :

If you can bear in mind the orders given,
 And never stint that flitting with your gun,
Till all mosquitoes from your tent are driven,
 YOU'LL NEVER GET MALARIA, MY SON !

That summer I became quite badly ill. Feverish, headaches and diarrhoea and inexplicable pains around the body. The doctor sent stools for testing and the answer came back that at least it was not amoebic dysentery. So I was confined to my tent for the time being with whatever drugs he prescribed. My notes from the "malaria" course said that DDT could be handled dry! I had been breaking up lumps of the crystalline yellow white concentrate and trying to dissolve it in paraffin.

ACROSS THE RIVER TO AGRA

I had become familiar with travel by train, from Wah and then from other localities in the north where we were stationed amongst the hills. I cannot say that I knew the train driver, but I was well accustomed to and enjoyed a symphony of sounds on journeys which took days. The train had its individual character, the engine's sighs and expletives, its whistle a little "toothless" and spluttering if steam was not up to full. Many years later I was to meet, in England, the man who might indeed have been the driver on some of the occasions that I journeyed through this marvellous countryside.

The responsible position of engine driver on main lines was entrusted to a European. He had ample help with firing but it was a demanding, dirty and often a very hot task. Some became Indianised. All were respected as important members of the Indian Anglo society and the pay was commensurate with the skill and responsibility. Their children often went to fee paying private schools in India.

Trains moved leisurely, securely and kindly with a feeling for me of that sense of proprietorship – like the relationship one has with a holiday cottage that one returns to annually.

I watched from my open train window fearful of missing something intensely interesting. There was the chance of seeing dynamic birds and daunting reptiles. Or it may have been an unrepeatable scene of water buffaloes wallowing in a water hole – not wild ones but accompanied by their handlers or owners, being scrubbed and well cared for after a hard day of cultivating or carting with great heavy wooden wagons.

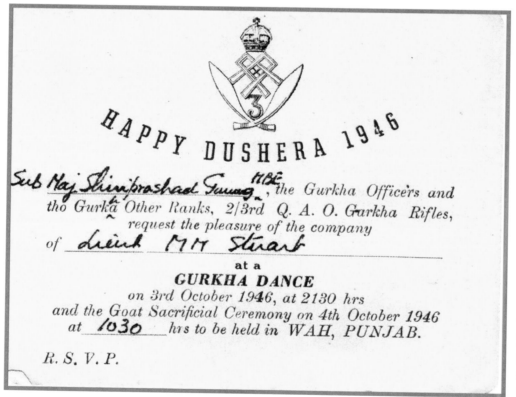

HAPPY DUSHERA 1946

Sub Maj Shivprashad Gurung MBE, the Gurkha Officers and the Gurka Other Ranks, 2/3rd Q. A. O. Garkha Rifles, request the pleasure of the company

of *Lieut M M Stuart*

at a
GURKHA DANCE
on 3rd October 1946, at 2130 hrs
and the Goat Sacrificial Ceremony on 4th October 1946
at 1030 hrs to be held in WAH, PUNJAB.

R. S. V. P.

Water buffalo have a permanent expression of being badly done by anyway. They are beasts of burden and milked as well. Hindus see them as not being "cows" and they may therefore also be eaten. We used to kill one for Dushera; the act of slaughter being granted to a deserving young member of the battalion. An extra large kukri was sharpened specially for the occasion and the head had to be severed with one blow. The body remained standing headless for what seemed a long time before crumpling at the knees.

204

A wild rhythmic rumbling sound announced the bridge on the Jhelum. The sound alerted me so that I crossed the gangway. Looking down, the pink image of the Taj Mahal was reflected in the broad sweep of the river on its steeper side. On the near side, on the flat bank, were several women dhobying. Clothes swung up over one shoulder and slapped down on flat stones. Swing, up, down, slap, up, down, dip, rinse and swing up, down slap and then scrub a little. Only feet away from them stationed still in the moving water, nostrils in the air or submerged slightly, but seen by me from my high vantage point was an incredible number of turtles. They seemed to be of one size, about that of large Victorian tea trays.

My daughter views the Taj Mahal from Agra Fort.

The huge fort at Agra covers acres. About ten Edinburgh Castles would fit inside. One motors around it. There are football pitches and huge barracks within and all is surrounded by a massive red stone wall which must be mostly a couple of hundred feet high and more in places. I stayed there for part of the course but I forget now any of the detail about messing.

My daughter is a pony girl and achieved modestly in pony club and some point to point events. It was a sad experience for her to see abused animals, in particular the gharry ponies, with sore blistered mouths and bare ribs about the entrance to the Taj Mahal.

The west has moved rapidly to become a society that is most caring regarding animals but perceptions vary between great extremes throughout the world. Human suffering must be borne with stoicism where there is no help for the disadvantaged. There is no choice. A woman may give birth in a doorway on the street as the world walks by as one may see in Bombay. But she will rise soon and carry the baby off with her – somewhere, back home?

JANGLA RAILWAY STATION

I was on my way to the hills more centrally in India than my previous wanderings. Sometimes I wonder, now more than ever, how on earth I found my way around India. Small detail surfaces such as the memory of some loud Americans in a tiny waiting room at a railway station surrounded by unbroken jungle. All around closed in by the greenest most lush jungle trees in an atmosphere of tropical moistness. The sky so blue above; the tiny waiting room, the ticket office – a glass window with the station master thickly bespectacled within; and the Americans.

They were all gun cases, topis, shorts and talk. Somehow they assumed that Indi-ahh was there for big game killing and their childish excitement was unconcealed. Dear knows where they were going and at who's behest and if they were paying for their pleasure. One has to remember that at that time Hollywood was still making films, in black and white, in which it was not uncommon for the hunter to become involved in shooting the "natives" as well as any wild creature that moved; but most of those films were located in an African setting.

When my train came in I sat in an airy compartment with slatted wooden seats. I remember that it was clean and it was light. There were no other passengers. It was not too hot, but then I was becoming better accustomed to the heat. The window was down or perhaps there were no windows at all. There was a long wait. The engine was some way ahead, three or more small carriages away, and it pulsated quietly for a steam engine. Perhaps the line was owned by the local maharajah. India was very different from Africa for here the local social and political structures were acknowledged and observed. British dignitaries to the top level of governor, and even the king and emperor beyond the seas, paid homage to local ruling figures.

The blue sky met the lush green of the jungle canopy and in a little clearing on a loading line were dark skinned dhoti-clad men filling open wagons with large heavy bundles of cut sugar cane. As almost everywhere else that I travelled in India my smile was reciprocated and I indicated by hand gestures that I would like a piece of cane to chew. It was easy to indicate between my two index fingers the size and I was given a generous piece through the window. The coolie was almost reluctant to take any money for the meagre little stick but was appreciative of the couple of Annas which I gave him; the smile was vast, sincere and friendly.

I chewed and sucked the sweet juice – and spat out the splinters. They say that sugar taken naturally in this way does not lead to tooth decay. I wonder why! There is good cause to believe that the teeth actually benefit from the exercise. I shall always remember the ready smiles of children throughout the Indian sub continent with their healthy white teeth. They appear all the brighter because they are set in a darker skin. No tooth brushes or fluoride but perhaps just a rinse for some of them with water after meals.

I was to be struck by the dreadfully miserable expressions on my return to Britain; so much so that I once stood at the corner of Hanover Street and Princes Street in Edinburgh in 1947 in order to observe the grim looks of the passers by and to wonder if it is perhaps a matter of scarcity of sunshine, mineral and vitamin deficiency.

SCIENCE

Now that I cannot even remember what it is that I have put in the microwave and have to open the door to see what I am having for lunch, how is it that I still know that there are two distinct kinds of mosquito – anopheles and culices! Some of my tutors throughout my learning life of school, the armed forces and then university and teachers' college are memorable. The malaria instructor must have been gifted. I cannot even remember if he was European or Indian; meaning – of the race. For I am an Indian by birth and my Indian birth certificate is the only record to show that I exist. I believe the registry records may have been lost since independence. Our instruction was important for one of the species carries malaria and the other does not.

It is astonishing just how much was known about both mosquitoes and the malaria bug. On the other hand no one seems to have studied the "knock-on" effects of the practices which we were compelled, encouraged, ordered to carry out. I suffered acutely and horribly for several weeks from exposure to dichlorodiphenyltrichloroethane. It is possible that a chronic condition continued for many years later.

But, then, I wonder too what colossal disturbance was caused to the food chains affecting the fish down river; and did the amphibian of my brief encounter suffer cold flushes and problems of food supply following the routine and extensive applications of DDT to the water courses around the camp. Perhaps its spawn no longer hatched. Its massive tadpoles no more to thrive with the enthusiasm which I had observed in their lively pursuit of their rightful expectations of life.

Did anyone, I wonder, ever know of that creature at all? Tell me, now, how many of them are still there, or anywhere, if any! If at all.

I stalked the camp at night with a small tin of water and if I should find anyone sleeping with their head outside their mosquito net a few drops of water on their face made them retract and cover up. It was taken with good humour by the men. It is a wonder I was not lynched for my unconventional methods.

Below the army camp the ground became more flat; gave way to a gritty desert with barely enough vegetation to keep goats happy. There was a fair sized river that curled about the camp and had originally carved out the pleasing features of the landscape on which the camp stood. It was possible to walk through most of the camp almost on the level. Somehow a whole battalion could disappear amongst the well spaced pine trees. Each part was cut about by gentle but deep ravines which created ideal dividers between the companies. Darkness came most beautifully and fairly rapidly. The sun set through the pines and created a gradation of gentle colouring and if my end tent flaps were propped open I had a marvellous view whilst sitting in my folding chair. And then I would lower the flaps and prepare for dinner in the mess tent.

I was probably one of the very last to equip myself with a wood and canvas folding camp bed; leather bound amidships and at the corners – presumably of camel hide. And there was the canvas and wooden folding camp chair with arms! These with my bedding roll went everywhere – on the back of a mule!

It was hot in mid summer although we were camped amid pine trees on steep ridges in the Himalayan foothills. The ground was cut about by deep gullies containing streams that were nearly dry – until the rains came – which they did not during our time there.

Rudyard Kipling, on whose works I was nurtured, would have travelled similarly – and what a trick of fate it was that I should relive that which I had romanticised from my childhood reading. Had I joined the Indian Army directly I would probably not have survived to tell this tale.

FLYING FOXES AND JACKALS

With a clean suit on, walking on quiet pine needles from my secluded vantage point I would hear the whoosh of something over my head. The sky was dark now and I was navigating by the dim lights which located the units. Then another whoosh followed by a scratching scrambling on a tree ahead of me. The moon became large and bright and illuminated the camp at times and it was at a time of full moon that I first saw the flying foxes. They are secretive and nocturnal and not given to fraternising with humans. I just wish I could have seen them more clearly but we never found an ailing one nor even a dead one. They seemed not to scavenge camp detritus and caused us no trouble. We did not see them during the day at all. One supposes that they would carry rabies though.

The full moon was one third risen toward its zenith at about bed time one evening. Between myself and the moon there was a knoll. The trees were spaced well enough to allow plenty of light through. Silhouetted on the knoll was a leading male jackal confirming its stake in the territory. It sat, head held high facing the plains, and howled every bit like a wolf – and this in the middle of several hundred sleeping men. This jackal issued a challenge and ruled supreme. At least it did on that night.

They are not like wolves. They have no harsh hoarse bark like foxes. And they cannot be said to sound like hyenas, but they have a high pitched scream and a laughter-like voice too. Many nights they would be within feet of my tent as I slept. A mighty chorus of hysterical jackals!

Saitbir entered enthusiastically into every aspect of my eccentric pursuit of life. We constructed a rock garden outside the end of my tent. Boulders and soil – ferns and grasses – and atop the lot a discarded drum

which he kept filled with water. There was a pin hole which allowed the slow escape of water to keep the plants alive. I do not remember a single day of rain all the time we were at the camp; it being the dry season. An unobtrusive toad took up residence in the lee of one of the boulders and no doubt contributed to keeping my patch more free of insects.

Charlie was still with me. He enjoyed a good diet supplemented with praying mantis and other insects but may have missed the geckos which are so juicy. It was on one of my forays to collect mantis that I had an incredible experience – well two!

I had left the camp by the "gate". There was no fence or enclosure; the whole camp was open but the duty guard manned a point on the track not far off the main public road and it was called the gate. I climbed the hill which lay to the north of us, towards the real Himalayas. Between the trees the grass is grazed by flocks of sheep and goats well tended and herded at all times. Sometimes the boy herders would yodel to one another across great distances. Hills and wild animals intimidate juvenile hearts and it seems that with such terrain anywhere in the world yodelling is the means of communication and providing reassurance and comfort. It locates the other herders. The sound was pleasing and musical – more so perhaps than local formal song and music. There was not any means of recording sound then other than in a gramophone studio. How I wish that I might have recorded their song that I might later have understood the words.

It was on that day that the seven jackals walked past me and soon after that I met Mohammed.

I was only several months with the unit before I became headquarter company commander. We were fast approaching Indianisation. Officers with a career to pursue were tending to go to staff college. The army was looking after its own. There were now only eight officers where the normal compliment was probably sixteen or more. "Hostilities only" officers like myself would soon be expecting to be released – demobbed.

The Viceroy Commissioned Officers would all become full officer ranks in the forces of either the Pakistan or Indian armies. We already had by then a Sikh brigadier.

General Auchinleck confers the MBE on Subedar Major Siriprashad Gurung.

The General turned to me and referring to my camera said "that will be worth something one day."

The Auk – General Auchinleck – would stay with us. He

210

liked the picturesque location and I believe he found our mess relaxed and unpretentious. I know that it was and I considered myself most fortunate to be with this particular battalion. Our Colonel had spent years in Canada on what was called "procurement"; purchasing weaponry for British or Indian troops. Perhaps he was that kind of guy anyway. He certainly was good company at all levels and went on after he left the army to do great work with "cross my heart living bras". I visited him once after he had established "Playtex" in London. I read later in our regimental newsletter that he had applied to the garment "latex foundation" company in USA where he was classed as untrained and inexperienced and given little hope of work or achievement. But he was offered the challenge of getting out and selling without much more than a suitcase full of samples. He sold and succeeded. His employers deduced that his success was the result of having not received any training. Anyway, he was promoted to set up "Playtex" Canada and then to "Blighty" across the Atlantic to launch living bras on the British. The Indian experience equipped many for a later interesting and enterprising life.

My company was dispersed around about – Pioneers, Signals, Intelligence, Police and HQ Coy platoon. Each platoon seemed to have its own individual character. The police were like police anywhere; quiet – almost secretive. Probably intimidating to others. Did we recruit "the type" to the platoon? Did suitable personalities present themselves for the job? The training may have established the appropriate attitudes.

I suppose I was attracted to the signals platoon. It was where I started in the battalion. Semaphore and Morse were my main strengths since I was removed from the sea and the skills which went with it. And of course it was Subedar Budibhal's platoon; he who had been first to approach me and welcomed me warmly to that party on my first evening.

Yet much of the pioneer's endeavours were akin to the practical tasks we had undertaken during naval training. Negotiating the near impossible – moving immovable objects – solving survival situations at sea, now became navigating jeeps round perilous corners with one inch of road between success and death down the khud side. Improvising bridges where small streams ran. Wherever there was something requiring a handyman, they did it.

"Intelligence" provided my essential back up. We interpreted maps and calculated. When we were out, on the move, one man would keep me informed of the passage of time – and warn me at intervals of the need to change the pattern of behaviour. Something similar to ships altering course to make an attack by torpedo less effective. Our moves now were for the confusion of tribesmen in the hills above us who might lay ambushes or plan sniper attacks on the column passing through their territory.

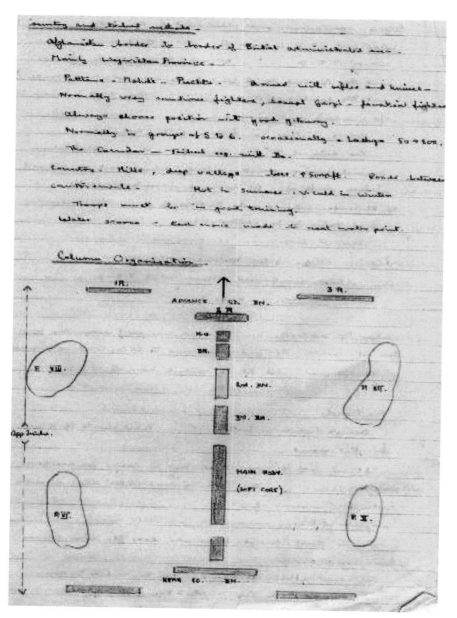

Each time we moved forward all the salient and commanding positions, the hill tops, had to be taken and occupied. So the column moved forward like some great slow slug. Behind the core of the unit, the piquets were withdrawn from their commanding positions as the column moved on to safety beyond rifle range or out of sight.

Occasionally just to ensure that the "enemy" were not waiting to reoccupy a vantage point we would do a mock retreat and then race back to the top of the hill. In the event of such a ploy our platoon or section would be in a position to bring effective fire to bear on the tribesmen now rushing up the hill on the other side. It never actually happened while I was there, but it was an essential insurance procedure that had to be carried out at intervals.

Then we had a mountain battery unit. Once to demonstrate our expertise we laid on a demonstration for the benefit of a visiting senior officer. In those days everything was judged by eye, estimating the range, and setting the sights. The first shot would be fired. If it fell short then one upped the range and tried again. It was hoped that the third shot at least would be on target, but the enemy had had plenty of warning by then. This applied to both mortars and guns. Indeed I had been doing it with 6 inch guns at sea which used shells weighing 100 lbs. Now, across hills, the breech, barrel and block were carried on one mule. A second mule carried the two solid iron wheels. It was astonishing how quickly the team could off load, assemble, aim and fire almost before the mules were being led to cover. It interested me that the little shell could be seen travelling wobblingly to its target. It certainly could be heard in flight and there was a considerable lapse of time between firing and the arrival of the missile at the target. For practice we would choose a harmless bank across the valley.

I wonder if the commanding officers knew about the subterranean mills that operated in the hills. The first really widespread mechanical device in the world must have been the mill. In the Himalayan range those that I saw were driven by a strong jet of water which gushed from a short pipe onto horizontal paddles. The small chamber was entered by a little door and the whole covered over with turf on stonework. The miller had no more than enough height to squat inside with his head bent as he fed handfuls of the grain into the central hole in the millstone. It was easy to pass them by quite unnoticed.

RIDING "DR" BY PONY

A Gurkha hat is the same as the Canadian Mountie's or a Boy Scout's hat. Broad brim with dents in the crown and around it a semblance of a cloth pagri with a green felt patch on which to mount the regimental badge. With the leather chin strap under my chin I never once lost the hat even at great speed. And we did travel. The air rushing past cooled and refreshed. This was preferable to our swims although I admit I enjoyed our occasional dips in the snowy river. There was another battalion some miles away to our west. I cannot now recall which regiment it was but I think they were not Gurkhas. My colonel would ask me to have papers taken there sometimes and I had been arranging this with a DR (dispatch rider) who could just negotiate the rough desert ground on a motor cycle.

Beside forty-five mules we had three ponies. Most respectable and well trained they were too. If I was to go on my own I chose the blond. I liked to think of it as "her" but in reality it was a gelding. Red with fine blond mane and tail that blew out like silken hair as we galloped across miles of unobstructed wild country. "She" loved an uncontrolled gallop and expressed her obvious joy at an opportunity to demonstrate her speed. She seemed to be laughing with the exhilaration and the exhaustion as we pulled up to report at the neighbouring battalion's camp some five or so miles away. In this climate and with the weather of that season little time was spent inside tents. We drew smiles from the more senior officers who would be sitting in a circle in the shade of a large pine tree as I dismounted and handed over the documents.

It is easy to remember the better moments, but thoughts of the coolness generated by the cross country gallops remind one also of the oppressive heat. There were times when my chatti needed much filling and I "collapsed" on my bed, the tent flaps open to allow a slight through movement of air. I had two saucers on the ledge by the bed. One contained salt and the other cayenne pepper. Salt has to be replaced to prevent real heat exhaustion or "stroke". Cayenne promotes sweating which is the body's cooling system. And then there was the cool water. When it was really hot – too hot even for the collared doves or the crickets to sing, then everything ceased.

"Ji nai, sahib" said Saitbir when I asked him if he had seen the toad. No sahib "do din pun". He had not seen it for two days. I presumed that it had to take walks or seek water or procreate, and I did not worry. Well, after all I had not made a pet of the dry brown lethargic creature. It could look after itself. Saitbir

filled the galvanised tub for me to bath in my second tent.

Charlie perched on the middle pole and when he was not asleep would wide eyed watch all that went on. But I did not usually know what it was that he was thinking. A loris must be primate? It knows only food – usually fresh "on the hoof" – and sleep, and occasionally he made sounds, usually of complaint if I teased him; little throaty sounds. He could take my finger in his mouth and although he had sharp little teeth like a kitten he knew that he should not bite so hard that I would be cross with him. We did have to provide the fresh part of his diet whilst living in a tent. Geckos do not run about on canvas at all.

Next morning Saitbir drew my attention to the bath tent. He had emptied the bath and put it out in the sun. In the middle of the oval depression on the ground was one flattened dead toad!

CORN, GRAPES, FIGS, TOMATOES AND OTHER GIFTS

On both sides of us the pine clad hills stretched forever along the three to five thousand foot level. Above, it tended to be bereft of trees, and the lower ground was farmed where there was soil. Much was desert – gritty, dry, hostile and useless. Throughout the lower levels of the tree clad parts were gullies, nullahs, mostly dry and I never saw them in the rainy season. On their banks grew wild fig trees much as in Britain do the elderflowers. The small fruits ripened and although still green skinned, the centres were turning purple and they were delicious. The stools of the local population became quite coloured at this time.

Another useful "wild" plant that served to extend the diet was the tomato. These, I think, were not indigenous but the seeds survived the journey through the human digestive tract. They found moisture and sustenance where they were deposited and the seeds are able to withstand great heat too and the plants grew well. The figs were too high for goats to reach and I found the tomatoes only where domestic animals did not graze in areas being kept for the "hay" crop. There was not one single fence or wall apart from those enclosing the yard or garden adjacent to most dwellings. For hundreds of miles around only natural features such as rivers and cliffs prevented passage. Livestock was herded continually – by young peasant boys.

Mohammed brought gifts to the camp for me. Corn cobs and seedless grapes. He would not come into the camp, not ever, but asked that I be called to the "gate". I enjoyed the extras and the cooks prepared the cobs which I shared with my colleagues.

No one ever questioned my peregrinations from camp. It did not occur to me that there might be any danger. I had no fear of the local populace. I forgot about cobras. I did not know if I should be afraid of jackals or that they were frightened of me. A rabid one would be a danger but I had not known much about rabies and hydrophobia at that time.

One day Mohammed brought gifts and asked me for a sheet. Although I had received Rs250 language payment for my Urdu I was now talking only Gurkhali. It was some time before I understood what he was saying and even then I did not know why I should give him one of my sheets.

Was it perhaps his idea of my gift to him in exchange for the presents he brought me? It worried me a little that I was down to one and a half pairs of sheets and it might not be easy to buy another when we were 100 miles from any sizeable town. I have since learned that I need not have doubted the generosity of these people and especially that of my friend. The sheet came back within days bordered with multicoloured embroidery. I was ashamed of my lack of trust – language!

22. LANGUAGE STUDY.

"When the officer has passed the Elementary Urdu examination he must neither think, nor be allowed to think, that he can relax his efforts to improve himself in the language. His passing of the Elementary standard indicates nothing more than that he has attained the minimum permissible standard in Urdu ; and so far from proving that he is justified in thinking that he knows the language, it must be continually kept before his mind that the knowledge he has acquired is only a foundation on which it is his personal duty to build."

This extract is taken from Para 27 of A.I.T.M. No. 18 dated December 1942. It is republished in order that it may be kept in view. It holds good even more now than it did before.

Facilities have been offered in A.I. (I) 198 of 1943 for officers to present themselves for Part II Oral of the Higher Standard examination, and it is expected that the fullest use will be made of these facilities.

In units for which a regimental language is laid down in Language Regulations, officers may take their Regimental Obligatory examination provided they have passed the Elementary Urdu.

Another present I received from Mohammed was a pair of chaplis – open sandals. For these I had to give him pieces of worn used car tyre. I wore them for some considerable time.

Electricity came much later. The Chinese provided financial, architectural and management services and constructed the Tarbella Dam and Power Station. A whole valley disappeared under water. Prior to that people were self sufficient. Not only did they make everything themselves –

216

they made the tools as well – and that is self sufficiency. It is also sustainable. I wonder if the aids to modern living such as electricity are demanding and are consuming too rapidly the resources of the planet. It provides us with the means and the temptation to indulge great debt. We may be brought to a painful halt one day.

An acquaintance of mine maintains that it was the precious cow in the west highlands of Scotland that made life unbearably focussed on a creature to the detriment of humans, he thought. It is interesting to note that the cow's interests take precedence over humans in Hindu India. Humans could not have colonised northern climes without the milch beast. It provided milk, butter, cheese, and skins to wear as clothes and sandals and many other hunting and domestic utensils including water or wine containers. Thongs for tying and sinews for weapons and for early musical instruments too. And we have to remember transport, cultivations, water raising, and every other chore, now overcome once humans' mental capacity has enabled the transfer of drudgery from the human yoke to the stout and uncomplaining shoulders of some humble creature.

I have seen yak caravans arrive with amethystine rock salt after hundreds of miles of travel over snow and precarious tracks from Tibet. The yak drivers wore hats and coats of long haired fur – from yaks. The tropics support many races unaided by animals, on nuts and pulses, fruit and vegetables. But move higher into the hills or just a little towards the poles and we need to team with a goat, a sheep, a cow, a yak, a reindeer, a lama. An animal between us and our limitations, and our extinction, an animal to whom we owe everything.

SHOOTS

Our shoots were enjoyable. Mohd and I would potter about his family's land and finish the afternoon or evening with perhaps a brace of grey partridges, green pigeons or a hare (khergosht).

Then sometimes he would bring a boy and I asked Saitbir to come with me and the two extras would help to flush and carry the game and it was a sociable event. We were young then. Saitbir would have been the oldest. It seemed so natural that we should be together enjoying the sport. A Scot, a Nepali – veteran of war in Africa and Italy – and two Muslims, in India which was British! Come the time when the cake is to be cut and the portion sizes are not predetermined, then there is a cause for warring and carving out the best part that may be obtained by force.

When there was just the two of us one day, Mohd and I saw and heard some collared doves in pine trees shading the burial ground. I hesitated but Mohd encouraged me to go ahead to see if I could get a shot at them. I made as if to decline thinking of the need to respect that it was the village burial ground, but Mohd nodded me on. I would have had a dove, or even two, but the gun's two barrels fired together with barely a touch on a single trigger. The kick near sent me flying backwards to the ground. I explained to Mohd what had happened. He had seen that something was amiss. He decided that Allah had warned.

TRIP TO DIV HQ

My father said in a letter to me that he had read about DDT. He thought that I ought to be careful. News from the USA reported ill effects to workers both in its manufacture and use. I pondered my illness and some aspects of my condition. I told the Colonel of my concerns. His prompt reply was that if I could find anything in "orders" regarding precautions whilst handling the stuff, then we would implement such order.

The Quartermaster detailed a driver and a 15cwt Chev. I set off for Divisional Headquarters. This was some 200 miles away I think. I was quite impressed by the building but in no way intimidated. Upstairs I was directed to an office with some WAC(I)s, the women equivalent in India of ATS, and some relatively senior officers who pretended a disinterest.

I was still just a very young lad but something to do with my Indian origins made me believe that I was privileged and had a right to make reasonable demands provided that I respected authority. I did notice a few coy smiles from the girls in the office some of whose complexions were distinctly dusky and most attractive. I had seen no women for months and months!

In the regular issue dark green metal filing cabinets I soon found the relevant order. I have no idea how we copied papers in those days, but I was given a copy to take back with me. The Colonel approved my indent for the appropriation of clothing.

VILLAGE HOSPITALITY

The charpoy on which I was invited to lie Roman-like would be surrounded by men and boys. This was in the small village near the army camp and home of my friend Mohammed. We were outside. My audience squatted. I do not believe that any other officers would fraternise with the local populace. Perhaps it was not entirely wise either as we were soon to be engaged in a campaign against a marauding crowd of about 3,000 tribesmen all armed with rifles whose leader later became my friend's father-in-law!

WATER AND ITS ABSENCE

On some of our excursions and sweeps through this wild, unrelenting country I was interested to see examples of the ingenuity and determination of the local people to survive and live reasonably well.

Forty years later my daughter and I were to travel these routes once more.

Roads sometimes were only passable in the dry season for they used a dry river bed for much of the way. We would stop at night and bed down in the river bed. I became adept at wriggling a hollow in the gravel for my hip and I always slept marvellously well, unlike some of the others who seemed not to have shed their expectation of home comfort. But then I had roughed it in the navy.

There were places where water was conveyed to quite distant paddy fields by channels chiselled in the rock bed and then carried over bridged gaps in hollowed tree trunks.

There was an occasion one night that I shall never forget. Our battalion was out on its own. Still a sizeable unit with many mules. I was exceedingly tired. I was commanding HQ Company and was also i/c signals, and intelligence and the other platoons of my company. So the route was chosen by me to use the terrain sensibly, to avoid human habitation and to achieve the object of our journeying. The Colonel decided

on a rest. It was in the middle of the night and we were travelling on the line of a low ridge. One of those long low hills that transverses the arid land; not too far from Abbotabad I should think.

I found a cleft in the rocks. Without a thought for whatever creature might already be in there, I crawled in, wound my khaki scarf around my head and neck for it was really quite cold and went to sleep. I woke refreshed but was dismayed to discover that there was not a sign of the army! It had gone. Not even the rustle and jingle of mule harness. Nor a whiff of animal or person. It was not quite dark although it was well past the middle of the night.

Fortunately it was my route that they would have gone and I set off feeling more than a little lonely. After hastening along for half an hour or so I could just hear the chinking of mule harness and I knew that I was safe. I resumed my place close to my company HQ. I said nothing. No one it seemed had noticed my absence!

And back to Wah camp for a short spell.

3. PAKISTAN REVISITED – FORTY YEARS ON

To Lahore
The Ywca
Bribery
Coach Travel
Suzuki
Arrival
Progress
Tarbella
Peshawar
Ransoms
Violence

TO LAHORE

My daughter would have been about twenty years old at the time. I had three ambitions then; to do the four British Isles rugby internationals, to visit Venice, and thirdly, to return to a little village in Pakistan. The first two I was prepared to forego. I became too old to stand uncomfortably with a poor view at a rugby ground when I may more easily watch the match on TV. If I find someone able to guide me easily and efficiently through overnight stops, airports and customs as marvellously as did my daughter in India, then who knows, I may yet see Venice.

We could not go by train they told us in Delhi. Much troubles. Too much troubles. It is totally quite impossible. Forty years before I knew all about the troubles. I was in the middle of the carnage. The enmity between the two factions broke suddenly as the third power prepared to relinquish control, discipline, law and order, and reasonable justice.

The return fares by air from Delhi to Lahore took much of our spending money. The two "warring" countries provided alternate flights. It was the turn of Air India to provide our plane.

I was interested to see the irrigation channels and endless cultivated paddy fields as we circled around Lahore. The plane touched down in an opalescent still afternoon haze and halted some hundreds of yards from the airport buildings. One was aware of trees, palms, shrubs, well spaced suburban housing and the soft atmospheric colours of October. We waited – nothing happened. It was getting warmer. The pilot broke the silence by announcing that he could not see much sign of activity. "There's nothing much happening here." And then corrected – "I am thinking someone is coming now." And they did; wheeled out some steps manually and parked them at our exit door.

THE YWCA

I liked Lahore Airport; light and spacious. We were quickly moved through immigration and pointed in the direction of an exceedingly smart tall young man advising on tourism and further travel. He was impressive, good looking and I felt that he might warrant more than a single glance from my daughter. He advised us that the safe place for us to stay in Lahore at our price was the YWCA – he explained that men accompanying young ladies may stay there. He spoke good correct English in thoughtful sentences.

Cars and taxis circled around the broad exit away from the airport side in orderly fashion. The taxi driver may have known where to take us but then one is never quite sure if vagueness is planned to extend the journey and enhance the fare. A hire is a hire and has to be made much of. Fortunately I had a little idea of where we were to go and recognised some of the main streets and buildings. I had not before been to the YWCA!

The taxi drove up to a grey sheet metal double gate about nine feet high with spikes on top and a bell at the side. The ring brought the chokidar who opened the gate and bid with his hand for us to drive on the circular drive to the front door of the sprawling single storey buildings. We were to be accommodated, so the taxi departed. We were safely inside.

A diminutive dark lady in a sari was the warden. She was rather shrivelled with age and spoke set phrases in English but obviously understood very little. During our stays there, travelling in both directions, although she said "yes" each time that I explained that I was with my daughter, she did not once vary from referring otherwise than to "your vife".

We shared a go-down on the periphery of the main building which comprised a small twin bedded room with adjoining tiny wash room.

A door opened on to the yard which was the playground for the Christian day girls' school which was probably the main function of the establishment. I was not permitted to be seen at any time in the main part of the building by any of the lady guests so we had to have breakfast one hour before the others rose. Purdah extended to Christians too.

A pretty Japanese girl was lodging in the "YW" so we invited her to join us. She had advised us that there was a fairly good Chinese restaurant somewhere down the main road. I was a little ill at ease. That feeling that one has to watch one's back. Probably I need not have worried, it being broad daylight. But the previous time I had been here, there was arson, shooting and darkness.

BRIBERY

A Sikh in the midst of swirling smoke, rising sparks and some gunfire, had pleaded with me to put a platoon or section in his house for he feared for his life and that of his family. He offered me 3,000 rupees; about six months pay before deductions. No British I knew in those days could ever stoop to bribery or even favouritism. An Indian would have entrusted his life savings to a British sahib with absolute faith. Both factions now sought protection from us.

COACH TRAVEL

I sent a telegram to say that we hoped to arrive a few days hence, and would find our way to the village and then we booked and prepaid for an air conditioned coach for the 200 mile journey. Never, ever again will I willingly travel by coach in that part of this planet.

We assembled as bid at Faletti's Hotel which also housed the Air India office. It was not far from the YWCA – turn left outside the high gates, then to what used to be called the Mall but had become Shahrah-e-quaid-e-azam, and then half right a short way on Egerton Road. From the start a rather dapper man stood at the front of the coach. His self appointed task would seem to have been to wrest the steering wheel from the driver should we be seconds away from disaster.

The driver was demented. He was not the only mad person in charge of vehicles. Perhaps all drivers that day were acting out some transport death wish ballet. The tarmac was three quarters the width of two vehicle lanes so if passing or overtaking someone had to put wheels on the rough shoulder. Everyone drove slightly right of middle in order to intimidate oncoming vehicles and then swerve at the last minute to avoid a collision. India and Pakistan drive on the left! I will swear that our driver nearly lost his nerve once and thought to swerve to the right as the oncoming vehicle held its line, but our dapper guardian angel made to grab the steering wheel and we moved to the left just in time to avoid a collision. All this at some horrifyingly great speed – it seemed like 70 mph. I had lost all sense of reality and proportion – perhaps it was 90 mph! Hitchcock used to be my indulgence for fear and suspense. He had not produced a fear as intense in any of his films such as I experienced mile after mile that day. We made the midway stop at Gujranwala. At a street side restaurant which was dim, dirty and derelict. I took a mug of tea out to the coach for my daughter.

There was a dual carriageway for part of the journey. Our driver now refreshed and probably phased with pheru foods re-entered the fray. With renewed vigour he forced everything off the road and held the middle line. That is until we met a string of camels coming towards us on our lane. We slid past with no space to spare with the scream of the horn held down. And then, next, we could see it coming from a mile away, a buffalo herder ran back across the two carriageways. Half his team had already crossed; the other black lumbering beasts were beginning to follow, emerging from shrubs and palms. Would he turn them back or try to hurry them across before we levelled with them. I shut my eyes and prayed. My daughter said she saw a dead camel by the roadside.

There was still a few hours of daylight when we arrived in Abbotabad. We needed the next coach to take us further into the hills to the market town nearest to my friends village. We had time to eat. A taxi took us to the Chinese restaurant recommended by the driver; and the food was good. Rather than lose the return fare our taxi waited outside for about an hour. I shall never understand the economics of trade and business. A shop keeper may sit more than all day amidst a stock which can hardly be worth in total any more than would keep us for a couple of days. Infrequently he will reach out for something and occasionally rise to fetch it from a higher shelf and take a few annas.

I nearly left my camera bag which also had our passports, papers and money in it under the table at the restaurant but the Chinese waiter came running out and handed it to me as we were about to drive off.

The sky was colouring when the second coach disgorged us just before sundown. Another earthy uneven park area with a horde of mixed males, excited or totally disinterested. The sort of village gathering where nothing in particular ever happens – but just might. We were the big event of the day! That we should wish to proceed to the village I named was met with disbelief, almost ridicule.

SUZUKIS

Suzuki "taxis" were parked around and their drivers physically pushed to gain places near enough to negotiate with me for the hire. There was a quieter man, the others made too much noise and were quite disturbing. My concern was that the driver should at least have understood me and knew the village that we sought, and if possible had knowledge of my friend. Mohd is a man of some standing. The quiet man nodded and said "Ji". Then we agreed the price. I chose a figure which was a little more than half that which the others were asking and the quiet man agreed so he was hired.

As we cleared the town the road begins to twist and rise. It is still tarmac but far from the smooth surface that Barber-Greens lay. The Suzuki's lights were on now and I had difficulty in

recognising the way in the dark. And yet, now and then, there was a bend or a steep part and a place where the water always seemed to run over the road that was familiar even after forty years. Suzukis are common here, almost the sole form of transport. They barely accommodate three inside the cab – including the driver. The engine sounds like that of a small motorbike. The back is an open pick up. I was concerned that I should keep an eye on our bags in the back but we did not stop anywhere. Conversation ended when it became apparent that the driver spoke only Hindko. He seemed not to wish to try much Urdu.

ARRIVAL

For the rupee equivalent of a few pounds we were deposited at the "hotel" in the row of half a dozen shops which lined the main road. I withheld payment pending our transfer into the safe custody of my friend Mohd. The hotel was square and it had a low flat ceiling with exposed beams strung with 8" plastic pennants alternately yellow and brown. But everything was covered in a thick veneer of smoke both from tobacco and the charcoal burning clay "stove" in a corner. I suppose there may have been a dozen or more charpoys; wooden framed with ropes sparsely strung lengthways and across. One always took one's own bedding on travels beyond the cities.

We were bid to sit on a charpoy in the dim light of a single low watt bulb as more and more of the men and boys gathered. We were given cups of tea. On asking for directions to my friend's house, it was made clear with hand wagging and head pivoting that no one knew of him. Cautious as 2,000 years of occupation by one or another emperor made them, I was asked if I had any written evidence of this friendship which I claimed.

The Suzuki driver waited patiently entertained by the most unusual scenario in years. In my camera bag I had all our correspondence. A letter was scrutinised and passed around a little. I was unconvinced that there was anyone who could read anything but Urdu script, or perhaps Hindi. My sincerity perhaps was sufficient conviction. "We send boy to see if anything can be done." The driver waited. We all waited. By now the hotel was packed out. A "sea" of white or standard grey clad men, some whose heads nearly touched the dangling pennants that adorned the room. Interspersed were a dozen youths. We waited. I became concerned. My friend lived not that far from the main road. I remembered that I had sat with them in the middle of the village – twenty or so houses dispersed over less than half a mile of the rough dirt road up the hill.

Then a stir, a way cleared in the ranks of curious onlookers, and Mohd entered. He was older, of course. He wore white perfectly starched clothing and his best astrakhan grey hat and slightly dense spectacles. The recognition was spontaneous given the requisite six seconds for the "photofit" to become the reality of today. The face, now lined where youth had been before. The shoulders stooped a little but still the proud man who had welcomed me so enthusiastically to his "family estate" forty years before. It was he who opened his arms to embrace me and we patted each other's backs to an accompaniment of "oohs" and "aahs" from the audience. The Hindko driver was paid and departed fairly expressionless in his Suzuki. My friend said, "He no good man."

PROGRESS

Electricity had arrived. Most houses sported at least one bulb but many had two. One on a pole on the roof – to light the way? To dispel ogres, or just to show neighbours that one has electricity. The houses I had known before were still there – mud bricks, flat roofs requiring refurbishment after each rainy season; plastered with mud.

Additionally however was a rash of new houses made of concrete. Expansion joints did not come with the instructions so buildings were completed without them and then cracked with the changes in temperature. It could be very hot in summer and it snowed in winter but there was little frost.

So little frost in fact that the water pipe through the village has not been buried. As a result the water would become extremely hot in the pipe unless the water is left to run continuously. Householders on higher spurs frequently disconnect the pipe and hammer in a temporary bung. Later the owners of the houses at the bottom of the hill have to come up to remove the bung and reconnect the pipe.

TARBELA

My daughter and I were treated to a very special outing. We were driven many miles to see the Tarbela reservoir.. This had been created by the damming of the Indus in a narrow valley. Here for the first time

230

ever, miles from the sea and in the absence of lakes, a boat may be seen. An entirely new form of transport. We were given a brief ride in one; a few hundred yards and then back to the shore. Forty years previously the narrow road had followed the valley floor through Amb. My Colonel was invited to dinner with the Nawab at his palace there. I was asked to select ten of our best shots because half a century earlier a British officer had similarly been invited and then shot during the meal.

My wise Colonel negotiated that there were to be ten armed men from each faction on the balcony surrounding the hall.

PESHAWAR

My daughter went by car. I was to travel by bus with my friend next day. It was not seemly for me to be in the car with the womenfolk. Apparently my daughter saw the lower end of the reservoir; the impressive dam and the electricity generating building. However the bus did not travel that way. It was a long and uncomfortable journey but trouble free. We had loo breaks and the

men squatted to urinate at the side of the road. Gone now was the sniping and military presence. Transport mostly passed freely. Violence there still was and some of it connected with the drugs trade. I am uncertain if the perpetrators of the bombings knew in what cause they acted or indeed if the victims understood why they should be the target.

RANSOMS

We dined out one evening during our stay in Peshawar. My daughter came too although they had to be reminded by me of her presence. Their women did not go out at all it seemed. The meal in a street side tikka was excellent; tender lamb, cucumber, "seven up" and etceteras. There was shooting in a street nearby, but as my friends explained, it may not have been a violent act but merely excitement at a wedding.

Truck drivers stayed at the Tikka restaurant, overnight or longer, awaiting the next load. If business was poor they would resort to kidnap. Children, babies usually, yielded considerable sums but if the money was not forthcoming then sale or gift of the kidnapped to wealthy and influential persons would be considered.

We left Peshawar by train. About 400 miles to Lahore; cost £4 each. We had no comfort breaks and many delays on the way. The driver sensibly reversed to the previous station if he should become bored with lack of progress. My friend had wished to pay our fares but I insisted that he should not; he having been so hospitable for nearly a month.

232

The railway line out of Peshawar. Unfenced all the way?

On arrival at Lahore in the packed jostling station we scurried to cover in the sanctuary of the YWCA once more. We read that a bomb had gone off in the very same train the next morning.

We must have passed quite close to Wah camp on our way. I have since heard that there is a vast munitions factory there.

There is a widespread brotherhood of people covering both sides of the border with Afghanistan. Sometimes some of the "clans" may not be speaking to one another, and there may be open war between them, but when others threaten, their strength is in acting together. I was proudly presented to members of the mujahideen who were "refugeeing" on the Pakistan side of the border. They assured me that Mrs Thatcher was a very fine person. She approved considerable sums for the support of refugees in Pakistan at the time when Russia was involved.

4. WHILE AT WAH

The Camp
Hypnosis Perhaps
Dushera
Rice, Aluminium and Nutrition.
Frontier Warfare
British Influence in India
Darning Socks and Train Travel
WVS Girl and Ciphers
Runaway Mule

THE CAMP AT WAH

Charlie Loris perched on the bamboo curtain rail in my room and slept during much of the day. I had purchased a considerable length of folk weave cotton material in a good shade of green. I paid the durzi to run up some curtains for the window in the room which I shared with a fellow subaltern. Charlie became more active in the evenings and I assisted him to reach geckos that strayed across the wall. These he caught one-handed deftly, then chewed them from the head down to the last morsel of the wriggling tail.

Wah was not far from the railway line that runs beyond Rawalpindi to Nowshera and Peshawar. It was mainly a vast cement factory with an adjacent brick built army camp outside its perimeter fence. I am told that today there is a massive munitions factory there.

Doc was Indian; a sociable young man. A Hindu, I presume, as the Gurkhas are Hindu. He and I played singles on the concrete tennis court. I believe there was an arrangement for officers to borrow the key to the gate in the cement factory fence.

HYPNOSIS PERHAPS

Doc must have been something of a hypnotist for I have never before nor since played a game as perfectly as on that day which was my twentieth birthday. Doc won, of course, but I was surprised and elated with my sudden new found skill in skimming balls low over the net. Nearly all my serves were in and at speed.

It was hot so I called at the mess afterwards and downed a couple of gin piaz before I went for my bath; a galvanised hip bath so my feet were outside but I fell fast asleep. The colonel sent an orderly who politely informed me that dinner was served. I went back to sleep, missed my dinner, and went to bed; – that was my twentieth birthday!

While we were at Wah Doc took leave to be married. We asked him if he had yet seen his bride. He had not. When he returned we asked him if marriage suited him and had all gone well. It appeared that he was ecstatic but he was too modest to elaborate.

The dozen or so games of tennis was one of only very few leisure or recreational activities during my time with the regiment. I did not take leave. There was a games pitch at Wah. The surface was gritty natural desert hard earth. It was used for hockey and football. A battalion of some other Indian regiment joined the brigade; perhaps they were Rajputs or Punjabis – fifty-five years on my memory dims. I was invited to join them for hockey. They wore no shoes. How they weaved and dashed and slashed and drove a hard competitive game – in their bare feet.

VCOs and KCOs at the nautch dance From left: Kishan Sing Thapa, Subedar Major, a VCO from the Dogra Bn.,
Tilbahadur Thapa, Birbahadur, David, Lilabir, and Mac.

Ann wrote to say that wrens are going on release and her mother has been demobbed. She said "Fog. Can't locate the ships. Ration increase for Christmas." A later letter stated; *"visual signalling is a thing of the past."* It took all of the war to replace Morse with verbal communication. We still used mostly Morse with lamp, heliograph and flag here. I wondered how the navy would function if it lost power. Its batteries all run down. Our trouble was the weight of the batteries. Quite a short range wireless set and its batteries were as much as a man could carry.

DUSHERA

We were in Wah both before and after the Oghi punitive expedition. We celebrated Dushera at Wah. A square temple was constructed from poles and branches. The sides were fifteen feet high with several horizontal rails and a space for a doorway. All was decorated with greenery – something resembling laurel that must have come from the screening shelter shrubbery around the cement factory. It was like Christmas.

A conjuror was engaged to entertain us and the Gurkha families who were resident in this camp.

We, the King's Commissioned officers, each received a beautifully printed invitation from our Subedar Major, Siri Prashad Gurung MBE, to dinner in the VCO's mess.

On the following day at the "temple" goats, one by one, were led out to be slaughtered. I was not privy to the process for selection of honorary slaughterer's. Beheading the Dushera sacrifices was obviously important and pride of place went to a strong young man who was to behead the young water buffalo.

Cows may not be harmed but the buffalo is meat, milk and is also burdened with all hard haulage tasks. Our mess was supplied with dairy produce from the local government dairy – water buffalo. For some months until I decided that I could not afford the luxury, I had a carton of cream at breakfast with my porridge. Buffalo's milk is 12% butterfat. British dairy cows provide 3% with a struggle.

Buffalo bulls are wild and unpredictable. At the dairy they were well tethered. There was also an experiment to determine if showering the animals was a substitute for wallowing.

The goats and the young buffalo stayed on their legs for what seemed quite a time after the head was severed; a single clean blow with a very sharp kukri. As the body crumpled to the ground someone took the hind legs and dragged it round the outside of the temple. A dark streak on the sandy soil soon surrounded the temple. This practice would improve the quality of the meat – the Dushera dinner for a festive day.

We were most hospitably entertained in the Gurkha Officers' mess. The rakshi was special; the meats delicious and we had quality rice. It was usually unwise to chew rice for fear of breaking ones teeth on the small stones. I ate in the mens' lines with one of my platoons once when we were in the hills beyond Oghi because the Officers' Mess khansaman had loaded paraffin above the food in one of the boxes. Travel on a mule's back liberally sprinkled the paraffin over the food. It repeated all day. Curried aloo (potato) and rice with the Pioneer Platoon was delicious but their jemadar commander said "No Sahib, not bite. Just swallow." Rice that was "every-day" had stones in it.

The much prized "offals" were served on a vast brass platter. Every part of the animal was there;

chopped, crisped and flavoured with dozens of condiments. One was expected, and encouraged, almost compelled to take some of each. How would one's nutrition be otherwise complete? It was necessary to partake of every part of the body, and we must not presume to decline that which had been sacrificed for our own good health.

RICE, ALUMINIUM, NUTRITION

Gurkhas were particularly advanced in their thinking about nutrition and health. They had declined aluminium as cookware so iron pots were essential in spite of being heavy. Our rations were bought locally, whole and unprocessed; the meat, mainly goat, on the hoof. The rice would have been threshed with flails and the feet of bullocks as they endlessly circled the heap. Then it was tossed in a breeze to winnow out the chaff and straw but stones the size of rice grains remained.

I ordered the condiments each month for my company. Other stores came via the quarter master but companies were given the privilege of selecting their own condiments.

There may have been over thirty. The cooks and the clerks prepared the list for my approval. The food was delicious and much to my taste then and even now. The simplicity of cumin, coriander and turmeric with other subtleties varying between ginger and cayenne produced appetising meals from limited bulk ingredients. It was all healthy and unprocessed.

FRONTIER WARFARE

This was 20 Brigade in the 10th Indian Division. It had served through North Africa and Italy when I was in the Royal Navy. My Gurkha story began after their withdrawal from the Mediterranean and as they anticipated moving to the Japanese theatre.

10th. Indian Division. Christmas card 1946.

240

And then the atomic bomb was dropped so our training changed from "Jungle" to "Frontier".

To move through, live in, and support the civil administration within the northern part of the Indian subcontinent required special attitudes and skills. Between the limit of administered India and as far as China and Russia 200 miles beyond to the north was "tribal territory".

There were permanently snow-clad ranges; deep gorges and wide valleys. The Indus river runs north and then eastward behind the Himalayas. Hillsides were endlessly and often precipitously terraced for growing crops; mostly rice and millet. Opium too but that was none of our business.

In this view I counted twenty-three villages; each with a tower that served as a lookout post and for defence. The valleys warmed well in the summer suns so that peaches and apricots, maize and grapes would grow well. We were camped at the lower reaches in the pine clad foothills. Beyond was Dir, Swat and Chitral. Then further still were the "Shangri-Las" of Gilgit and Hunza.

The only Europeans (British) amongst these constantly warring tribes were the officers of the Frontier Constabulary. I met only one; he came from Glasgow. That was when we attended at the Oghi affair. He wore the same clothes as did his riflemen in order to avoid being an obvious target. They were out on the ground patrolling for a week at a time and carried their meal and salt with which they made gruel (porridge). They were very mobile and carried easily all that they required for their Spartan existence. I suppose that they were Pathans. We met up with them to receive intelligence regarding our "enemy's" disposition.

A patrol of the Frontier Constabulary.

BRITISH INFLUENCE IN INDIA

I have a great regard and respect for India for it was there before we were a gleam in a Roman's eye, and they were adept at sports even then. An Indian woman politician interviewed on radio during a debate on human rights declared that India, she believed, legislated thus 3,000 years previously.

The British did – with Roman, Viking, Norman coaching – make a marvellous job of administering this vast country; developing transport and communications; of establishing law, order and the judiciary and encouraging trade and industry.

A tradition of trust had evolved in India so that my parents provided security for workers on the tea estate. Monies for weddings, inheritance and savings would be entrusted to their safe keeping until required.

My family in diverse occupations became committed to the care of many people – the uncle by marriage managing the bank in Bombay. My father's brother in the Indian Civil Service was District Commissioner at Chittagong when the Japanese were within artillery range. It was he who persuaded the merchants to sell their hoarded stocks of rice and prevented starvation during a post war famine. My mother's brother died of cholera whilst in the Nilgiris working in the coffee business. Father's cousin managed the tile factory in Mangalore.

Scotland exported whisky, wool, herrings and people. The 1920s and 1930s offered little in the way of secure employment at home so the colonial services had a need and provided the answer. The British fostered responsible attitudes in India so that many historical buildings and artefacts were preserved for posterity. In the hills colonial disciplines exist to this day such that a tree may not be felled without a licence. Unfortunately corruption has now become a way of life which dissipates public funds intended for the common good.

DARNING SOCKS AND TRAIN TRAVEL

I wore chaplis much of the time. One day I took out a pair of clean socks and found that Saitbir had darned the holes in the toes with four different coloured wools – green, red, blue and yellow. They would look most peculiar in the open toes of my sandals. I asked him "Why?" His simple reply – he thought it would look pretty!

A pin-up picture came with each copy of "The Sketch". These were daring for that age. Some even exposed the breasts. The artist was David Wright. At any one time I may have had a dozen drawing-pinned to the wall. One went missing. I had been hoping to achieve a complete collection and it was discouraging to find that someone had removed one. I asked Saitbir if he knew where it had gone. His perfectly sincere and honest reply was that he had borrowed it and would return it quite soon. So all was well.

Once each month I travelled by train to Delhi. A .45 revolver loaded; compartment on the train reserved for me. Timber carriage with four bunks and an ablution/wash "en suite". There was no corridor. The floor of the wash area sloped towards the centre where there was a plug hole with no plug. It had a brass surround and I could see the gravel between the rails passing underneath. I was saddened by the memory that mother had told me that she had dropped her wedding ring on just such a train twenty years earlier. It had inevitably rolled to the middle of the floor and dropped to the track through the plug hole. I still wonder how my father had reacted. It is unlikely that he was gently compassionate.

WVS GIRL AND CIPHERS

My reason for visiting Delhi was to collect the ciphers. They were encoding books so that wireless communication could be transmitted secretly. It was not really difficult and I would not have been surprised if the printers sent copies to interested parties anyway. On one occasion I was waiting in Delhi Station for the train to depart. The train was becoming full. The RTO walked past my compartment several times accompanying a young woman in WVS uniform. Eventually, having found nowhere for her he took courage and asked if I would consider allowing her into my compartment. It was a high security errand that I was on. I pretended a degree of reluctance and then acquiescence, so she travelled the two days with me – and darned some of my socks.

It transpired that she had lost her fiancé who had been an RAF pilot and decided that some kind of service to the forces would have a palliative or at least a distracting effect at her time of loss. She was a sweet and kind young woman in her early twenties. I was fairly certain that the Brigade Major was not the kind of company she sought or needed. However, we decided that it would be politic if we emerged separately from the train. I did not see her again until I was on my way "back to Blighty". I called in at Poona and we sat and talked beside the swimming pool on a sunny afternoon before I made my way to Bombay and the ship home.

RUNAWAY MULE

The road out of Wah camp was straight. The land was flat. Nothing punctuated the flat arid land to the west of Wah camp. The road faded into the distance. At each side of the road there was a constructed depression, a ditch, dry of course but ready to take the run-off when it rained. I was half a mile out of camp. I suppose I was looking for signs of life, such as ants, or plants, or lizards but there seemed to be nothing to interest me and I was about to walk back into camp.

PART TWO : TRAINING IN GENERAL.

10. HOW TO CATCH RUNAWAY MULES.

The necessity for chasing mules can be greatly reduced or almost eliminated by a little training.

The method consists of hand feeding animals.

Drivers should carry a nose bag and commence each feed by hand feeding. Even the shyest animal will very soon associate a nose-bag and an outstretched hand with a meal.

Should a mule break loose, it can generally, if trained as above, be induced to come up to anyone advancing with a nose-bag and outstretched hand.

Animals should be trained to both British and Indian troops as some are "topee shy".

11. HOW TO GET MULES ACROSS RIVERS.

All mules and ponies should be allowed to grow a "mounting lock" to facilitate control by men in the water.

They should have their feeds put on to whistle blast. A whistle may then be used to induce them to cross the river.

Mules MUST be fed after swimming across a river. During training, swim them before a feed is due and give the feed on the far bank.

A rattling, crashing sound emerged from among the camp buildings. It was a mule yoked to an ammunition cart. These carts were all metal; wheels, floor slats, sides and shafts. All was metal and it made such a noise that between fifty and a hundred Gurkhas and muleteers had soon emerged from camp to watch the fate of the runaway mule.

I was the animal man. My reputation was to be truly tested. A mule in panic, a noisy cart and what seemed like an open space between it and Karachi somewhere 1,000 miles away. One supposes that a mule has a brain although it is hard to prove it. I assumed that the mule might have enough sense to stay on the road. Did it anticipate anything at all. Would it, could it, consider the result of galloping into the ditch? It must surely have been killed or certainly been severely injured if it did anything other than stay on the road. I stood in the middle of the road with my arms outstretched. Its speed did not reduce until it halted with its steaming nostrils not a foot away from my chest. It had sense after all! I believe it was truly grateful to me for saving its life as I took its bridle, turned it on the road and led it back to its muleteer; totally docile.

The muleteer was much relieved too. So was I! I had not at that time had access to the training manual with recommendations for training mules – but in any case it did not say anything about catching or stopping one in full flight.

246

We used rifle ranges somewhere out of camp. I only mention it because in this part of the world it was necessary to dig all the spent shots out of the butts. This was done to prevent the lead being taken and used to make bullets for the tribesmen's home-made rifles and used against us.

In November the snow line was descending. For reasons unknown to me we had to make an incursion into the hills. A brigade is a massive crawling caravan of men, mules and munitions. As it moves among the mountain ranges every high ground and hill top overlooking the route has to be piqueted; to be occupied by us to prevent sniping by tribesmen.

We were traversing a broad high slope. A ridge to our right rose sharply. I saw on its near vertical face a broad white scar, a gash running obliquely for more than a hundred yards. I moved to it and discovered that it was a substantial thick seam of mica. Sheets of it large enough to equip masses of electrical goods with insulation.

The Indian Army was originally officered entirely by Europeans – British. Many were Scots. Now Indians were being granted King's Commissions, KCOs. Soon the British would be gone and all the Viceroy Commissioned Officers would be given full officer status in the army of whatever the country became following independence.

So for a time we were greatly under-officered. Although I was a novice, but because there was no one else, I was thrust temporarily on occasions into the role of acting brigade intelligence officer. Map reading was familiar to me and something I enjoyed from an early age. Now some parts of the map were not detailed, perhaps not surveyed. Most of the map was coloured purple; the higher ground. Low ground started with pale buff, through darkening shades of brown to purple; then above was white, uncharted or permanent snow!

The Colonel challenged me once. He bet me a bottle of whisky that we would not arrive at our intended destination. He had a knack of getting the best from each of us. The night was clear and starlit. I had sneaked out earlier to make a bit of a reconnaissance. The way ahead appeared to be without problems. I had told the duty company at our part of the camp perimeter that I was going out, and we knew the password of the night so that I could safely approach on my return. I sometimes wonder how I have survived, considering my irregular behaviour and individual peregrinations. The moon was bright and I could see the way ahead for several miles.

For overnight stops we chose a flat area large enough to accommodate the brigade in a square. It had to be that it could be defended easily and that it was not overlooked by higher ground. Stones were gathered to make a low wall along each of the four straight sides. My battalion was allocated the north west corner. It would be manned by alert riflemen all night.

In the middle of each straight side was a "gate". Roads between opposite gates crossed in the middle of camp. In the softer centre were the mule lines. Literally lines; strong parallel wires were pegged out to which the mules, and our three ponies were hobbled by a hind and a forefoot. The ponies were for casualties – non-

walking wounded. They were fed and watered and eventually settled down to rest and sleep. Mules are very silent creatures. Not at all like rowdy donkeys.

Our mess tent was quickly dug out with parallel foot trenches so that we could sit each side of the raised centre on which was rolled out a canvas and slat "table". We were fed by the mess cooks and a bar was at hand. An orderly fetched drinks as requested. There was snow all around.

At Brigade HQ somewhere else in the camp, the Brigadier with senior officers dined and discussed plans. We waited for the outcome of their deliberations. It was my twenty first birthday. Two hurricane batties hung from the tent ridge pole. I played shanties and popular songs, very badly on my mouth organ and we sang, also badly. It was in the wee small hours that the adjutant arrived with the orders for the following morning. I expect that I stood a round of drinks

The brigade moved out two hours before daylight. The stones had been quietly dispersed and the camp area cleared of almost all signs of our overnight sojourn.

Apart from the harness sounds and occasional scuff of boot or hoof there seemed to be relative quiet. It was a still night. There were some trees and scrub but we proceeded steadily without the delay which day time piquetting would have required. For a time we were on the route that I had reconnoitred. Some dogs started barking so I was able to locate a small village unseen in the dark and I knew where we were. It was then that the Colonel made his challenge. Dawn broke and the coldness eased up as we came to the end of the ridge. We veered to our left downwards to a broad sweep of a sizable river. It was shallow here and we crossed to the shingle beach which was vast enough to accommodate everyone. Some of the men gathered branches and tree limbs and lit a large bonfire. The warmth was very welcome for we were feeling the cold in spite of our jerseys, scarves and the leather sleeveless jackets which had been issued.

I doubt if there is anymore spectacular way to travel in such mountainous country. To walk in it, sleep in it breathing the air. Glimpsing the higher snow peaks with sun coming on to them. Using routes which were not established ways.

Three or four of us, subalterns, were confined to camp at Wah for three weeks by the Colonel for behaving unseemly on our return from a dance in Lahore. We presented the adjutant with a vast bunch of flowers on his upturned bed, with him underneath it, as we sang "happy birthday to you." I think it *was* his birthday, but I do not remember. In any case we were not likely to be going anywhere for we were earnestly preparing for the Oghi punitive affair.

It was said that about three thousand men had gathered for the fun and the pillage. We, a whole brigade with Divisional headquarters backup, were sent to discipline the area in what would be termed a punitive operation. Half a century or so earlier there had been a campaign here "the Black Mountain" – and a medal struck to confer on participants.

We were to implement the imposition of fines. Sixty nine thousand rupees, sixty nine rifles, and the return of the three girls who had been abducted. Presumably, had we failed, we would have advanced into tribal territory to demolish a dozen or so villages which in winter would make life difficult for the dispossessed.

In retrospect, I believe that the rising was a planned ploy. It had been designed to tie up the military whilst the partition violence sought to gain more territory for the new nation of Pakistan across the width of the plains. But we were soon to be needed down there.

As far as I am aware I never met Khan, the leader of the marauding tribesmen, although I was once confronted by two ornately dressed gentlemen on the track we were building from Oghi over the pass to the tribal territory beyond.

The Black Mountain – site of an earlier military campaign for which a medal was struck.

For some time I had been packing snow around my tent each night but now spring was beginning. Everything still froze at sundown – in five minutes, it seemed. The sun awakened each morning an astonishing and colourful array of alpine flowers. I had names for none of them.

I was exploring the otherwise desolate hillside cut all the way up by endless terraces used for growing rice or millet. I could not tell which from the crop residues after months of snow cover. We met perhaps less than a mile out of our uncomfortably perched tented camp. They were tall, erect, proud, beak nosed, elaborately dressed and much adorned with beaded waistcoats and belts with gold trimmings; wrapped around with bandoliers and a weight of ammunition, and knives at their belts. Each carried a long rifle, home made locally, of course, the barrels wound in copper wire perhaps torn from the telephone line to Hunza. The rifles must have been cumbersome and heavy to carry. A vision handed down over centuries from Mogul and other old empires.

I moved, as we approached, to the higher left side. It is advantageous to occupy the higher ground as do ibex and the like. In another place one would seek a cliff, a rock, a wall or tree at one's back. There was none here. So we kept about ten or twelve feet between us and engaged in a peaceful discourse – with

250

Urdu and a few English words and gestures. The reasons for our military presence, they pretended a conviction, was to investigate Russian infiltration? It was at the time when membership of the communist party in India was growing noticeably. This might have influenced elections following independence. I believe, now, that they knew better than us precisely why we were there. Their plan had worked very well.

Temporary Officers' Mess. Part way up the road we built. Near Jal Gali.

I suppose we used about a quarter ton of rice every meal time – if it wasn't the turn for chapattis, that is. Supplies were being dropped – sometimes even our water – by Dakota planes. We would have laid out our orange cloth markers for the DZ – and over would come the pilot and buzz me – he would see us all and then rain down solid bags of rice and jerrycans of water packed between bags of straw right over our heads or else half a mile away!

Well! You can dive for cover when you see them coming – but it does cause a panic when everyone decides to run in different directions. Then there is absolutely nothing worse than asking weary men who have walked miles all day, since the early hours of the previous morning, to come half a mile to collect dinner as yet uncooked. There is! Worst luck. There is one thing worse – and that is asking the muleteers who have just settled the poor beasts and got them all hobbled to their lines – to get them up and harnessed to go off round the next bend in the dry river bed to collect air dropped supplies.

So it would sometimes be nearing darkness – as night comes quickly in the hills away in the deep valleys of the north. It was preferable to get all the activity over before dark and before the paraffin cookers started up their roar, as the cooks pumped up the pressure in them. It was an invitation, and a

251

target, to snipers to have lights and cookers alight in the dark in that tribal area.

Everyone from Norfolk would say that the terrain here was mountainous. We were in what were known as the foothills. The ideal site for Gurkhas to hold their annual "khud race". Khud is presumably the Nepalese for hillside. To fall over the edge meant tumbling down the khudside. The race took place over a course which would be chosen for its incline and distance. The Nepalese have incredibly well developed legs albeit short. Their calf muscles are notably powerful. Their health is exceptional and their staying power something in which they take much pride. Ascent of what seemed to be a forty five degree slope was taken at the double. Descent was by leaps and bounds with the feet touching ground only briefly and with much space between. For humans it was more impressive than mountain goats or ibex. I did not hear of any injuries. I believe I was rather busy that day and was not able to pay close attention to the event.

For more than a year the only time I lived in a building was when we were briefly stationed at Wah.

Brick buildings with doors and windows. Some single rooms and some twin. I shared a sizable room. With my curtains and other comforting touches, it was a popular room for fellow officers to visit. We had access to the camp shop and I remember that we over indulged on Gordon's gin, bought by the bottle with the colourful "export" label.

After so long in tents, on the move, demanding work schedules, it was natural that there should be

252

some relaxing "hi jinks". Garth may have been a captain. He was certainly large. With a glass clutched close to his chest he came through the door without opening it. The wood was feeble – kutchha. One evening Tommy's room door and his window were quietly bricked up as he slept – without mortar. It was the electric fan placed face down on the floor and then switched on from outside that caused consternation and panic. We had also removed the light bulb. He was most displeased.

Permanent picquets were built at base camps.

Letters from Ann suggest life in Blighty is not at all easy. Permit to paint the woodwork of the house was not granted. She had her 21st birthday at the lodge. She was pleased to have her sister home and demobbed from the navy – a Petty Officer. Ann is training in horticulture.

5. HOTTING UP – RUNNING DOWN

The Frontier Mail
Decimation
Unrest
Bodies, Camels and Disposal
Partition, Problems, Murder
Back To School

THE FRONTIER MAIL

There are one or two east-west ranges of hills to the south of Wah. They are arid, hot and not much frequented except by an occasional herd of goats. Mostly the life there is wild; lizards and snakes and a few buzzards. Perhaps there is more activity at night. My daughter and I saw a very large lizard, at least four feet long, from the train on our return from Peshawar to Lahore.

The train has to pass through these hills either in cuttings, or embankments or in tunnels. There has, in violent times, always been trouble with the trains there. They can so easily be ambushed.

Vernon Beck drove the engine regularly between Rawalpindi and Lahore. On my monthly mission to Delhi it was he who would have driven me from Wah to Lahore (where he lived) and then the next driver took the train on to Delhi. On main line railways, such as the North West Railway, engine driving was entrusted to a European. They were, in Indian terms, well paid and I have met several children of the mixed marriages of railway families. The daughter of one attended the boarding school in Coonoor (where I was born) which was a long way from her home in Calcutta and she now lives in Kent.

Vernon's widow also lives in Kent and the daughter is married and is presently singing with an amateur choral group, having retired from a responsible post – matron in an old folks home. It was Vernon who drove the train that was the big massacre event during the height of the violent unrest – the riots prior to independence. His family recall that he said he just kept driving. There was nothing that he could do. On arrival at the station, perhaps it was Lahore, it was unbearably horrible. They said that he compulsively washed his hands for many months afterwards.

Although nothing, by this time, was happening in Wah, we were hearing of trouble. It was supposed that the rifles of a whole army section had been thieved in the night. The rifles should have been chained and padlocked around the centre pole of the bell tent in which the sepoys were sleeping (not our brigade or regiment). Is it possible that some silent and very daring and determined persons managed to secret them away without wakening the sepoys (sipahis).

DECIMATION

The task which I have liked the least, in all my life, was to recommend serving soldiers for retention in the army down to only two thirds of our strength. *I had to recommend the retirement of one third of my company*. This might have been acceptable in some regiments – there will have been some who would have been recruited to the Indian Army solely for the period of hostilities. But the Gurkhas – although some were recruited as war reservists, to a man *they were all in it as a career*. Each serving rifleman was the pride of his family. Nepalese families strove and competed to get a son into the Gurkha Brigade (meaning the ten Regiments). Certainly the numbers had been increased to meet wartime needs, but the Gurkha riflemen and his havildars and Naiks did not, and could not, see themselves as "surplus to requirements". My father had been surplus to the needs of the Royal Navy in 1922 – I became an embarrassment to the navy along with a hundred other C/W candidates in 1944 – but then I was HO ("Hostilities Only") and I moved sideways to the Indian Army before finally returning to my civilian status.

Some of these young and aspiring Nepalese men were devastated. I do not know what happened to them. It was an unwise and cruel act but we were ordered to cut short the careers of some of the best. Perhaps it was resolved better in the end than I could ever have hoped. In retrospect, I have thought that the Gurkha Brigade should have become the United Nation's peace keepers. They would have revelled in that role and been unbiased in their application of forceful justice wherever there was turmoil and disaffection.

I did not stay long enough to discover what transpired. It is possible that verbal instructions about the way ahead were being passed around the battalions by the clerks. I did get a hint that my orders, those selections so impossibly made, about who might serve on were being put on hold until the time we, the British, left. I give full credit to the clerks for carrying out their work with respect and patience towards us, the remaining KCOs. The future of the new armies of Pakistan and India were to be shaped by the promoted VCOs who must have known their soldiers so much better than did we.

Not much later than this I gave thought to my own future. I did not relish permanence in the army – any army – I longed to return to my home and family; and then marriage and a fireside that I could call my own. The thought of moving about the world and living with WD furniture, and socialising in a mess, appalled me. One way or another I had been away for nearly five years. My greatest desire was that we should be a family once more.

UNREST

On one of my visits to Delhi "things were hotting up". I collected the ciphers from Government House but the train was not due to leave for several hours. I went to a forces (European) recreation club not too far from the city centre. It was a low isolated building with not much more than a snooker table and a refectory. I could hear a murmur of people coming closer as I was sitting on the loo but I was quite unprepared for the half brick which came through the glass window above my head.

In no time we had (all six or so of us) shared out the billiard cues ready to defend the building and our lives. I had my loaded .45 too. The crowd passed on their way shouting "Jai Hind", "Quit India". By this time it was a foregone conclusion that the British were leaving India – the politicians were arguing about the detail of partition – and then quite suddenly our role became one of protectors of life and property. We were in considerable demand.

Whilst I was at the leisure centre it transpired that a company of some other Indian regiment, commanded by a contemporary of my training days in Bangalore, was involved in the city centre of Delhi. The mob attacked a bank and the demonstration was turning to looting. After the requisite warnings the young officer ordered the shooting of a rioter who was about to enter the bank through a window. Such scenes were repeated across the width of India from Calcutta to Karachi. The indigenous population became embroiled in a primitive battle for territory; Muslims to the north in the new nation of Pakistan; Hindus to the south, to be called India.

On return to Wah it was evident, and certainly propitious, that we should defend the cement factory. I moved in with part of my company. My bedding roll was unrolled in the testing laboratory – on the floor. It was cool. Stone shelves lined the walls and ceramic containers filled with water had small round discs of cement samples in them. The setting time and quality was to be judged under water and continuously. Benches were set out with laboratory scales and testing equipment. I was woken in the early hours of the morning by a knock on the door. It was Budibhal. He asked what we should do with some injured civilians – one with a serious stab wound in the abdomen. The injured man was sitting on a bench and it seemed best that he should remain there holding his stomach. He did not look at all happy but had put himself in our custody for help. It is extraordinary how humans with all their intellect can flip into a blood lust mode and kill others who are suddenly suspected of being *an enemy*. We sent for transport. A military ambulance came and the injured were removed in the night.

Back in our own billets in Wah camp we were not to dally for long. It became apparent that the whole of the army was going to have to move in to the middle of the worst conflict areas and attempt to keep the warring parties apart. We moved to Gujar Khan.

Wah was less than thirty miles to the north of Rawalpindi. Gujar Khan was about the same distance southwards from Rawalpindi. This is the main route, the only route, from central India, Delhi, through Lahore and northwards to the important towns of Nowshera and Peshawar and on through the Khyber pass to Afghanistan and Kabul. The road and rail run parallel with each other and not far apart for most of their length sharing crossing points on the rivers Indus, Jhelum and Chenab.

All the views are spectacular, none more so than at Attock on the Indus. A memorial to those killed in a previous battle stands out in the sunshine. Mounted slightly above river level, across the bridge, there is a stone replica of a rifle bullet (a round) pointing skywards. Beyond there and you are in different territory altogether.

BODIES, CAMELS AND DISPOSAL

"The Colonel wants to see you" someone said. What now I wondered. "Something about camels" my messenger said. We were camped between the road and the railway line; a rectangular barbed wire enclosure in a part of the maidan in Gujar Khan. Camps were set up and taken down without my participation. I would be busied with other company matters. Saitbir showed me to the tent which he had pitched and was to be mine.

There was something of a village at Gujar Khan. I did not see any of it but knew that there were habitations about and people. There was the usual passage of laden donkeys, buffalo drawn carts and an odd camel. I do not remember or perhaps I ignored the passing trains. There must have been at least two each day. It was quiet, except one night in darkness I was asleep in my camp bed in the tent. I was really fast asleep and completely relaxed from exhaustion. Like an explosion two cats shot into my tent round it in what seemed to be like a wall-of-death circuit of the canvas and then out again. All accompanied by screeches and spitting and the worst catty expletives in any language. They went as quickly as they had come and were gone and it was silent before I had become conscious and realised what had happened.

A bullock cart brought three civilian bodies to the camp one day. The carter expected us to dispose of them. The colonel ordered a truck to take them out on the road in the other direction and dump them. We were mostly occupied in rounding up miscreants; murderers, arsonists, thieves, poisoners. We took about 300 each week to Rawalpindi jail. I did the jail run once. In the back of a 3 ton truck filled with what were purported to be miscreants. My hand near my .45 – and a Gurkha with a Sten. The clerks were kept very busy typing up statements to accompany all the accused. It was not an easy time for anyone.

"You're the animal man" the Colonel started flatteringly "There are three camels at the gate." The gate was merely the truck-wide gap in the barbed wire – well sentried. No one but our own men would enter easily. "Get rid of them. Try the police station." I am sure he spoke in a kindly manner. I admired the Colonel and respected his decisions. He commanded respect whilst projecting a sense of equality in his relationship with others. His orders were clear, fair, concise and for the good. This time for the sake of the camels – and I was the animal man!

I went to the gate and checked over the camels; three, sitting one behind the other, still with about 6 cwt. each of rice, lentils or other goods on their backs. Although not distressed it was obvious that camels could not sit there loaded too long. I must have looked foolish but I do not remember noticing that there was anyone watching. I lifted the halter of the leading camel and made a noise such as one would to a horse. I gave the halter a tug and made horsey noises again. The camel raised one side of its blubbery upper lip. I retreated a little having heard that creatures of the camel and llama tribes spit.

Obviously the camels were going nowhere on their own and certainly not with me. Then I had the brainwave that should have been my policy from the start. I went to my company and asked three riflemen to accompany me. I ordered them to bring the camels and accompany me to the police station which was on the far side of the maidan across the main road. "Ji Sahib" they said in unison. They looked as if they welcomed the diversion, a relief from boredom in the barbed wire enclosed camp – in the sun.

Each went to the head of a camel and I did not detect any look or gesture between the three of them. As if on a word of command each picked up a halter; moved to the rear of each camel; and as if choreographed and timed perfectly they booted the camels' bottoms. The camels groaned, grunted and squealed their chorused complaint – BUT all rose, see-sawed front and back and then up on to four legs.

I knocked, almost too tentatively, on the police station door at the side entrance in a small courtyard lined with outhouses. The door opened a little and then quickly shut. The police were not becoming involved evidently. There was certainly going to be an awful lot of adjustment – we had a Muslim munshi teaching us Urdu in Bangalore – for him that would become four days travel by train to his new country in the north. There were Hindus and Sikhs in what was to become Muslim territory and there was open warring between the peoples of the two main religions. We walked the camels round and back into the yard. My toe went in the door this time and I ordered the policeman to offload the camels, water them, and do what ever he wished with the loads. They took them.

PARTITION, PROBLEMS, MURDER

Does partition provide security and peace? Cyprus, Korea, Ireland? I was not aware at that time of the political wrangling; of Jinnah and the Muslims' desire to take control of their own destiny – to have their own country. There were many Muslims who had hoped for a unified multi religious sub continent (all India) and they were members of the Indian Congress. The fear was that the Muslim voice would be outvoted by a Hindu majority in a single nation. Religiously there is the widest gap between these two factions – one, the oldest; the other, the most recent.

So the deadline was set. Mountbatten appointed by the Labour Government in Britain to assume the post of the last ever Viceroy of India. The task was to deliver millions of people, many who enjoyed, and were loyal to British ways into the hands of whatever sort of Government became agreed by the politicians of the time. And chaos reigned.

There were reports of poisoned village wells. Bodies were thrown into wells. A practice quickly caught on; that of locking the occupants in their house and setting fire to it. One of our companies was out on a vast sweep of large territory – our battalion was covering an area the size of Yorkshire and with probably as many or more people in it.

Rifle companies were being overstretched so the Colonel asked me (HQ company) to go into the hills with a company and offer safe conduct to anyone who wished it. We were to bring them in so that they could be accommodated in a refugee camp. It was beautiful country; a few hundred feet higher than the plains. Well spaced pine trees allowed grass to grow between and it must have been seen as an enviable life for those who lived on the plains, to be a goat, sheep, or herder with shade trees in these undulating hills. Looking back across the vast lower area that day I counted thirty fires burning – and each was probably a small village.

We went to all properties amongst the dispersed trees and rough grazing land. The houses had accommodation for the people above and the ground floor was for their animals. It had been easy to set fire to them with all the feed and bedding. Some people stayed and some elected to come with us until I had a strung-out column of two or three hundred yards long. The Gurkhas surrounded the civilians who were leaving home with just a few possessions – but their lives were intact.

Some of the Gurkhas were having a self conscious laugh amongst themselves. I enquired what the joke was. Eventually they owned up to insisting that women needing the loo would have to do it where they were – and then they could watch. Gurkhas find fun and amusement in coarse "naughty" behaviour. I had to devise a system of privacy, by distancing them, from those who needed to relieve themselves. Eventually, by the end of a long day, we made it back to a road where transport was waiting to take the refugees to their camp and us back to Gujar Khan. There was much unrest and no security for a mass of people. Partitioning vast lands brings much trouble.

BACK TO SCHOOL

The Colonel asked me to take a small convoy of vehicles and a platoon of men southward. I was to stop the Frontier Mail before it reached one of the tunnels. There was concern for the thirty or more girls who were returning to boarding school after the holidays. All went according to plan. I had a truck load of cotton-frocked teenagers singing all the way to Murree where there is a Catholic Convent School. It's still there today, I am told. (But the Brewery has gone).

262

I waved the train on. Perhaps Vernon was the driver that day. We made for the hills in convoy. A 15cwt. Chevrolet leading, then the 3 ton truck with summer frocked girls lining the tail boards and swaying with the movement over the not too even road. Behind that I came in the second Chevrolet. The motor cycle went forward and back acting as a scout. We were a force to be reckoned with. The Gurkhas would have been out of the "chevs" at the slightest provocation. Many of them were well battle seasoned.

We climbed the lower hills which were dotted with trees. We could see marauding groups armed with spears; poles with knives tied to them. There was no evidence of any fire arms. It was a strange and perhaps slightly unnerved party that I was escorting to the safety of the convent school in the hills. They sang "Money is the root of all evil" and was it "She'll be wearing pink pyjamas when she comes" – all the way.

Murree sits high in hills with great distant views over the plains to the south west. There are substantial buildings and streets. How did our drivers navigate so expertly? Of course they were from Divisional Head Quarters and so probably were familiar with all the roads although it was all new to me.

Some months previously, one peaceful day, I took the bus to Murree. After crossing fairly level ground for about twenty miles we reached the bottom of the real hills and there, although it is the lesser distance of the journey, we weaved on endless hairpin bends in a low gear and covered many miles. I should think the bus needed new brake linings often each week, for, unbelievingly the driver switched the engine off on the downward journey and free wheeled using only the brakes all the way to the bottom of the hill. We lurched and swayed at every vicious hairpin bend.

From my lowly position it was not possible to appreciate the political and territorial manoeuvres. In retrospect I am fairly certain that there were several incidents which had been planned by the politicians to support their strategic aspirations. Our call to Oghi drew us away from the lower land around Campbelpore, Rawalpindi and southwards towards Lahore. Then there was bloodshed, I was told, in Rawalpindi – something to do with the Sikh regiment stationed there. Sikhs would have to move south to the new independent India. From south of Lahore northwards, all would become Pakistan and mainly Muslim.

We moved most rapidly into Rawalpindi one day – arriving in the dark. The town was enveloped in smoke and it seemed that a battle was raging. I was put into a large bedroom in what might have been a guest house. I think we requisitioned anything we could. I wonder who, if anyone, paid the bill! I think that it was a four poster bed for the room would have suited one! I had no idea where all of the battalion was. Indeed, I did not know where any of my platoons were. My company headquarters knew where I was. As the gunfire raged around and the smoke grew more dense a petrified civilian Sikh was brought to me. He asked that I put a platoon of Gurkhas in his house for the night. He believed that he and his family would be murdered that night. He was probably right. He offered me Rs 3,000 for one night's protection; that would have been equivalent to six months pay. But the British were incorruptible; of course.

Next morning the whole battalion was trucked in convoy up the hairpin road to Murree. The army unit stationed there had run out of ammunition during the night. I think that the Catholic Convent was not endangered, for the battle was now entirely Muslim versus Hindu. Our task was to do a house to house search through the whole town. Gurkhas were expert at this. Many of them would have excelled at it in Italy. They were not trigger shy either.

An excited Gurkha havildar came to me with the news that he had found the arsenal. All the spears, swords and even firearms, he said. This was the centre of all the trouble. I went with him a couple of streets away. It was a town built on hills so one could look out over roof tops in many directions. Some of the houses were built on such steep ground that the ground floor on one side was the second floor from the street below. The building that I was taken to was stone built, substantial. I believe it was circular and there were tall narrow glazed windows. A petrified chokidar had against his will been forced to unlock the heavy wooden double door. I had not the slightest idea what to expect. It seemed most unlikely that the murderous hordes milling about bent on violence had such a respectable building for their use.

I entered, with the havildar and a couple of riflemen, the chokidar like a broody hen fluffed his arms about but the very nature of the building compelled a respectful silence. It was totally quiet inside. Through the next door from the surrounding circular passage, we entered the round chamber. Yes! The walls were covered in collections of all sorts of armoury.; swords, spears, perhaps firearms – I do not recall. Hard for a man from Nepal to see this collection's role in peaceful pursuits – it was the Masonic lodge. We left quietly and I thanked the chokidar who was most relieved to lock the large heavy studied wooden door once more. Could I have explained to the Gurkhas, hill men from Nepal, that this was indeed a permitted, a wholly legal and a peaceful, organisation.

My mother's brother was a Freemason, he had come to South India from Argentine. He was found to be unsuited to telecommunications. He came to work in the coffee business and I remember that he sent bags of green coffee beans to us in Edinburgh after we had returned from India. My father roasted the green beans. The oils oozed as little golden beads on the skins of the beans and the house smelt most marvellously of quality coffee. My uncle died of cholera. Then no more coffee beans came.

We did however continue to receive our supplies of tea in plywood boxes. The boxes that were stamped "untouched by hand" but were more often packed with the aid of a pair of feet.

This was Nilgiri tea: quite superb – and a friend keeps me supplied with it today. It is different because unlike ordinary Indian tea which is fermented until it is quite black, this is dried when it still retains a touch of its greenness. So it is part way to being like China tea. It is so much more refreshing than all those "popular" brands – and the taste lasts to the end of the cup.

During the partition troubles one of our rifle companies was tidying up an outbreak of violence in the town. As they moved along a street one of the rioters ran out of a doorway. Whilst doing so he threw a knife at the nearest Gurkha rifleman – who shot him. David, the Company Commander, just a youngster and not one of the battle hardened officers from the Mediterranean and North African war, was asked to write a report of the incident for the Brigadier. He was quite upset and more than a bit worried. The Brigadier was by now a Sikh. Many of the VCOs were being promoted to full officer status for the new armies of India and Pakistan.. It was obvious that this hasty promotion required delicate handling and our Colonel was kindly when the Brigadier came to ask "Now Leslie, what do you think we should do here?" I give the Brigadier his due too for good "man management". When he went over the report with David – he thanked him and, to put David more at ease, said "Come back, when you've got six more." And it did help to relieve David of his anxiety. We were there to do the job – and to do it well. Gurkhas do not mess about.

D Company lost a naik (Dilbahadur) whilst there. I did not see the report nor did anyone give me a first hand account of the incident. The platoon, or section, was patrolling amongst houses in one of the villages. In those days all houses were of mud bricks and flat roofs. The size of houses was dictated by the length of roof timbers one could afford. By the time I returned with my daughter in the 1980s there was an increasing proportion of concrete houses being built. Unfortunately instructions about expansion joints did not come with the cement. Many new houses had open cracks in the walls. The rain came through but it did not seem to upset the occupants much. My friend asked if my house in Scotland was made of concrete to which I replied "No." He was disappointed for my sake when I told him that part was of stone and part of brick. He believed us to be backward and perhaps not at all wealthy.

The patrol moved through the village. It was said that the naik became separated from his section; and that he went forward to 'parley' at the request of the villagers. Usually at close quarters the Gurkha is not slow to wield a kukri when threatened. This time it was the Gurkha who was beheaded.

"Dulce et decorum est pro patria mori." The Gurkha served anywhere and would go with honour everywhere. It was for the honour of his family and of his country that he served others.

Letter from Ann asks if the reason for the increased time for mail reaching me is because I have been in more remote areas. She is attending the Midland Agricultural College on a horticultural course.

6. BACK TO BLIGHTY

A Foreign Power
Posh
Liar Dice
Redirected

A FOREIGN POWER

I was packed, tin box crated in timber slats. I remember being critical of the joiner's work when he hammered the screws right in without recourse to a screwdriver. My camel skin suitcase WOV (wanted on voyage). A beautiful shade of leather such as I have not seen elsewhere. Neither coffee nor cinnamon – but something better and in between. My rank and name blocked in capitals, in white, consigned to my new home address. It was a new home that I had heard a little about but did not really visualise. Cousin Elspeth seemed to think it was a lovely place and "Marilyn Munro" Marie wrote to say that she had been to see it too. She and my sister were now both physiotherapists.

Two years had passed since I was last in Poona – no monsoon this time, but a good time of the year. I was on my way from Nowshera, via Dehra Dun, then to Bombay to join a returning troop ship and back to "Blighty" and I was an officer now. In Poona I had an assignation with the young WVS lady who shared my train compartment between Delhi and Wah the year previously. I travelled so effortlessly; where was my luggage, where did I sleep en route – of these details I have no memory. I was directed to the swimming pool by staff at the camp gate at Poona. She must have warned them that she expected a visitor. She was there – sitting in the sun in her bathing costume. No one else, it seemed, was in sight. How do some moments seem so specially one's very own. Where are you now? I hope life has been kind and rewarding to you. My final year in India was spent in tents and muchly male – then the awful upset to my body with DDT. It left me antisocial, agoraphobic in reverse, politely nearly speechless in the presence of company. We chatted for only a short time. It must have been very special for me for the memory has lasted.

Bombay was bustling. The quayside was crowded. I lost my Gurkha hat, a very precious part of me, in the sheds on the dockside. It was on my tin trunk whilst I signed some papers consigning my worldly goods for transit – and then it was gone. So I wore my beret which I lost later in the Waverley Railway Station in Edinburgh. I began to feel that there was not a great deal of me left.

Throughout my war service I felt that time was marking. I anticipated that when the war was finally resolved we would all return to our rightful place in the world that we had known before; to the security, to laughter, to loving and a settled family. It was not to be. I should have realised that. There was virtually no family – not ever again together; a rift between parents – a different house.

The whole of India was an exciting adventure. I knew well that I had been born there and I did feel a sense of belonging. I was treading familiar family territory.

My father had given me, before I embarked, a little address book which contained the names of the people he had known in India. Additionally the end page had a quotation regarding the inadvisability of mixed marriages. He believed that he should, and could, direct me – in the straight and narrow. What *he* considered to be right for me.

So I went on a lengthy taxi drive to an address, out of town. Was it Lahore? We went by unmade road although it was at times lined by smart bungalows and two-storied European style houses – detached, with gardens, reminiscent of suburban London. We passed under some large trees at one point where the road was particularly uneven, even severely undulating and the taxi had to proceed gently. The branches of the trees met overhead and a large troop of monkeys cavorted and played tig in them. Some watched our passing almost disapprovingly and grimaced from above. It was an open car.

Finally we arrived at the house of the correct number. The path and garden was like any in mid price Swanley or Surbiton. The shrubs and flowers were mixed, but many were also as familiar as those in Surrey or Middlesex.

My knock failed to bring someone to the door for a considerable period of time. Eventually an Indian woman, well dressed in a sari opened the door. She spoke no English. I enquired about my father's friends, she had no knowledge of them at all. I did not search for any more of those on my father's list. I was twenty years too far away and India had changed. It seemed once more that I was breaking new ground. The past was an irrelevance.

And, yet! On my return I have discovered that many of my family know their way around not only India, but about half of the world. My Uncle in the bank in Bombay was not a "one-off".

Aunt Lina, in 1914, returned to the East. She went to India and spent some time with her step brother, Herbert, seeing Delhi, Meerut, Lucknow, Cawnpore and Agra. She wrote home to say that she had visited all the mutiny places.

All the daughters of James Stuart, tea planter in Assam, were born in India. Lina trained as a nurse at Edinburgh Royal Infirmary about the beginning of the century. Her son has a Christmas card sent to her by Florence Nightingale. She then became a doctor, in Edinburgh, married a doctor who served in Karachi, (1914 – 18 war) then Travancore in the Indian Medical Service. Leelie acted as M O to a leper colony near Poona.

There is more than a sprinkling of the Stuart family throughout India and Europe – I am sure that all of them saw their lives as a service to King, Country, and to those people of the Empire where there was a need for medicine, education, banking, and civil engineering and administration. Then there were the planters, tea and coffee mostly, rubber and cotton — perhaps a church missionary too.

On my return to Scotland in 1947, my mother told me she had made friends with a family in the village. On telling the wife that one of her sons is in the Gurkhas, the woman replied that it was indeed interesting as her husband had been in "leather". She may have confused Gurkha with gherkin!

I know that I saw my role in both the navy and the Indian Army entirely as service to my country – to the

King – and for the common good of both the British and, latterly, also Indians.

By early 1947 I realised that my pay would soon be coming from the Indian Government. Not from the country which validated my contract of service by presenting me with a shilling from the King. I had signed on as a "hostilities only" member of His Majesty's Service. The hostility had come from Germany, USSR for a time, and Italy and Japan. It had little to do with India and its problems. Even if I had an Indian birth certificate I considered that the end of my contract with the Indian Army was now nearing an end. I told someone so. They said, "You had better go then." So I did.

Back at Regimental Headquarters in Dehra Dun the doctor ran out of prime muscles for all the injections I had to have before returning to Blighty. I collapsed on my bed in the large tent with the thatch. My body seized up and I may have hallucinated a little. When the full moon shone in through the tent entrance it made deep shadows across the earth floor. I became convinced that there was a black panther lying at the edge of the shadow. And then I fell asleep again for another twenty hours.

I made a one night stop in Lahore to say good bye to friends from Bangalore days. The hoopoes cooed from palm tree tops above the formal borders filled with colourful cannas in Flashman's Hotel grounds. The weather was pleasantly warm. I was given a room in the garden lodges which had a little balcony and I slept in the late afternoon. A young house boy, work starts at a young age in India, sat outside below the window. I assumed that he did not realise that I was in residence as he masturbated just a few feet away.

I was complimented on the smartness of my dress drill suit at dinner. Having come almost direct from the hills and tent life my friends expected someone dishevelled. But now with a suit case in place of the kit bag of navy days it was easy to fold and pack suits. We stowed items of clothing in the navy tied between cardboard ends. Bell bottoms were concertina folded and emerged most beautifully pressed. I made my farewells.

POSH

I had always thought that POSH meant "Port side Out, Starboard Home". The side away from the searing sun in the Red Sea and crossing the Indian Ocean in days before air conditioning. It is disappointing to find that dictionaries suggest that there is no evidence to support this origin of POSH. We would have travelled posh, and my ayah who accompanied us back to Britain in the 1920s would have gone steerage and on the hot side. I was starboard side going to India and now in 1947 I believe that I was starboard coming home.

Accommodation on the return journey was more comfortable. After all I was an officer now. Travelling, with his wife, was my father's cousin. He was a brigadier. Two deck chairs marked clearly in block letters "Brig Boyd" remained permanently in place on the boat deck. He offered me their use. I was sitting in one on a sunny day half way between Bombay and the Persian Gulf when a fellow subaltern warned me of the severe trouble I would find myself in if I was caught there! I didn't offer the explanation of my relationship with the "brig" and therefore my legitimate use of the chairs.

I remembered being the page boy at his wedding when I was about ten years old. I wore a little kilt in Royal Stuart tartan. I was partnered, the bridesmaid, by my cousin Elspeth, affectionately known as Eppie. She and I were very fond of each other both then, and long after. It was she who met me in London on my first day back. She was at university and took me to a concert that evening after a meal in her student refectory. I do not remember where I stayed but I was a member of the Overseas League and may have stayed there in the Park Lane area.

The first year of the Edinburgh Festival was 1947 and I was able to return the compliment by inviting her to several concerts. She insisted that I should follow the music scores which she brought with her.

LIAR DICE

There is so very little to see at sea. We passed much of the time, day and evening, playing liar dice. The loser of a "hand" bought the next round at the bar, or we played for cigarettes which we had become accustomed to receive free in tins of fifty. It was a game that I thoroughly enjoyed and consequently became not only an enthusiast but something of an expert. Some hands went to high stakes in spite of a limit of starter for three; but stakes could be doubled. Once with finally four aces I gained a whole fifty tin of "Players".

There must have been several dining rooms, messes, for I only occasionally came across my relatives, the Boyds, during the journey. I made good use of the deck chairs.

For several months apart from the partition riots I had been living on the edge of the snow line. Well wrapped up and with water rationed to a pint for washing and shaving I had remained pale skinned. I thought I should do something about a sun tan. We were passing Aden in the Red Sea. It was hot. I tried stretching out in swimming trunks and achieved a mild burn in no time. Then prickly heat developed.

A colleague suggested, wisely, that I should not report to the MO for fear that I would be detained for treatment on arrival. I soon recovered but the prickly heat recurred almost annually for several years.

Much worse, more debilitating and quite worrying, although I did not at the time know what it was, was the effect of my exposure to DDT. It was to be several years before some papers from the USA described the symptoms and warned of its poisonous effect. There were to be times when I found it hard to concentrate. I became timid and uncomfortable in company. So much so that I would hasten out of Crawford's restaurant in Edinburgh's Hanover Street with what is called a hot flush as it became crowded at lunch time.

Sutton Bonnington   17 - 6 -47

Dear Mickey,

Have burnt my boats. Am not returning to the place. Have always wanted to go to Reading for the degree course, so hope to start in the Autumn Frightful family opposition, but I hope they understand now. Went home last weekend, but the subject was never mentioned Can't say that there was much opportunity as I was out most of the time!

This term has been hectic. I cut down on everything to the barest minimum, and wrote to no one, or hardly anyone. But feeling rather stale with swotting thought I'd write instead

As I said, went home. Travelled up on Friday night Was awake pretty well from Appleby onwards, and it was grand to see the dawn breaking over the borders. The spring flowers were out, tho' they have been over for some time here Edinburgh is just the same, and being cleaned up for the Royal Family, and for the Festival in the autumn Owing to rather a good party, went to bed at 0500 on Sunday. Sunday equally hectic. Took Luke out in the morning That always includes the unexpected One never knows what he will do.

We are trying to organise a Garden Fete, and were very busy thinking up the various side shows. Barnton is a lot nicer now. It has been cleaned up and we are putting down the lawn again You could call it switching over to Peace Time production!

This is an incredible year. All winter we were breaking records the coldest and longest etc. Now we have had a heat wave which beat all others Temperatures were recorded which have never been known before. Alas, Edinburgh had the usual easterly haar, tho' the rest of

Scotland had it. This weekend was some much needed rain, so the present outlook for the fruit is good.

Exams are on us on Thursday. There is a week of them. Then three months holiday. Have many plans afoot, which probably means that I shan't do any of them! Family are going to the Dublin Horse Show, but tho' I wanted to go at first, have backed out when I thought of what it would entail. Milling crowds in a crowded town. No thank you. Then they are taking the car and are going places, but I'd just rather not.

Hope some time to go NW, not to the islands, for I think that they will be a trifle full. Then I also want to go to the lodge. Don't have to be at Reading until the 1st October, so, really, I ought to be able to do quite a lot.

Shan't be sorry to leave this place, but what I wonder is, am I going out of the frying pan into the fire? Next year I don't touch Horticulture at all, which is rather sad. At least, that is what I am told.

Are you making the army your life, or are you coming back to do something else?

I don't seem to have written a very interesting letter. I suppose it is because have done nothing really, since I came back. And, as usual, now that the exams are upon me, I realise that I know nothing. It is only at these times that that particular realisation becomes a concrete fact to me, tho' others are telling me so all of the time. Hey me.

One diversion has been bee keeping. It wasn't compulsory, but I thought it might come in handy some time. So once a week we put on rather Victorian like hats and veils, and cover up all holes such as sleeves and trouser legs, we have to wear trousers to protect our legs. It is a most interesting task. Quite bee minded now, I am. The sad part about it is that we shan't be here for the honey. You have no idea how intriguing the whole business is. There just isn't time to be scared. Mercifully, the college doesn't go in for fierce bees.

Best love   Ann

Instructions on how to use this Book

1. The holder's name, full postal address and National Registration Number must be written in the spaces provided on page 1, in INK, before this book can be used.

2. When shopping, you must not cut out the coupons yourself, but must hand this book to the shopkeeper and let him cut them out. IT IS ILLEGAL FOR THE SHOPKEEPER TO ACCEPT LOOSE COUPONS.

3. When ordering goods by post, do not send this book—cut the coupons out, and send them with your order by registered post.

4. All clothing books of deceased persons must be handed to the Registrar of Births and Deaths when the death is notified.

5. If you are recalled to Service and have not obtained extra coupons against the application form on page 8, see that it is kept safely until your return to civilian life.

6. This book is the property of H.M. Government, and may only be used by or on behalf of the person for whom it is issued. TAKE GREAT CARE NOT TO LOSE IT.

Page 2

Page 5

It looked as if I would need to be patient, very tolerant. I would be setting out on an entirely new way of life.

Severe rationing and restrictions. Control, for years to come. Post war deprivation was serious. Cigarettes had to be searched for – one had to follow the delivery van or cart into the shop.

I had absolutely no idea what lay ahead. It was likely that I would enter university and then rethink my direction thereafter. There seemed to be a state of confusion in my mind. Complete a degree course and then see what transpired. Between my release from the army and the October start of a university year I added to my qualifications with what was called pre-registration certificates. My botany, physics and chemistry knowledge advanced greatly. I was ready and later graduated BSc at Edinburgh University. My student grant from the government was £180 per annum rising to £200 in the third year.

Someone in India owing me money sent a British Postal Order issued in Dehra Dun in September 1949. Two years and more after independence! I suspect that they owed me a great deal more than just six pence!

Relative freedom arrived with the end of petrol rationing although I received a letter declining my application for an extra allocation two days previously.

". . . having regard for the continuing need for economy in the use of petrol."

A letter from Ann to India followed me back to Blighty. She was attending an agricultural college. Then she moved to Reading University – a degree course in agriculture

Marie went off shortly after my arrival in Blighty to marry someone in the RAF. We never did have that party.

Ann sent me a packet of "National Dried Cocoa" – somewhat reminiscent of kai in the navy. Years later her sister asked me "were you the cocoanut?"

There were loves and there were losses. Hi jinks and heartbreaks. There were those who lived on and there were some that were gone. We all became redirected – like my mail. The world was a changed place. We were changed. Not one of us was as we had once been.

Food rationing continued and increased in severity for many years and was extended even to the feed for farm animals.

On disembarkation at Southampton I had sat in the train with my back to the engine. I looked up at the vast side of the ship at the dockside. My father had left here at the age of twenty two, twenty five years earlier. Parcelled off to Naga country in the back of beyond. He must have felt that the world, his world, had come to an end.

I was exactly twenty one and a half years old. I was back home now. Back in Blighty, and my life, my real life, was just about to begin.

Reading University   21 . 1 . 48

Dear Mickey

Remember I promised you some National Milk Cocoa? If a parcel of indefinite shape arrived about a fortnight ago that was it, only I forgot to say so inside Maureen promised to send it off for me It may well be that it is not worth drinking

How are things? Spect you are pretty busy at the moment I know that we are You remember I failed Zoo last term, so I hadn't really much hope about my essay But the Gods were merciful, and the great Goddess herself, told me that it was good, and awarded me an alpha minus, so I feel that things aren't as bad as they were In Botany we are doing Algae, which I find extraordinarily interesting In zoo, we've done the Amphioxus, and are in the middle of the frog and doing Histology of us at the same time.

What with one thing and another, never saw you to say goodbye Things were frantic at home, it was as well I left when I did My basher hasn't returned this term, is to be married in the spring so there is rather a gap by my side I am now completely unicellular, but sometimes like bacillus radicula, I join up with other organisms Do I really put symbiosis on your envelope? Never can remember whether you are Road or Place The first Sunday here, I was a terrific High Brow for I was asked out to bear

281

Bachs St Matthew's Passion on records, a most heavenly evening Last Sunday, I went to my cousins (?) where I became low brow and extremely knowledgeable on the latest American records And midweek, I always sing Madrigals So with my wireless and one thing and another, am having too much music But I feel that I've earned 'cos I'm well on the way to understanding the Ionic Theory.

We get five weeks at Easter, coming down on March 18th Haven't the vaguest idea what I am doing and for how long I am to be in Edinburgh. Family are going to fish in Ireland, so I may in that case go straight home. Yet, on the other hand, it is easier to do my relations at the beginning not at the end of the holidays, as in spite of every thing I find it difficult to leave Barnton

Had meant to write much more but it is 0030, and I must go to breakfast tomorrow. It'll be the first time this term, but, you see, I have to clear it away. A wretched waste of time, but I console myself with the thought that if I do pass Inter, then I shall try to go into digs.

Love   Ann

India Office,
Whitehall.

21st May, 1947.

Sir,

Now that the time has come for your release from active military duty, I am to convey to you the thanks of the Secretary of State for India and of the Government of India for the valuable services which you have rendered to your country at a time of grave national emergency.

At the end of the emergency you will relinquish your commission, and at that time a notification will appear in the London Gazette (Supplement), granting you also the honorary rank of Lieutenant.

Meanwhile, you have permission to use that rank with effect from the date of your release.

I am, Sir,

Your obedient Servant,

Lieutenant M.M. Stuart.

283

Ann - 1925 to 1994
A singular signaller Wren

Try: www.bothymedia.co.uk for books by the same author

"I'll Tell You About Harry" *"Your story of Harry is true touching and a lesson to all who would understand more about the world in which they live "* Dr. Nicholas Dodman author of "If Only They Could Speak".
A compact much illustrated documentary of a relationship between a completely wild creature and a human.
45 pages   £5.49 in shops.
ISBN 978-0-9563034-0-0

"The Mimee Tribe" The events, characters and locations are the product of the authors imagination.
Any likeness to persons alive today is entirely intentional.
It shows that nothing much has changed in a very long time.
90 pages   £5.49 in shops.
ISBN 978-0-9563034-1-7